A Measure of Fairness

A Measure of Fairness

THE ECONOMICS OF LIVING WAGES AND MINIMUM WAGES IN THE UNITED STATES

Robert Pollin, Mark Brenner
Jeannette Wicks-Lim,
and Stephanie Luce

ILR Press AN IMPRINT OF
Cornell University Press
Ithaca and London

First published 2008 by Cornell University Press
First printing, Cornell Paperbacks, 2008
Printed in the United States of America

Library of Congress Cataloging-in-Publication Data

A Measure of fairness : the economics of living wages and minimum wages in the United States / Robert Pollin ... [et al.].
    p. cm.
  Includes bibliographical references and index.
  ISBN 978-0-8014-4558-3 (cloth : alk. paper)
  ISBN 978-0-8014-7363-0 (pbk. : alk. paper)
  1. Minimum wage—United States. 2. Living wage movement—United States. I. Pollin, Robert. II. Title.

  HD4918.M57 2008
  331.2'30973—dc22   2007033006

Cornell University Press strives to use environmentally responsible suppliers and materials to the fullest extent possible in the publishing of its books. Such materials include vegetable-based, low-VOC inks and acid-free papers that are recycled, totally chlorine-free, or partly composed of nonwood fibers. For further information, visit our website at www.cornellpress.cornell.edu.

Cloth printing   10 9 8 7 6 5 4 3 2 1

Paperback printing   10 9 8 7 6 5 4 3 2 1

To all the organizers who built the U.S. living wage movement

*Their commitment to economic justice has forced communities,
policymakers, and researchers alike to think hard
about our society and values.*

Contents

Tables and Figures

FIGURES

Preface

ROBERT POLLIN

This volume brings together a representative sample of the research work my co-authors and I have done on living wage and minimum wage measures since the publication of my 1998 book with Stephanie Luce, *The Living Wage: Building a Fair Economy.*

There is some irony in the fact that we have collected seven more years of research work since the time of the earlier book. The first book was a by-product of the research Mark, Stephanie, and I did with other co-authors on the Los Angeles living wage proposal that the Los Angeles City Council approved in March 1997. After that ordinance passed, I received several requests to conduct new studies for different cities similar to the one we did for Los Angeles. At the time, I thought that, practically speaking, we could not possibly keep doing more city-specific research of this sort. It seemed like the best way to address the different requests was to write a book that attempted to generalize from our findings in Los Angeles. Our aim for *The Living Wage* was that it could be used as a broadly relevant reference, serving as a substitute for additional city-specific studies.

I think the earlier book did serve this function, at least to some extent. At the same time, I was completely unprepared for the persistent spread of the living wage movement and for the corresponding needs of all those involved in these new campaigns for more and better research. For example, the next study Stephanie, Mark, and I did was in 1999 for the proposal in New Orleans. This measure had very different features than the Los Angeles ordinance. In particular, it was designed to apply to all workers within the city of New Orleans, not, as with the LA measure, a relatively small number who happened to be employed by businesses holding city service contracts. This feature of the New Orleans proposal alone required substantial extensions as well as departures from our Los Angeles–based work. Next, along with other colleagues, Mark, Stephanie, Jeannette, and I considered in 2000 a proposal in Santa Monica, California. In undertaking that study, we realized that we had not previously considered seriously an appropriate working definition of the term *living wage*, the very term that was the object both of our study and the entire communitywide debate. This was a rather serious gap that we tried to close while doing the Santa Monica work.

More generally, what became increasingly clear since 1998 is the need to continue to examine the detailed features of various proposals. In addition to the immediate need for these studies to address the specific debates in various cities, this kind of detailed analysis also seemed like the most reliable path through which to gain a more general understanding of how living wage and minimum wage laws work. This is why we thought it would be of value to bring together these distinct studies, as we have here, into one volume.

The format of this book is a hybrid between an edited and a jointly authored work. The various chapters were written either by one of us or by different combinations of the four authors. Thus, as with an edited work, we have listed separately the authors of each chapter. Moreover, as with an edited volume, I have played the role of choosing which selections to include from our full range of work since 1999 and how to order these selections to produce a coherent whole. I also wrote the introductory sections for each part. Jeannette made large contributions working as an effective co-editor.

On the other hand, unlike most edited books, this volume has only four contributors. In addition, the four of us have worked closely together for the past seven years to develop and improve the general methodological approach that carries forward through all the studies. As such, each of us has had at least some hand in producing every chapter in the book.

A Measure of Fairness

Part 1

WHAT ARE THE
QUESTIONS?

In this part, we present the range of major issues and the breadth of the debate around living wages in the United States, without plunging just yet into too much detail. We proceed with the more detailed analyses in part 2. The three chapters in this part were all written by me.

Chapter 1 provides an introduction to our work on this issue and also offers some preliminary guideposts to some basic issues at hand. I start with the most basic question of all: What is a living wage? We, of course, return to this topic later in the book. I, then, distinguish the difference between living wages and minimum wages, both as a matter of substance and in terms of the range of measures that have become law. And, finally, I distinguish between different types of research that we and others have conducted on this topic.

Chapter 2 is an updated version of a lecture I delivered at the University of Tel Aviv in December 2001. I had been invited to deliver the Tel Aviv lecture months before the September 11, 2001, terrorist attacks in New York. After September 11, I asked one of my hosts, Chaim Frishmann, whether people in Tel Aviv were really still interested in hearing about living wages in the United States. Chaim insisted that indeed they were—that people in Israel had heard about the U.S. living wage movement and were eager to explore ways of advancing a similar movement in Israel. As it happened, I had given similar lectures only weeks before my departure to Tel Aviv in Syracuse, New York, one at Syracuse University and the other in a local church social hall. Evidently, in Syracuse as well as in Tel Aviv, many people were not deterred by the terrorist attacks and its aftermath from continuing to explore ways to create more egalitarian societies. This lecture sets out some basics about how effective living wage initiatives can be toward achieving that broader goal.

Chapter 3 offers a highly critical review by Paul Krugman of my earlier book with Stephanie Luce, *The Living Wage: Building a Fair Economy*, and my response to Krugman. Krugman's review and a shorter version of my response were published in the *Washington Monthly* in September and November 1998, respectively.

In one sense, the 1998 exchange with Krugman is clearly dated. He wrote then that our earlier book contained "much that is silly," and he predicted that the living wage movement was "doomed to fail." This was because the movement's supporters, along with us, the authors, did not sufficiently grasp the maxim that "the amorality of the market is part of its essence, and cannot be legislated away." I have no idea whether Krugman still thinks that our book is silly. But given the history of the living wage movement since 1998, I am confident that he would no longer stand by his prediction of the inevitable doom of the living wage movement.

Regardless of how Krugman may now feel about living wages—he now voices strong support for raising the minimum wage and for countering rising inequality more generally in his regular *New York Times* op-ed column—the fact is that his review has acquired a life of its own among living wage opponents. It is frequently cited to confer credibility on anti–living wage arguments. These critics usually rely on a simple appeal to authority, as in "if Pollin and Luce can't even convince Paul Krugman, the distinguished economist and well-known liberal, that the living wage is a good idea, then surely their book and the whole movement must be flat-out wrong." Amid the frequent references of this sort, I have never seen a discussion that considers my response to Krugman—either favorably or unfavorably—even though it has also been available since 1998 in the pages of the *Washington Monthly*. Providing the full exchange here should, therefore, help clarify the basic matters in dispute. Beyond that, of course, individual readers will judge the debate as they wish.

—R. P.

1   *Introduction*

ROBERT POLLIN

The contemporary living wage movement began in the United States in Baltimore in 1994. I myself became involved as a researcher on this issue when I was approached in August 1996 by Madeline Janis, who was the lead organizer of the initiative then being considered in Los Angeles (and who remains today as director of the Los Angeles Alliance for a New Economy, LAANE). I was then teaching in the Economics Department of the University of California–Riverside, fifty miles east of Los Angeles.

Madeline called to ask whether I would be willing to provide a professional evaluation of the Los Angeles proposal, which was to establish a living wage minimum of $7.50 per hour, plus an additional $2.00 in health benefits for workers without private insurance, for all workers employed by business firms holding service contracts with the City of Los Angeles government. This would mean a 76 percent wage increase over the then national minimum of $4.25 per hour that prevailed in California, with health benefits on top of that, for workers employed by firms holding city service contracts.

At the time of her call, I had barely heard of the living wage movement. I knew nothing about the history of the term or similar movements in earlier periods. I also had only a superficial knowledge about many of the issues connected to living wages, minimum wages, or wage mandates of any sort. Given my background, my initial response to Madeline was that she might want to consider working with someone with more expertise in the area. Madeline explained that she had already called a few such people and that they had all turned her down.

After Madeline and I agreed that I could pursue the research with complete autonomy and was free to publish any and all conclusions without vetting them with her or other supporters of the proposal, I accepted the assignment. I then assembled a small team of researchers at the University of California–Riverside that included then–graduate students Mark Brenner and Stephanie Luce (who was a student at the University of Wisconsin but living in Riverside). Our thought was that we would do our best working on this project for 2–3 months and then return to whatever we had been doing before Madeline called.

Jump forward one decade, as I write now, to March 2007. There are today roughly 140 living wage ordinances in place throughout the country that are comparable to the Los Angeles measure, which itself was approved in modified form by the Los Angeles City Council in March 1997.[1] Another roughly 30 proposals are being debated, again in communities of all sorts throughout the country.[2] Moreover, in the national election that ended in November 2006, in which the Democrats took control of both houses of Congress for the first time since 1994, there were also ballot initiatives in six states to raise their statewide minimum wages well above the current $5.15 federal minimum. All six proposals passed, with overwhelming majorities in four of the six states—to $6.75 per hour in Arizona (66 percent majority), to $6.85 in Colorado (53 percent), to $6.50 in Missouri (76 percent), to $6.15 in Montana (73 percent), to $6.15 in Nevada (69 percent), and to $6.85 in Ohio (56 percent). These ballot-initiative victories mean that, as of January 2007, fully twenty-nine states and the District of Columbia, representing nearly 70 percent of the total U.S. population, are operating with minimum wage standards above the federal minimum.

Still more, the very next day after the Democratic electoral landslide, the incoming Speaker of the House Nancy Pelosi included the goal of raising the federal minimum wage—which had been stuck at $5.15 per hour since 1997—as her first-listed priority when the new Congress convened in January 2007. And indeed, on January 10, the House voted overwhelmingly to raise the federal minimum in three steps to $7.25 per hour as of mid-2009. The Senate approved the raise a few weeks later, after attaching tax benefits for business to the minimum wage increase. As of this writing in March 2007, President George W. Bush is expected to sign into law whatever compromise results from the House-Senate negotiations.

The raise to $7.25 is certainly welcome. At the same time, it is crucial to emphasize that $7.25 per hour as of mid-2009 is not close to being a living wage according to even the most modest definition that we propose in the following chapters. Indeed, after controlling for inflation, $7.25 as of mid-2009 will likely represent an increase of only about 4 percent over $5.15 as of 1997, when $5.15 became the federal minimum. As such, the issues that we raise in this book which refer to the $5.15 minimum wage that was law from 1997–2007 remain just as valid under a $7.25 minimum wage that will take effect in 2009. I consider this point further at the end of this chapter.

Beginning with our first 1996 project and continuing through to the most recent study that we present in this volume (on the 2006 Arizona proposal for a $6.75 statewide minimum wage), our working premise is that we take almost nothing about this issue for granted. Or to be more precise, we do take for granted that the supporters of living wage measures are committed to helping low-wage workers and their families raise their living standards. We clearly share their broad commitment, even while we have never regarded our openly acknowledged support for the aims of the movement as a barrier to our producing scrupulous and reliable research. We also take for granted that businesses facing increased wage mandates will experience higher labor costs and, as such, have an obvious and natural incentive to oppose such measures, whatever effects they may have on low-wage workers' living standards. This natural source of antagonism to living wage proposals is separate from a purely principled opposition, which holds that governments have no right to interfere in the private market decisions of employers and employees as to the wage rate both deem as adequate to induce the employee into the workplace. Research into the effects of living wage laws is irrelevant to adjudicating the merits of this purely principled opposition.

Beyond these most basic matters, we do not presume to know before doing our research whether living wage laws do indeed end up helping the low-wage workers they are intended to help. We take very seriously the claims by living wage opponents that these measures will end up hurting many of the very people they intend to help. Opponents assert that this "law of unintended consequences" will occur because, when faced with their mandated increases in labor costs, businesses will either lay off workers, hire fewer low-wage employees in the future, replace their low-credentialed workers with those having better credentials, or, finally, even relocate to avoid facing the increased costs being imposed on them. Opponents also claim that the fiscal burdens of these measures will force governments or other institutions affected by these measures (such as universities) to cut back on their other commitments, such as direct poverty-reduction measures or scholarships for students who cannot afford a college education on their own. The research that we present in the following chapters represents our best efforts at addressing each of these specific questions and several other related matters, all toward the general goal of providing some bottom-line assessments—that is, are living wage initiatives worth pursuing and, if so, under what set of circumstances?

Our general research finding is that the living wage laws and minimum wage increases that we examine in this book have been effective policy interventions. They have been capable of bringing significant, if modest, benefits to the people they were intended to help. The costs of these measures are also real, but, at the levels at which these raises have been proposed and implemented, they do not entail serious cost burdens for the affected businesses, governments, or other entities bearing these costs. Indeed, given the level of wage increases that have been implemented and proposed to date, the costs involved are widely diffused among the nonpoor segments of the affected communities—including nonpoor consumers, businesses, governments, and private institutions such as universities—so the burdens are almost always small, if not trivial. Probably the largest costs are borne by middle-class consumers when prices rise in restaurants and hotels by modest amounts. As we discuss at length in later chapters, restaurants and hotels have the highest proportional concentration of low-wage workers and thus face the largest proportional cost increases from living and minimum wage increases.

In the decade during which we have been accumulating research findings, we have also observed a decisive, if slowly evolving, transition in the arguments advanced by opponents. As I discuss in chapter 2, when we began our first research project in 1996 on the Los Angeles measure, the city's then–Deputy Mayor for Economic Development Gary Mendoza was already on record as having suggested that "entire industries could be wiped out or move overseas" if the living wage measure passed. Similar claims were made in this early period in Denver and Houston when measures in these cities were overwhelmingly defeated by voters. In Houston, the opposition Save Jobs for Houston Committee put out numerous ads and mailings with the message that the ordinance would lead to "Cops and firefighters yanked off the streets. Higher taxes. Thousands of jobs lost. Soaring prices for such essentials as food and prescription drugs. The wholesale destruction of small businesses. Streets riddled with potholes. Swollen welfare roles."

By the beginning of 2007—after approximately 140 municipalities had passed living wage measures and with twenty-nine states and the District of Columbia either already operating with minimum wage levels above the federal level or poised to do so—claims such as those made a decade ago in Los Angeles and Denver have clearly run their course. Indeed, in the Arizona debate leading up to their November 2006 vote on the $6.75 initiative—a debate in which Jeannette Wicks-Lim and I participated—opponents advanced almost no economic arguments at all. They had rather shifted to a new terrain, claiming that the minimum wage law would threaten the privacy of the state's residents. This would occur because workers eligible for wage increases could enlist outside representatives to defend their legal rights. As it happens, such opportunities were already available to workers and their representatives under the federal minimum wage laws. But these matters aside, the broader point is that by emphasizing this sort of critique, opponents have clearly retreated from their earlier economic-disaster scenarios.

Should we infer from this retreat by living wage and minimum wage opponents that the economic issues—that is, in particular, whether the intended or the unintended consequences of living wage laws tend to prevail—are no longer in dispute? Of course not. In fact, even if opponents of the 2006 Arizona measure were disinclined to debate the economic effects of a $6.75 statewide minimum, this does not mean that they would have the same reaction if the proposed increased minimum wage were $8.00 or $9.00—that is, an increase to levels closer to the living wage standards that have been set throughout the country at the municipal level. In short, whatever the prevailing politics of the moment, the most fundamental question of whether living wage standards can be viable in the United States remains very much alive. Of course, if my coauthors and I did not think this were true, there would be little justification for producing this book.

SOME PRELIMINARY ISSUES

Before proceeding with the detailed discussions of the various issues at hand, it is useful to briefly consider some preliminary terminological issues. These questions include the differences between the research methods we use in the upcoming chapters; the meaning of the term *living wage*; the distinction between living wage and minimum wage initiatives; and, finally, some initial thoughts, spurred by the federal minimum wage increase to $7.25 as of 2009, on how to move the federal minimum toward something that is closer to a living wage standard.

Distinguishing Different Types of Research

There are two basic ways of characterizing the research we present in this book, as well as the work of other researchers on this issue: prospective research and retrospective research. Prospective research, which we present in parts II and III, establishes what is likely to happen when a new living wage or minimum wage law is passed. Retrospective research examines what actually did happen after a measure has been operating over some reasonable period of time. In principle, retrospective research is a more reliable approach because it is guided by observing past experiences rather than anticipations of the future. However, in practice, prospective research necessarily plays a crucial role in formulating policies. By definition, researchers cannot conduct retrospective research on a policy that is still under debate. Communities and policymakers have to make decisions on whether to support such proposals; prospective research is necessarily their guide.

In practice, the distinction between the two types of research is not as clear-cut as the difference in time dimension may suggest. This is because a major component of prospective research, including our own, is the available evidence of past experiences that are relevant to the current policy debate. Moreover, the results of both prospective and retrospective studies should correspond to one another if they have both succeeded in accurately portraying reality. Retrospective findings, therefore, serve as a means of corroborating the methods used in prospective studies.

We can also distinguish research in terms of the underlying data being used. In all of our studies, a substantial part of our work is based on publicly available government statistics, the same types of data that form the empirical backbone for all public policy deliberations. However, in some of our studies (including the New Orleans study in chapter 4; Santa Monica in chapter 8; and Boston, Hartford, and New Haven in chapter 10), we also conducted our own surveys. These surveys certainly provide depth and perspective to our findings. However, as we demonstrate, particularly in chapter 5 on Santa Fe, we have still been able to provide estimates on the impact of these measures that are highly accurate when we have relied entirely on publicly available data.

The issue, then, is not simply the types of data that are used in research but rather whether the researcher uses the best available data at hand in appropriate ways. Thus, in chapter 14, we are critical of the research approach taken by two other scholars, David Neumark and Scott Adams. Neumark and Adams relied on the U.S. Department of Labor Current Population Survey (CPS) to establish their conclusions about the impact of living wage laws on wages, as well as on employment and poverty. Our argument with their approach is certainly not about the validity of the CPS data, on which we also rely heavily at various places. Our critique is that they used this indispensable tool in an inappropriate way.

What Is a Living Wage?

We address the question of what is a living wage in later chapters, beginning more informally in chapter 2 and with greater detail in chapter 7. But it is helpful to introduce the issue up front and, in particular, to identify two largely distinct ways of addressing the question. First, what is a wage rate that is minimally adequate in various communities, in the sense that it enables workers earning that minimum wage and the family members depending on the income produced by this worker to lead lives that are at least minimally secure in a material sense? What wage rate, correspondingly, can allow for a minimally decent level of dignity for such workers and their families?

The second, equally legitimate, question necessarily places the issue of material well-being and dignity to one side. It instead asks, How high can a minimum wage threshold be set before it creates excessive cost burdens for businesses, such that the "law of unintended consequences" becomes operative?

Any serious examination of living wage laws has to keep both questions squarely in front of us.

What Is the Difference between Living Wage and Minimum Wage Standards?

People generally use *living wage* and *minimum wage* to refer to distinct types of initiatives. But, in my own discussions, I find that people tend to use the terms, and the distinctions between them, to mean different things. What is at issue here?

As a simple matter of terminology, a *minimum wage standard* refers to whatever the standard happens to be at a given place and time. Thus, as I have mentioned, the new federal minimum wage as of mid-2009 will be $7.25 per hour. However, few if any observers would consider $7.25 a living wage, in either of the senses I have mentioned. In fact, as I discuss in chapter 2, the energies of the living wage movement, operating at the municipal or statewide levels, has been motivated first and foremost by the premise that at least the present federal minimum wage standard, and probably the statewide minimum levels as well, cannot be considered to be close to a living wage standard.

At the same time, when a living wage movement is, in fact, successful at getting a living wage ordinance passed into law, that new standard becomes the legal minimum wage that businesses have to pay workers if these businesses are covered under the law—the living wage standard becomes the minimum wage standard in these cases. Living wage initiatives are therefore essentially ways of raising the minimum wage among the businesses covered by the law.

As the living wage movement has advanced over the past 12 years, the roughly 140 municipal measures that have become law can be characterized according to two key features. The first is that the living wage standard was substantially higher than the federal or even statewide minimums. Thus, when the Los Angeles law was passed in March 1997, the living wage standard was $7.25 per hour, 45 percent higher than the then prevailing statewide minimum of $5.00. Similarly, the initial Baltimore living wage law was for $6.15 per hour, 45 percent higher than the federal minimum wage of $4.25 prevailing then in Maryland.

The second key feature is that the number of workers and businesses that were covered by these municipal measures was very small. Typically, they applied only to businesses holding service contracts with cities, such as firms providing janitorial, parking, or landscaping services for city buildings. The remaining businesses in cities with living wage laws were under no mandate to raise their employees' wages to the living wage minimum. For example, in the case of Boston that we examine in detail in chapter 10, the living wage law provided a living wage minimum of $9.11 to approximately 2,000 workers. But there were about 171,000 other workers employed in businesses in Boston earning between the state minimum wage of $6.75 and $9.11. I have termed these narrowly targeted measures *contractors-only* living wage laws. I emphasize the term because it underscores that what is distinct about these measures is not the minimum wage rates per se but, rather, the manner in which businesses are established as being covered under the law.

Of course, the benefits flowing from contractors-only living wage increases are real and welcome to the limited number of workers who receive raises. But in addition and perhaps of even greater significance, these limited measures have been the grassroots platforms that have launched broader discussions about what should constitute a fair minimum wage in various communities. In particular, it has been through such discussions that political coalitions were formed to advance various statewide initiatives as well as broader initiatives in some cities.

The statewide minimum wage increases that stand as law or are scheduled to be implemented in twenty-nine states and the District of Columbia as of this writing generally apply to all businesses within a state, not simply to businesses holding service contracts with the state government. In addition, in New Orleans; San Francisco and Santa Monica, California; Madison, Wisconsin; and Santa Fe and Albuquerque, New Mexico, measures that apply to businesses, regardless of whether businesses hold city service contracts, were all approved at some point by city council votes or referendum initiatives. The measures in San Francisco, Santa Fe, and Albuquerque are operating today as laws. Thus, we can call both the statewide measures and these city ordinances *area-wide* measures.

Statewide measures typically set the minimum wage standard well below what we would reasonably consider a living wage standard. Thus, at the end of 2006, the statewide minimum wages that were set above the federal minimum ranged between $5.85 and $7.63 per hour. However, the area-wide measures now operating in San Francisco and Santa Fe *can* reasonably be called living wage measures—the minimum in Santa Fe for businesses with more than twenty-five employees is $9.50 per hour, and in San Francisco, all businesses must now pay at least $8.82 to employees who work at least 2 hours weekly. The overall point is that two types of distinctions are in play when discussing living wage and minimum wage measures: the wage standard that they set and the extent of their coverage. These two types of distinctions are laid out in table 1.1 with some examples.

This is not simply a matter of taxonomy. What has generally occurred in discussions on these issues is that people call only those measures that fit into the upper right-hand cell of table 1.1 living wage measures—that is, the narrow contractors-only measures with relatively high wage standards. Meanwhile, minimum wage laws are often seen as applying to businesses much more broadly, based on location. In other words, the way the terms are used implies that living wage standards cannot be applicable for all businesses within a city, a state, or the country as a whole—that is, the lower right-hand cell in table 1.1 is not a discussable option. But, in fact,

Table 1.1. Distinguishing living wage and minimum wage laws

	Wage standards	
Range of coverage	Lower minimum wage mandates	Higher living wage mandates
Contractors-only measures	Narrow coverage; low wage standard • Baltimore 1995, at $6.15	Narrow coverage; decent "living wage" standard • Most 140 municipal measures • Los Angeles 2006, at $9.39 + $1.25 in health benefits, or $10.64 without health benefits • Boston 2006, at $11.95
Area-wide measures	Broad coverage; low "minimum" wage standard • Most statewide 2006 minimum wage laws, ranging between $6.15 and $7.63[a] • New Orleans proposal 1999, at $6.15	Broad coverage; decent "living wage" standard • Santa Fe 2006, at $9.50 • San Francisco 2006, at $8.82

Source: ACORN Living Wage Resource Center, http://www.livingwagecampaign.org/index. php?id=2071.

[a] We exclude the West Virginia $5.85 minimum wage from this range because its coverage is exceptionally narrow due to the exclusion of businesses that engage in interstate commerce.

such broadly based living wage initiatives are certainly feasible. There is no reason in principle why a standard that applies to only a small number of businesses holding municipal city service contracts cannot also be applied to an entire geographic area. In fact, they are already being applied in Santa Fe and San Francisco.

MAKING THE FEDERAL MINIMUM WAGE A LIVING WAGE

It is important to emphasize, as I have already noted, that the increase in the federal minimum wage to $7.25 as of 2009 is a welcome step forward but that this cannot be considered an adequate living wage for any community in the country. The issue is partially that $7.25 as of mid-2009 is likely to represent an increase in real, inflation-adjusted dollars of only about 4 percent over $5.15 as of 1997, when $5.15 became the federal minimum.

But the inadequacy of the $7.25 minimum becomes clearer still when we consider the combined effects of inflation and the rise in labor productivity—that is, the total basket of goods and services that the average worker produces in a year. The rate of inflation between 1997 and 2009 is likely to be about 3 percent per year. This means that the buying power of a $5.15 minimum wage will have fallen by about 40 percent over these years. Meanwhile, average labor productivity will have grown by well over 30 percent in 1997–2009. This allows businesses to pay their low-wage workers 30 percent more (in real, inflation-adjusted dollars) and have enough money left over for their profits to also rise by at least 30 percent. The fact that the minimum wage has been falling in inflation-adjusted dollars while productivity has been rising means that profit opportunities have soared while low-wage workers have gotten nothing from the country's productivity bounty.

In light of these considerations, it is useful to now sketch out a path for establishing a decent federal minimum, even before we proceed in the next chapters into the details about what might constitute both a desirable and feasible living wage standard in different communities.

In fact, the Santa Fe ordinance provides a model of how we might proceed cautiously toward a national living wage standard. This 2004 measure established raises from the federal $5.15 standard to $10.50 as of January 2008, to be implemented in three steps. But before progressing with each scheduled raise, the city first determines whether the previous raise caused negative employment effects. The Santa Fe minimum rose to $9.50 in January 2006, after the city established that employment growth under a $8.50 minimum had been healthy.

A federal government variant could entail implementing the newly established $7.25 minimum as of mid-2009 and also allowing for increases every 2 years thereafter, once it is established that no negative employment effects resulted from the previous raise. The 2011 increase could be to $9.00, that is, to roughly the low-end living wage standard in communities throughout the country. Increases beyond this could then be tied both to inflation and average labor productivity. This would mean a roughly 10–12 percent increase in the federal minimum every 2 years, if inflation and productivity trends were to continue as they have for the past decade. The raise in 2013 would then be to about $10.00.

Even a $10.00 federal minimum in 2013 will not be adequate for most of the country. Local communities and states will need to continue setting their own living wage norms. But the idea of providing raises in line with average productivity and inflation, after taking account of employment effects, should at least move the country closer to what voters have demonstrated they support, what the economy can readily absorb, and what low-wage workers deserve.

PLAN OF THIS BOOK

This book is divided into five parts. Each part includes its own introduction, so I provide only the barest roadmap here. The remainder of part 1 comprises chapters 2 and 3 and presents broad overviews of the main issues at hand. Part 2, comprising chapters 4–6, includes three prospective studies evaluating the impacts on business firms of measures that were proposed in the cities of New Orleans and Santa Fe, and in the state of Arizona. Part 3 then presents another set of prospective research in chapters 7–9, estimating the effects on workers and their families of measures that were proposed in Santa Monica and again in Arizona. Part 4 consists of chapter 10, a retrospective study on the contractors-only measures in Boston and in Hartford and New Haven, Connecticut. Part 5 comprises four separate technical studies. Chapter 11 focuses on estimating the ripple effects of minimum wage increases—that is, the extent of wage increases that businesses provide to workers beyond what the legal mandate requires. Chapter 12 presents a detailed look at whether minimum wage increases have the unintended effect of reducing employment. Chapters 13 and 14 present critiques of the works of other authors who estimated the effects of living wage laws on wages, employment, and poverty.

2 The Economic Logic and Moral Imperative of Living Wages

ROBERT POLLIN

I begin by recalling the two epigrams with which Stephanie Luce and I began our initial book on this question, *The Living Wage: Building a Fair Economy*. The first was from the book of Deuteronomy: "Thou shall not oppress a hired servant that is poor and needy" (Deuteronomy 24:14). I think that certainly anyone who takes seriously a commitment to Jewish values, or any other religious or ethical values, should be thinking about how to create labor market conditions that provide living wages for working people. That is a basic principle motivating my own work.

The other epigram was from a book called *The Living Wage and the Law of Supply and Demand*, written way back in 1895 by Robert Blatchford: "Whenever you hear a speech or read a paper, which tells you that the living wage is against an economic law, ask the speaker or writer these questions: 1. What is the actual working of the economic law? 2. In what book on political economy can the law be found? In every case the speaker or writer will be unable to tell you."

My own work on living wages tries to capture the spirit of both of those epigrams—the moral imperative behind the living wage and the economic logic behind it, whether it is economically viable in the United States, Israel, or anywhere else.

As we have seen with the quotation from Blatchford's 1895 book, the living wage issue in the United States has been around for a long time in some fashion or another. In its contemporary phase, the movement in the United States began in 1994 in Baltimore, Maryland. The reason it began there was very straightforward. It was not begun by academics, nor by unionists, or other social activists. It was, rather, started by religious workers operating in soup kitchens, homeless shelters, and the like. These people committed to serving the poor had begun to increasingly observe two things in the early 1990s. The first was that there was a rising demand for their services; the second was that a high proportion of those who were using those services were people who held jobs—people who went to work every day, coming with their families to homeless shelters and soup kitchens.

So, these religious workers reached a straightforward conclusion and they did not need economists to help them figure it out. This was that, if people are working, often full-time, and are still bringing their families to a soup kitchen, then the wages these workers were earning at their jobs were not a living wage. Their wages had to be well below a living wage. Yet these same workers were earning the legal minimum wage. That led them to recognize that the legal minimum wage was by no means a living wage.

That was the spark that started the living wage movement in the United States in 1994–1995 in Baltimore. The movement has since spread with such remarkable speed that in roughly 12 years around 140 municipalities in the United States now have some version of a living wage law. In addition, in 2007, at least twenty-nine states, representing roughly 70 percent of the country's population, are operating with minimum wage standards above the $5.15 federal minimum. I have been involved as a researcher and consultant in several of the cities and states since 1996. I have seen firsthand that to get from the point where a few living wage activists have an idea to the point where something becomes law takes time and a lot of working through politics, the drafting of legal documents, fighting through the inevitable legal challenges, and other blocking tactics. So, the fact that in 12 years we moved from being a nonexistent phenomenon to something that is pervasive throughout the country is remarkable.

Of course, there have also been major opponents throughout the country. Probably the most visible and persistent opponent is a group in Washington, D.C., financed by various business groups called The Employment Policies Institute. But even this major opponent has been forced to recognize the successes of the living wage movement. In 2001, the then–public relations director of the Employment Policies Institute, a man named John Doyle, observed that "the phrase living wage is seeping into the vernacular and changing the dynamics of political discussions" (Debare 1999, B1). Doyle obviously did not think this was a favorable development, but the movement had grown strong enough that he had to acknowledge the reality.

As I have noted, the idea of the living wage goes back a long way in the United States. Indeed, the concept of a living wage was the motivation behind the passage of the initial minimum wage laws in the 1930s—minimum wage laws were established to create decent living wage standards. In fact, the movement that led to the passage of minimum wage laws in the 1930s was inspired by, among other things, a 1906 book by a Catholic priest, Monsignor John A. Ryan. Monsignor Ryan's book was titled *A Living Wage, Its Ethical and Economic Aspects*, and it was a best-seller.

Move forward to the 1930s, when the initial minimum wage laws were passed, first at the state level and then for the United States as a whole. In 1934, a well-known U.S. political figure, advocating the passage of these initial minimum wage laws, asserted that "No business which depends for its existence on paying less than living wages to its workers has any right to continue in this country."[1] This is a very strong statement—that no business has any right to continue in this country if it does not pay living wages to its workers. The person making this argument in 1934 was President Franklin D. Roosevelt. Can you imagine George W. Bush, or for that matter Bill Clinton, George Bush Sr., Ronald Reagan, Jimmy Carter, or Richard Nixon making such a statement?

Moving now into the 1940s, and considering the issue on a global scale, the Universal Declaration of Human Rights of the United Nations, article 23 paragraph 3 says that "Everyone who works has the right to a just and favorable remuneration ensuring for himself or his family an existence worthy of human dignity and supplemented, if necessary, by other means of social protection."[2] (If they had been writing today, the drafters of this statement would, of course, have explicitly recognized that women workers deserve the same rights as men.)

So the living wage idea has been around for a long time, both in the United States and globally. But why did the contemporary movement spread so quickly in the United States? There have been basically three factors at work. The first is just that there are activists working on the issue, people who care and are willing to fight for economic justice. Without their efforts, nothing whatsoever would have happened.

The second factor is what we call the outsourcing of government jobs to the private sector. This is when public entities such as city governments or universities that used to hire workers directly to perform a wide range of services began to contract this work out to private firms. Initially, when this sort of outsourcing started in the United States in the 1980s, proponents offered a straightforward analytical justification. This justification was that the private sector is more efficient than the public sector—governments are bad at doing things, whereas the private sector is good at doing things. Because of this, outsourcing to private entities the performance of public-sector services will enhance efficiency.

As it turned out, the factor that was crucial in achieving these "efficiencies" was that workers' wages went down when the same jobs were done by private firms as opposed to public entities. There was no trick here. The magic of the market was that wages just went down, often dramatically, when the same services were provided by the private, as opposed to the public, sector. In Chicago, for example, a 1997 study found the following for these jobs categories that had experienced outsourcing: from 1990 to 1995, wages fell 25–50 percent for watchmen, elevator operators, cashiers, parking attendants, and security guards. That is, there were massive cuts in the living standards of these workers. That was the magic of the market (Mason and Siegel 1997, 5).[3]

The third factor is even more straightforward. These are the basic facts about what has happened to the minimum wage in this country over the past 40 years. We can see this with some simple figures. Figure 2.1a shows the movement over time for the U.S. minimum wage (expressed in constant 2005 dollars, and thereby controlling for inflation). Looking at this picture alone shows us the fundamental force behind the U.S. living wage movement. As we can see, there has been a huge decline in the value of the federal minimum wage in the United States. In 1968, the minimum wage was $8.98 (expressed in 2005 dollars). What does this mean? It means that the lowest-paid person coming to work at a McDonalds somewhere in Texas, for example, an 18-year-old on her first day at work, was paid almost $9 per hour, if McDonalds was obeying the law. That was 37 years ago. The same worker today would get $5.15 per hour. So, we observe an absolute decline in the minimum wage over these years. Let us be clear: there has *not* been a slowing down in the rate of increase in the minimum wage over the past 37 years but, instead, a dramatic *absolute decline* in its value of 43 percent, from $8.98 to $5.15.

So we can see from figure 2.1a alone that there has been a major transformation of U.S. society. But perhaps still more to the point, figure 2.1b shows us the minimum wage relative to the government's official poverty line for a family of three. The question I raise here is, if a worker is employed full-time (which itself is a strong assumption) and is earning a minimum wage over the course of the year, where do this worker's earnings fall relative to the official poverty line (which is an extremely low threshold, a point to which I return)? What a minimum wage worker earned in 1968 was certainly not princely but his or her family lived 20 percent above the poverty line. Today, as we can see, this worker is more than 30 percent below the federal family-of-three poverty line.

I do not know how well you were tuned to the rhetoric of the Clinton years, but the Clinton rhetoric was about rewarding people who played by the rules; that is, "if you do your job and play by the rules, you should be rewarded fairly." The minimum wage workers in this example are playing by the rules; they have jobs and they are working full-time. But earning the minimum wage, even by working full-time, they are ending up 32 percent below the government's official poverty line.

Figure 2.1a. Real value of U.S. minimum wage, 1960–2005 (in constant 2005 dollars)

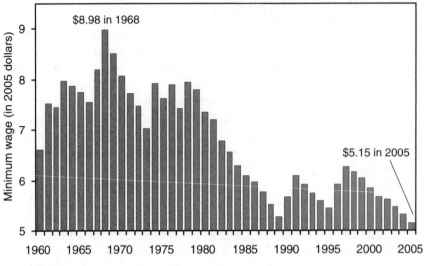

Source: U.S. Department of Labor, Bureau of Labor Statistics

Figure 2.1b. One full-time minimum wage income as a percentage of the U.S. three-person poverty threshold

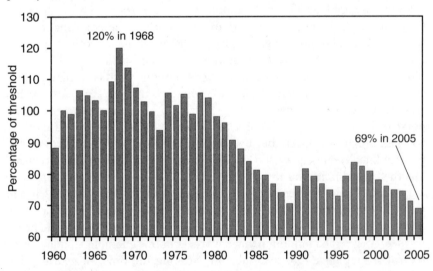

Source: U.S. Department of Labor, U.S. Census Bureau

18

Let me offer one more perspective on the minimum wage collapse over the past 37 years. One of the arguments frequently made in labor negotiations is that owners are willing to give wage increases to workers when productivity goes up. The owners will not give increases when there are no productivity gains, but they can give raises when productivity improvements create a bigger pie to split up. So the point I am raising is very simple. From 1968 when the minimum wage was at its peak until today, productivity in the U.S. economy has gone up quite substantially—by roughly 110 percent between 1968 and 2005.

So here is a little exercise. Starting at the peak value of the minimum wage of $8.98 in 1968, what would happen if policymakers increased the minimum wage, percentage point by percentage point, along with the rate of increase of average productivity? Not a penny more but raising it just exactly at the rate of increase of average productivity. This, by the way, would include the long period from the mid-1970s to mid-1990s when productivity improvements in the United States were very slow, although still on a positive trend. If we conduct this little exercise, the result is that the federal minimum wage in the United States today would be $18.86, more than three and a half times greater than the current federal minimum of $5.15. This exercise illustrates the extent to which the division of the country's total income pie—the fruits of productivity growth—has gone dramatically against low-wage workers over the past two generations.

My focus is on low-wage workers. But it is also important to emphasize that the patterns that we observe regarding the minimum wage reflect a more general trend for nonsupervisory workers in the United States. Figure 2.2 shows the pattern for the average (mean) wage for U.S. nonsupervisory workers (again in real 2005 dollars). The figure shows that the average wage for U.S. nonsupervisory workers peaked in 1972–1973 at $18.22 per hour. The average wage then experienced a precipitous fall from the mid-1970s through the early 1990s. Into the mid-1990s, under President Clinton, the average wage then stagnated at the low level to which it had fallen. The average wage then started to rise in 1997, with the increase extending to 2003. We frequently hear about the economic boom under Clinton. There were 3 years of real-wage growth under Clinton. There were 3 more years under Bush, before real wages started to fall again in 2004. But even adding up those 6 consecutive years of real-wage growth, as of 2005 the average real wage in the United States was $16.11, 12 percent below the peak levels attained 32 years earlier in 1972–1973. Meanwhile, average productivity between 1973 and 2005 rose by 79 percent. The long-term gains in average productivity are clear from the pattern of the upper line in figure 2.2.

It is useful here to offer one interesting perspective on this pattern of average wages. This is from Alan Greenspan, who from 1987 to 2005 was the

Figure 2.2. Average real wages and productivity level in the United States

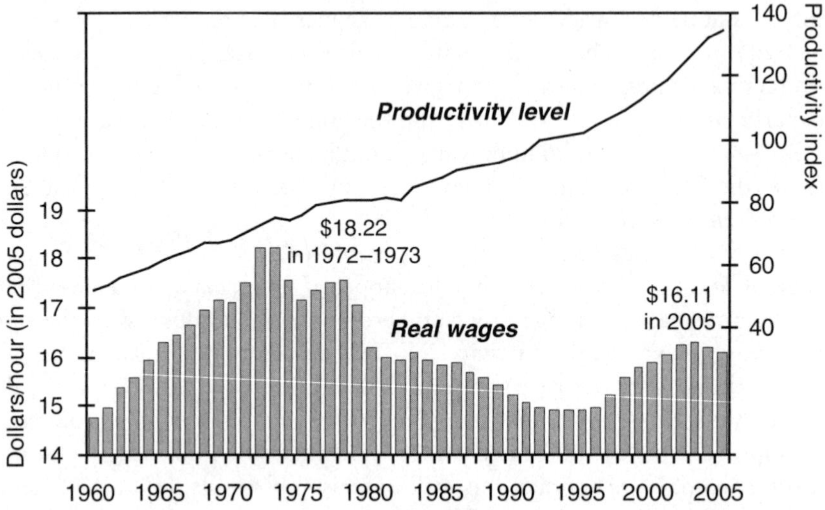

Notes: The productivity index measures output per hour of all individuals in private business. Wages are mean hourly earnings (in 2005 dollars) for nonsupervisory workers in the private sector.

chair of the Federal Reserve Board and universally recognized as the single most important economic policymaker in the United States. Greenspan was known for being deliberately cryptic whenever he made public statements—for sounding profound while not saying anything. Still, every once in a while something substantial slipped out of his mouth. In July 1997, when Greenspan had to make his biannual report to the Congress, he spoke about the economy's "extraordinary" and "exceptional" performance. He then tried to explain this "extraordinary" and "exceptional" performance. He said that a major factor contributing to its outstanding achievement was "A heightened sense of job insecurity and as a consequence, subdued wages."[4] So here is the most important economic policymaker in the United States, stating effectively that the reason the economy is doing so well is because workers are not getting wage increases. Greenspan drew a clear distinction between the performance of the economy and the rewards that should accrue to the overwhelming majority of people who were actually participating in the economy. Those people were just the wage earners; they clearly did not count in Greenspan's eyes when he described "extraordinary" and "exceptional" economic performance.

That, in my view, is the basic background, the motivating factors that have driven the living wage movement forward. The living wage movement is therefore not just about raising the minimum wage; it is about addressing the broad issues of income distribution and economic justice in the United States. The living wage movement is a means through which we can both protest and formulate a concrete alternative to the economic injustices that have prevailed in the United States for over a generation. The living wage movement has had some great successes so far. But there is still a long way to go.

WHAT IS A LIVING WAGE?

Figure 2.1 illustrates the relationship of the minimum wage to the official government poverty line. In the early stage of the living wage movement, the goal was to establish a living wage level that would at least enable a family of three or four to reach this poverty line. So, effectively, the living wage movement was initially saying, "Let's define a living wage as a wage that gets a family to the poverty line." But that definition became increasingly problematic as people looked into it further. This led to lots of careful study. Indeed, one of the things that the living wage movement has achieved is just getting people to think more seriously about what is going on in the low-wage labor market. And certainly, when we think seriously about these issues, a basic question that emerges has to be: What is a living wage?

A general answer to this question evolved over a century of activism. There is an excellent book by Lawrence Glickman called *A Living Wage* (not to be confused either with Monsignor Ryan's 1905 book of the same title or with my book with Stephanie Luce titled *The Living Wage*). Glickman's book is a historical analysis of the living wage movement in the United States as it evolved over roughly 100 years. Reflecting on what the living wage movement has been about over time, Glickman provides this definition: "It is a wage level that offers workers the ability to support families to maintain self respect and to have both the means and the leisure to participate in the civic life of the nation"(1997, 66). So, Glickman does not provide a number, a specific wage level, but rather a concept.

In reflecting on Glickman's definition, it occurred to me that it corresponded closely to the concept of a poverty standard that has been promulgated by the distinguished Nobel laureate economist, Amartya Sen. Sen has revolutionized the way we think about poverty, not in terms of an income number but, rather, relative to the achievement of what he calls "capabilities." For Sen, someone who is living above the poverty line is someone who has a certain set of capabilities. Again, there is no single income number in Sen's definition. He says the capabilities include such things as the ability to read and write, to lead a long and healthy life, to have freedom of movement, and—here we again pick up what Glickman says—"to participate meaningfully in the civic life of the community" (e.g., see Sen 2000, 89–90).

Again, it is a concept, and this provides the foundation on which we should think about how to define a living wage.

Still, we remain faced with the challenge of attaching some meaningful numbers to these concepts. People frequently ask me to put a number to the concept, that is, "What's your number for a living wage?" So let us give it a try. Here is an exercise I did in connection with the living wage movement at Harvard University after students occupied the university's main administration building demanding living wages for all Harvard employees. The starting point for trying to find a number is the official poverty line. At the very least, a living wage standard should enable workers and their families to live above the official poverty line. But we immediately confront a problem here, which is that the poverty line in the United States is completely inadequate as a measure of a minimum living standard threshold.

What is wrong with the official poverty line in the United States? The U.S. poverty line was established in 1963, during the early period of the John F. Kennedy and Lyndon Johnson eras. It was constructed as a means of having something to measure when the government began to pursue what Johnson called the War on Poverty. If the government was going to embark on a War on Poverty, it obviously needed to define the concept against which this war was to be waged. The accepted definition at the time was that the poverty line was to be measured according to the cost of purchasing a basket of food that would give families of different sizes a nutritious but monotonous diet, which the government called the "economy food plan."[5] The economy food plan was initially developed by the Department of Agriculture, drawing from their 1955 survey of household food consumption. They saw the economy food plan as being designed for "temporary or emergency use when funds are low" (Peterkin 1964, 12). The poverty line became simply the amount of money needed to purchase the economy food plan, multiplied by three. Why multiplied by three? Because it was assumed that poor people would spend one-third of their income on food. Basically, that has been the extent of the methodology for measuring poverty in the United States from 1963 until today. The only significant change since 1963 in the dollar threshold itself has been to raise the poverty line annually in step with increases in the cost of living.

What is wrong with this as a poverty measure? The main problem is that other expenses for poor families are not factored in and these costs have risen over time relative to the cost of food. What I am talking about here are the cost of transportation, the cost of housing, and most particularly the cost of child care. One of the major policy changes that led to an increase in the cost of raising children was the dramatic cut under President Clinton in the federal government's so-called welfare program. This program specifically provided cash subsidies to mothers who were caring for their children.

I do not want to debate here the merits of the old federal welfare program. But one point about the effects of cutting the program is uncontroversial. In cutting the program, the idea was that these mothers should go out and earn a living by holding a paid job rather than relying on government checks. Now, if these mothers go out and work, then somebody else has to take care of their children. These new child-care costs then become a major additional expense for these families because by definition, we are looking at poor single-parent households.

So, the costs of child care, as well as housing and transportation, have gone up relative to food, and this is not captured at all in the official measure of poverty. This problem is sufficiently serious that the National Research Council commissioned various distinguished researchers on this issue to come up with alternative measures of poverty. I will not go through all the work that was produced under this commission, but here is a simple summary of their results. The commission's report (Citro and Michael 1995) presented eight separate studies using different methodologies for coming up with alternative poverty measures. If we simply calculate the average of these eight alternative poverty lines, this average is 42 percent above the official poverty line. That is, according to the average of this research, the actual poverty line should be roughly 40 percent above the official line.

Another factor that is not taken into account at all in determining the official poverty line is regional differences in the cost of living. Regarding the case of the staff at Harvard, we need to consider the cost of living in the Boston area, which is about 25 percent above the national average.

So, we then bring together these two numbers: (1) that the poverty line should be about 40 percent above the official line and (2) that the cost of living in Boston is 25 percent above the national average. Adding these suggests that a true poverty-line minimum wage for Boston should be about 65 percent above the official poverty. But to be conservative, let us round this down and propose that a decent poverty line for Boston is about 60 percent above the federal poverty threshold.

How does that translate into establishing living wage standards? I bring some relevant numbers together in figure 2.3. Figure 2.3 first shows the $6.75 Massachusetts minimum wage as of 2005, a figure which is 31 percent higher than the 2005 federal minimum of $5.15. The figure then shows what the minimum wage would need to be to bring both a three- and a four-person family up to the Boston poverty line (i.e., 160 percent of the official line), assuming that one member of the family is working full-time all year (i.e., a total of 2,080 hours) for wages. As we see, the wages for 2005 are $11.97 and $15.35–roughly double the Massachusetts minimum wage of $6.75, to say nothing of the $5.15 federal minimum wage.

Figure 2.3. Alternative living wage standards for Boston area, 2005 (assuming full-time year-round employment; 2,080 hours)

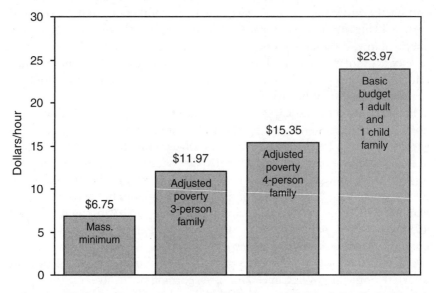

Sources: U.S. Census Bureau; Economic Policy Institute (2005) Basic Family Budget Calculator, http://www.epi.org/content.cfm/datazone_fambud_budget.

The last bar in figure 2.3, $23.97, is a representative number generated from the work of a group of researchers that developed out of the living wage movement. These researchers have been doing what they call Basic Budget Studies to establish the wage level necessary for a family to live above the poverty line but still at a very basic level. Here we see the lowest such figure that applies to the Boston area, generated by the Economic Policy Institute. This is the wage that applies to a family consisting of one adult and one child; this basic number is $51,540.

So, what is a living wage that would apply to workers at Harvard and throughout the Boston area? There is no way of defining this exactly, as our exercise shows. But a reasonable range is somewhere between the wage rates in figure 2.3—that is, between $12 and $24 (in 2005 dollars).

INTENDED VERSUS UNINTENDED CONSEQUENCES

Now let us get back to the issues associated with the second epigram from my earlier book with Stephanie Luce—whether the living wage can actually be workable. When opponents of the living wage discuss the issue, they do not generally debate what the exact living wage rate should be. One view they take is that *any* number given for a living wage is a bad number, that the very notion of the government intervening to establish a mandated minimum is against the precepts of free-market economics. Their view is that, rather than raising the minimum wage, we probably should just be getting rid of it altogether. Indeed, Alan Greenspan supported exactly this idea in congressional testimony in July 2001. Asked directly by Congressman Bernie Sanders whether he was "for abolishing the minimum wage," Greenspan answered, "I would say that if I had my choice, the answer is, of course."[6]

But this argument, that as a matter of principle all minimum wage mandates are bad, is actually not the most common position advanced by opponents. The much more frequent claim is that living wage laws are prone to creating negative unintended consequences—that living wage laws end up hurting the very low-wage workers they intend to help.

As I consulted in different cities on this issue, I heard this argument many, many times. The argument is often made most vehemently by business representatives, such as those from the Chamber of Commerce. In spinning out the unintended consequences scenarios, these representatives rarely, if ever, mention the fact that being able to pay workers lower wages might actually mean higher profits for the businesses they represent. Rather than acknowledging this obvious possibility, I frequently heard a sterile debate. Instead of acknowledging that they might have a bit of self-interest in preventing wages from rising due to a living wage law, these business representatives said repeatedly that a living wage law was going to be bad for workers. To this claim, the supporters of the living wage response was usually something like "You are just greedy capitalists and we know that, so we can't trust anything you say."

In fact, my position all along has been that, whatever the extent of deceptiveness by opponents of living wage laws, the arguments they make about potential negative unintended consequences are still quite serious. Indeed, the supporters of these measures need to take the oppositions' arguments more seriously than even the opponents themselves take them. So, what are the arguments of the opponents? There are basically three that come up all the time.

The first argument is that living wage standards are bad for the workers because they will create employment losses. We may succeed in raising wages through these measures, but we will also reduce the number of jobs that are available within the low-wage labor market. And even if the total number of jobs in this market does not fall, employers may still choose to hire better-qualified workers and lay off their existing low-wage employees because they are now being forced to pay higher wages. The second argument is that businesses are going to pick up and move out of the locations that have higher living wage standards and into places where workers can be hired for less money.

The third argument is that many entities that end up having to pay living wages are already doing lots of good things with their money. Paying workers living wages may not be the best use of their resources. Consider, for example, a city that is going to have to put lots of its budget into covering living wage raises. A significant part of such a city's budget may already be going to alleviate poverty. So, this city will have to take money out of its poverty alleviation budget and give raises to its low-wage workers. Moreover, perhaps a high proportion of these low-wage workers who get raises because of the living wage standard are teenagers from middle-income families who just want to buy iPods or fix up their cars.

There are variations on this third argument worth mentioning. I heard one at Harvard expressed by a well-known economics professor. If I may quote him from memory, he said something to the effect that:

> Of course we know we have a $19 billion endowment and we can afford to raise wages. But people didn't donate to Harvard to support the workers here. They gave money to Harvard to support education. If we take, say, $4 million out of our budget to cover wage increases, that may be a small fraction of our budget, much less our endowment, but it is still $4 million. It is lots of money that could be going to scholarships for poor children, or medical research or something equally important.

So, those are the three arguments. Again, even if opponents are making them only in a self-interested and cynical way, I think each and every one of them represents a serious challenge to supporters. Let us take them one by one.

First, employment losses. The argument here relies on a very simple theoretical premise. It is that when you raise the price of something, the demand for it will go down. Very simple. So, if you raise the price of low-wage workers, the demand for low-wage workers goes down. That argument is repeated over and over again. Now, is there anything wrong with that logic? There is nothing wrong with that logic as far as it goes, but the fact is it does not go quite far enough. There is one important detail here that is almost always neglected in textbook treatments and certainly in policy discussion. This is a *ceteris paribus*, or "all else equal," condition. That is to say, the theoretical premise is correct when everything else is held equal. So, if we increase the price of something, the demand will go down, if nothing else in the world changes at that time. But the fact is that things do change—living wage or minimum wage increases will take place when other things are also changing in the economy. It is also true that the living wage law will itself induce changes in the economy, including even the very workers showing up to perform the same jobs that they had before.

Let me give one example of this. In 1997, when the federal minimum wage was last increased, these arguments came up prominently, as always. But after the new minimum wage was put in place, there was a report in the *Wall Street Journal* of October 27, 1997. The story was titled "Chicken Feed: Minimum Wage Goes Up But a Fast-Food Chain Notices Little Impact." The story reports that "the minimum wage increase of 1996–1997 has turned into one of the non-events of 1997, thanks mostly to the economy's continuing strength" and "Low wage Americans, nearly 10 million of them, by some estimates, got a raise. But amid the current prosperity, hardly anybody noticed" (Wysocki 1997, A1).

Thus, when we consider other things that may change when the minimum wage changes, it is crucial to begin with the business cycle—that is, whether an economy is expanding or contracting when the minimum wage increase is implemented. When an economy is expanding, as the U.S. economy was in 1997, the demand for products is high. In such a situation, the relatively small changes in business costs generated by the higher minimum wage are manageable for firms. The businesses can absorb those costs because, on average, the demand for their products will be high. Reducing their number of employees would very likely entail scaling back their operations, at least in the short run, before they could replace workers with more machines. But businesses certainly will not want to scale back operations when demand for their products is high. In fact, the effects of business cycles on employment swamps the impact of minimum wage changes.

Readers may have noticed that I did slip in just now a crucial point without any back-up support, explanation, or even emphasis. It was that the cost increases for businesses from the minimum wage increase would be "relatively small." How do I know these cost increases will be relatively small? The entire tenor of the rest of my previous discussion would obviously have changed had I instead said that the cost increases were "burdensome," or even "large," or even if I had not mentioned anything about whether they were small or large. So the credibility of my whole discussion actually rests on my assertion that the cost increases are "relatively small."

The reason I know that the cost increases will be relatively small is that my coauthors and I have estimated these cost increases, over and over again. We have estimated them as they have applied to a wide range of city and state measures, and we have also used a variety of statistical sources and estimation techniques. In all cases, we have still found that the cost increases have been relatively small. This does not mean that costs increases would remain small no matter how high the living wage standard was pushed—for example, to $20–25 per hour. But within the range of increases we have studied—that is, from $6.15 in New Orleans and Florida up to $10.75 in Santa Monica, California—the cost increases have remained relatively small.

For example, in 2006 Jeannette Wicks-Lim and I considered the impact of a proposal for the state of Arizona to raise the statewide minimum from the $5.15 federal standard to $6.75 per hour, a 31 percent increase in the Arizona minimum wage. This proposal was supported with a 66 percent majority in November 2006 and became law in January 2007. We found that for the average business in Arizona, assuming this business kept all its employees and maintained its existing operations intact, the cost increase would be about 0.06 percent of their total sales.

Now, of course these cost increases will vary widely across the full range of industries, depending on how significant low-wage workers are as a proportion of the total operating budgets. For example, one industry in Arizona, as elsewhere, that has almost no low-wage workers as part of its operations is finance and insurance. The average finance and insurance company faced a cost increase of 0.02 percent relative to its total sales when the Arizona minimum wage rose from $5.15 to $6.75 per hour. By contrast, fast-food restaurants faced the largest cost increases because they rely so heavily on low-wage workers as a part of their overall operations. But even for fast-food restaurants, we estimated that the cost increases would be about 1.7 percent of sales. Even this highest industrywide cost increase is, thus, still within the range of "relatively small" increases.

What about a case in which the living wage increase is large? Here is the basic picture for Santa Fe, New Mexico, which raised its citywide minimum wage in 2004 from $5.15 to $8.50 per hour, a 65 percent increase. (Santa Fe raised its minimum again in 2006 to $9.50.) In this case, the average Santa Fe business experienced a cost increase of 1.1 percent relative to its sales. Restaurants, on average, saw their costs rise by 3.3 percent.

How can it be that, even with a minimum wage increase of 65 percent, as in Santa Fe, the average business would face a cost increase of only about 1 percent of its sales? There are two basic factors. The first is that for most firms, such as insurance companies, low-wage workers represent a small proportion of the firm's overall business operations, including their overall number of employees and their nonlabor operating costs. The second factor is that even most workers who receive raises when a new living wage standard becomes law are not themselves earning the rock-bottom minimum wage at the time the law is enacted. Thus, in Arizona, the average worker who would by law receive a raise to $6.75 was earning $6.00 per hour, not $5.15, before the measure was passed. The actual raise for this $6.00-per-hour worker was therefore 13 percent, not 31 percent. Even in Santa Fe in 2004, the average worker earning less than $8.50 was receiving $6.91 per hour, not $5.15. So the average increase was actually 23 percent, not 65 percent.

Now to return to my previous point. The reason the minimum wage increase in 1996–1997 amounted to no more than "chicken feed" according to the *Wall Street Journal* was that the effects of the business cycle expansion swamped the impact of the relatively small cost increases that even the fast-food chicken outlets faced—and now I can refer to the "relatively small" cost increases backed by evidence.

Moreover, the ups and downs of the business cycle are not the only other thing that can change. Two other factors that are likely to change along with the minimum wage increase, even if by a small amount, are the prices firms charge their customers and the productivity of their operations. Indeed, here we may expect to see modest price increases and/or productivity improvements precisely *because of* the minimum wage increase. Note that these changes are unlike the business cycle fluctuations, which occur independently of changes in the minimum wage.

With price increases, the situation is straightforward. If we consider Phoenix, Arizona, for example, our research told us that the average hardware store would have to raise its prices by no more than 0.1 percent to fully cover the cost increases they would face from the minimum wage rise to $6.75, assuming the same number of people continued to buy their products after they raised their prices by 0.1 percent. That is, the price of a hammer would rise from, say, $10.00 to $10.01. It seems likely that the same number of people would still buy hammers and would barely notice this tiny price increase. Even at McDonalds, the price of a Big Mac would rise by no more than 2 percent to fully cover the cost increases resulting from the $6.75 minimum wage. Would customers buy fewer Big Macs if the price rose from, say, $3.00 to $3.06, especially if all other fast-food restaurants also raised their prices by the same amount in the face of the minimum wage increase? The evidence tells us that customer demand is not likely to be affected by such small price increases, especially for discretionary purchases such as eating meals at restaurants.

With respect to productivity improvements, the crucial point here is that after a new living wage standard is implemented, businesses effectively get a new group of workers, even though the same individuals are showing up at the job. This is a very important point. Workers show up at work, but what they actually do when they get there is contingent on pay. When they are paid decently, they become better workers, and the productivity of the firm tends to improve.

We can talk about this in very technical terms, but one of the pieces of research my colleagues and I did early on was to just ask firms about this issue. We know that there are firms that pay higher wages than their competitors, and we simply asked these firms "How do you survive?"

In fact, when we did this in Los Angeles we went to a firm that was competing with a minimum wage firm that was actually getting massive subsidies from the City of Los Angeles—a very low-wage firm. The firm we spoke with was paying 30–40 percent above what the low-wage firm was paying its workers. We asked this high-wage firm how it could survive. The answer was "We survive through having higher morale among our workers." In specific terms, this meant that this firm had a low turnover of workers quitting their jobs, whereas the firm paying minimum wage had a very high turnover. The high-wage firm had almost no absenteeism and therefore had very low costs for administering, hiring, and training. So, that is another thing that changes when living wages go up—the "all else equal" condition does not hold.

I need to emphasize this point because, on several occasions, I have been accused of "repealing the law of demand" in arguing that creating a living wage standard need not induce employment losses. Again, I am not questioning the basic logic that when the price of something goes up the demand goes down, but I want to emphasize that it is an "all else equal" condition. That is a fundamental point. The people who neglect it are actually the ones being muddleheaded about the law of demand.

The second argument is that firms are going to move out of cities that implement living wage laws. When I first got involved in researching living wage proposals in 1996 in Los Angeles, I was told just this by the deputy mayor for economic development of Los Angeles. He was a sophisticated guy, with an MBA from the Wharton Business School at the University of Pennsylvania. He said that whole industries would move out Los Angeles if the living wage proposal passed. The proposal at the time was an increase in the minimum wage from the then federal standard of $4.25 per hour to $7.75 plus health benefits, but only for workers employed by businesses holding city contracts. I had to take the deputy mayor's claim seriously. It was certainly being taken seriously among policymakers and the press, as well as the business community.

My coworkers and I did lots of detailed calculations—lots of huffing and puffing—to get a solid estimate for this figure. The answer we came up with was that, for the average firm, the cost increase would be 1–1.5 percent of its total costs of doing business. These results included all the costs firms would experience through a living wage—including directly mandated wage increases and extra nonmandated wage increases, what we call "ripple effects." The ripple effect says if we raise the wage to $7.75, what happens to the workers who now are making $7.76 or $7.80 or $8? Are they also going to get a raise? The ripple effect assumes that they will also get raises, although smaller ones; there is no way to know how much of a raise they are going to get because, by definition, these raises are not mandated.

But we factored in this ripple effect. Our estimate of an average cost increase of 1–1.5 percent included all cost increases, including ripple effects and additional payroll taxes.

Based on that finding, we argued that most firms would not make any kind of big adjustments in their business operations due to such a small cost increase. They will rather make small adjustments. In fact, for the most part, they will absorb these cost increases themselves, especially if they are trying to win city contracts through competitive bidding. Contracts with city governments are desirable for the private businesses that bid on them. They are not going to walk away from the opportunity to win these contracts over a 1 percent cost increase.

Our conclusion on this point, which was a projection based on prospective research, has been borne out by subsequent retrospective research looking at what actually happened, as opposed to what we think is likely to happen. Would individual firms, much less whole industries, be motivated to move out of Los Angeles, due to this living wage measure? We concluded that the average firm would certainly not be moving. They might try to pass along their extra costs, but in a competitive bidding situation, they might not succeed. Again, these are desirable contracts. Firms are probably going to be willing to eat a 1 percent cost increase rather than lose the contracts.

Keep in mind that these cost increases are occurring in an economy in which productivity is rising, on average by 2–3 percent per year. This means that a one-time 1 percent increase in business costs can be absorbed by the average firm through 4–6 months of productivity growth. In other words, for a half year or so, the average firm's productivity increases all go to the low-wage workers who have not been getting raises for a generation.

But the next question is, fairly enough, "What about the nonaverage firm?" We found in Los Angeles that 86 percent of the firms would experience a cost increase of less than 1 percent. But some firms would experience significant increases, rising all the way up to nearly 30 percent. These firms are not going to eat a 30 percent cost increase. My position is very simple. The cost increases experienced by these firms need to be passed on, in the form of either higher prices for consumers or better terms for firms with city contracts, if the citizens of the community value what these firms do.

I have been faced with this question many times. I'd like to relate my experience in Rochester, New York. When I spoke there in 2000, the office staff from Catholic Family Services in Rochester came to the talk. The director of the agency raised a challenging question; she said, "We are all for the living wage in principle. But we can't afford to pay it. We would have to shut down our services. Give me an answer, so we can get out of this dilemma."

My first response to her was to ask, "What is your rate of turnover?" She said her turnover rate was 60 percent. So my response was, "One thing that is going to happen is that you will lower your turnover and will therefore save on administration costs." I did not claim that that the cost savings would fully cover the wage increase at Catholic Family Services, which was going to be 20–30 percent of the overall operating budget. I just said to expect some significant savings.

But she did not give up. So she then asked, "Fine. But what about the rest of it?" Here my response was, "If you have city contracts and let's say your overall cost is going to go up by 20 percent, then if the citizens of Rochester want this living wage standard to be implemented, they will have to pay for it. They will have to absorb the rest of the costs through higher taxes. It's as simple as that."

In Los Angeles, we found that no more than about 0.5 percent of all firms would have very large cost increases, on the order of 20–30 percent, like Catholic Family Services in Rochester. But if the community valued the services provided by these firms, just as the people of Rochester valued what Catholic Family Services does for their community, then most of the increased costs would just have to be absorbed through tax revenues. For example, there is a program in Los Angeles called Meals on Wheels, which delivers meals to mostly older, poor people who are homebound. I was told in Los Angeles that "We are going to have to cut out Meals on Wheels." I said, "No you don't. If the people of Los Angeles want both Meals on Wheels and living wages, then they will have to pay for both of them. There is no big trick here."

Again, generally speaking, the necessary adjustments for businesses will be small. But they are not nothing, and there is no magic trick that enables the adjustments to vanish. Yet if we believe in the living wage as a principle, we have to make those adjustments. Returning to 1968 for a minute, when the federal minimum wage was roughly $9 per hour (in today's dollars), the economy operated so that the lowest paid worker at McDonalds could make this $9 per hour minimum wage. The economy actually functioned quite well then. Unemployment was 3.6 percent and productivity growth was high.

Having considered all these points, the one issue I have not really touched on is how a living wage standard will affect workers themselves. I think we can assume that it is always going to be better for workers and their families when they earn a decent wage, so I did not think it was necessary to dwell on that point. But I would like to close by reading a story that was in the *Los Angeles Times* after the living wage law was implemented in Los Angeles in 1997. The story begins:

> Let the academics, politicians and labor leaders debate the definition of the living wage. For airport janitor Jose Morales, it means two concrete things—a bed and a car. Two years ago Morales was sleeping on flattened cardboard boxes in a Compton garage. Every morning before dawn he stumbled to the

corner bus stop for the start of a two hour commute to his job at Los Angeles International Airport. Twice on that corner he was mugged. Without health insurance he considered himself particularly lucky to escape unhurt. Now Morales stretches out at night on a soft double bed, with his commute time cut in half by driving. He can sleep until 5:00. He no longer feels vulnerable to pre-dawn assaults, and if he was to be hurt, his medical expenses would be covered by insurance. What has made the difference is a 1997 Living Wage Ordinance that boosted pay for the Los Angeles janitor and some 2,000 other bottom-rung workers in Los Angeles by nearly $2 an hour. Now, in exchange for 8 hours of sweeping, dusting and dumping trash, the 36-year-old immigrant earns $59 a day plus health benefits. Still far from princely, it is a 36% raise over his old pay and enough to qualify for what Morales calls a "salario digno." "Everyone thinks that working here at the airport we must earn a lot of money," says Morales, chatting in a closet size room where he and 45 other Terminal 2 janitors pick up mops and change into navy blue uniforms. "It is not true, but at least now with the living wage we can hold our heads up high."(Cleeland 1999)

3   Debating Living Wage Laws
Paul Krugman versus Robert Pollin

The first part of this chapter is Paul Krugman's book review of *The Living Wage: Building a Fair Economy* by Robert Pollin and Stephanie Luce, which appeared in *Washington Monthly* in September 1998. Robert Pollin's response follows, an excerpted version of which appeared in the November 1998 *Washington Monthly*.

PAUL KRUGMAN'S REVIEW: "MORAL ECONOMICS: WHAT THE CAMPAIGN FOR A LIVING WAGE IS ALL ABOUT"

Economics textbooks enthuse about virtues of a price system. In a market economy, nobody needs to order people to economize on a scarce commodity or make extra efforts to produce it: Scarcity leads to a high price, and sheer self-interest does the rest. Conversely, nobody needs special persuasion to take advantage of an underemployed resource: Abundance will make it cheap, and again self-interest will take it from there.

And yet there is a problem with markets: They are absolutely and relentlessly amoral. Labor, in a market system, is just another commodity; the wage a man or woman can command has nothing to do with how much he or she needs to make to support a family or to feel part of the broader society. Some conservatives have managed to convince themselves that this poses no moral dilemma, that whatever is, is just. And one supposes that there are still unrepentant socialists who believe that one can do away with market determination of incomes altogether. But after a century marked by both the Great Depression—which basically ended unalloyed faith in markets—and the fall of communism, most people support some version of the welfare state: a system that is based on markets, but in which the government tries to prevent too unequal a distribution of income.

But how is that to be accomplished? The standard economist's solution, which is also the main way the U.S. welfare state operates, involves "after-market" intervention: Let the markets rip, but then use progressive taxes and redistributive transfers to make the end result fairer. However, many liberals have always felt that this solution is unsatisfactory. Instead, they want to increase "market" wages, notably through support of collective bargaining, and through the imposition of minimum wage standards.

The "living wage" movement, which has attracted considerable support in several major U.S. cities, is a variant on this tradition. As described in Robert Pollin and Stephanie Luce's new book *The Living Wage*, it essentially involves putting a floor on wages not through a conventional minimum wage law, but by requiring minimum wage standards of firms that do business with a local government. Aside from novel enforcement issues (I know this lawyer who will explain to you about creating dummy companies for the contract work, leaving the rest of the business unregulated), this is basically a distinction without a difference: The living wage movement is simply a move to raise minimum wages through local action.

So what are the effects of increasing minimum wages? Any Econ 101 student can tell you the answer: The higher wage reduces the quantity of labor demanded, and hence leads to unemployment. This theoretical prediction has, however, been hard to confirm with actual data. Indeed, much-cited studies by two well-regarded labor economists, David Card and Alan Krueger, find that where there have been more or less controlled experiments, for example when New Jersey raised minimum wages but Pennsylvania did not, the effects of the increase on employment have been negligible or even positive. Exactly what to make of this result is a source of great dispute. Card and Krueger offered some complex theoretical rationales, but most of their colleagues are unconvinced; the centrist view is probably that minimum wages "do," in fact, reduce employment, but that the effects are small and swamped by other forces.

What is remarkable, however, is how this rather iffy result has been seized upon by some liberals as a rationale for making large minimum wage increases a core component of the liberal agenda—for arguing that living wages "can play an important role in reversing the 25-year decline in wages experienced by most working people in America" (as this book's back cover has it). Clearly these advocates very much want to believe that the price of labor—unlike that of gasoline, or Manhattan apartments—can be set based on considerations of justice, not supply and demand, without unpleasant side effects. This will to believe is obvious in this book: The authors not only take the Card-Krueger results as gospel, but advance a number of other arguments that just do not hold up under examination.

For example, the authors argue at length that because only a fraction of the work force in the firms affected by living wage proposals will be affected, total costs will be increased by only 1 or 2 percent—and that as a result, not only will there be no significant reduction in employment, but the extra cost will be absorbed out of profits rather than passed on in higher prices. This latter claim is wishful thinking of the first order: Since when do we think that cost increases are not passed on to customers if they are small enough? And the idea that employment "of the affected workers" will not suffer because the affected wages are only a small part of costs is a non sequitur at best. Imagine that a new local law required supermarkets to sell milk at, say, 25 cents a gallon. The loss in revenue would be only a small fraction of each supermarket's total sales—but do you really think that milk would be just as available as before?

They also argue that because there are cases in which companies paying above-market wages reap offsetting gains in the form of lower turnover and greater worker loyalty, raising minimum wages will lead to similar gains. The obvious economist's reply is, if paying higher wages is such a good idea, why aren't companies doing it voluntarily? But in any case there is a fundamental flaw in the argument: Surely the benefits of low turnover and high morale in your work force come not from paying a high wage, but from paying a high wage "compared with other companies"—and that is precisely what mandating an increase in the minimum wage for all companies cannot accomplish. What makes this an odd oversight is that the book contains a lengthy and rather well-done critique of attempts by local governments to create jobs through investment incentives, arguing that they mainly end up in a zero-sum poaching war; how could the authors have failed to notice the parallel?

But while there is much that is silly in their book, Pollin and Luce are diligent and honest—and as a result the book carries lessons and implications they may not have intended. The most interesting section is their estimates of the impact of living-wage proposals on the budgets of hypothetical families— estimates that perhaps give us the clue to what all this is really about.

Consider, for example, the effects of "Plan Y" (never mind) on the hypothetical head of a household, currently making $5.43 per hour. According to their estimates, as long as he or she remained fully employed, the living wage law would raise earned income from $10,860 to $14,500—and also mandate $2,500 in health coverage. (This is, incidentally, a 57 percent increase in the cost to employers; you have to have a lot of faith in Card-Krueger not to worry that some jobs might be lost.) According to their numbers, that family would currently pay less than $900 in taxes while receiving some $9,700 in benefits such as food stamps, Earned Income Tax Credit, and health care. Their calculations also show that most of the gains from the living wage proposal would be offset by reductions in these other redistributive programs. Indeed, only about one-fifth of the mandated increase in wages and benefits actually gets manifested in disposable income; the rest is taken away as benefits decline.

Now to me, at least, the obvious question is, why take this route? Why increase the cost of labor to employers so sharply, which—Card/Krueger notwithstanding—must pose a significant risk of pricing some workers out of the market, in order to give those workers so little extra income? Why not give them the money directly, say, via an increase in the tax credit?

One answer is political: What a shift from income supports to living wage legislation does is to move the costs of income redistribution off-budget. And this may be a smart move if you believe that America should do more for its working poor, but that if it comes down to spending money on-budget it won't. Indeed, this is a popular view among economists who favor national minimum wage increases: They will admit to their colleagues that such increases are not the best way to help the poor, but argue that it is the only politically feasible option.

But I suspect there is another, deeper issue here—namely, that even without political constraints, advocates of a living wage would not be satisfied with any plan that relies on after-market redistribution. They don't want people to "have" a decent income, they want them to "earn" it, not be dependent on demeaning handouts. Indeed, Pollin and Luce proudly display their estimates of the increase in the share of disposable income that is earned, not granted.

In short, what the living wage is really about is not living standards, or even economics, but morality. Its advocates are basically opposed to the idea that wages are a market price—determined by supply and demand, the same as the price of apples or coal. And it is for that reason, rather than the practical details, that the broader political movement of which the demand for a living wage is the leading edge is ultimately doomed to failure: For the amorality of the market economy is part of its essence, and cannot be legislated away.

RESPONSE TO KRUGMAN BY ROBERT POLLIN

In his review (September 1998) of *The Living Wage: Building A Fair Economy*, my new book with Stephanie Luce, Paul Krugman seeks to discredit the arguments we make on behalf of living wage legislation. There is much at stake here. Some form of living wage legislation has been passed in 20 cities over the past 4 years, and is now being considered in another 50 or so municipalities. The living wage movement thus represents the most widespread grassroots effort at reversing the sharp 25-year decline in minimum wages, to a level today, $5.15 per hour, that is fully 30 percent below its peak of $7.37 (in 1997 dollars) in 1968. But Krugman claims that our book contains "much that is silly" and, more generally, the living wage movement is "doomed to fail" because neither we authors nor the broad living wage movement can get our economics right. In fact, Krugman's review demonstrates the opposite of what he intends. If we allow that Krugman's arguments represent the strongest case that living wage opponents can muster, then living wage supporters can move forward in confidence that economic logic—if not always political power—is on their side.

Will city government budgets necessarily bear the full cost of wage and benefit increases due to living wage legislation?

Our research showed that most firms holding municipal government contracts, and thus falling under the terms of a living wage ordinance, would face a negligible increase in their total costs (on the order of one percent) once they comply with the living wage laws. We therefore argued that most affected firms could readily absorb these small costs rather than passing them on to city budgets through winning more expensive contracts. This is a crucial point because it implies, for example, that workers in Los Angeles could get a total of $50 million in annual wage increases but that the city's budget need increase by only a small fraction of that total.

Krugman, however, calls this "wishful thinking of the highest order," stating that firms will always pass along their added costs to customers, even when they are small. Of course firms will *try* to pass on these costs. But whether they succeed will depend on the competitive environment in which they operate. If firms are bidding competitively for city contracts, city governments need not cave in to business demands for better contract terms to cover their living wage costs. The firms can either absorb a 1 percent cost increase to win a city contract or relinquish the contract to a competitor. It is notable that in both Baltimore and Los Angeles, studies show that the passage of the living wage ordinance has had no significant impact on post–living wage contract bidding patterns.

Will living wage ordinances, like all minimum wage laws, only produce unemployment among low-wage worker?

Krugman rehashes what he terms the standard Econ 101 argument that when you raise the price of anything (like low-wage labor), demand must fall (businesses hire fewer low-wage workers). But even Krugman acknowledges, if only as an aside, the qualifying feature of this law, which is that it holds only when *all else is assumed constant*. In fact, in the real world, all else is rarely constant. As one important factor, the impact on jobs of fluctuations in the demand for goods and services produced in the region will overwhelm any effect stemming from a municipal living wage law. As we argue in the book, when demand for goods and services is strong, unemployment will be low among low-wage workers, regardless of whether cities have municipal living wage laws. By the same token, jobs will dry up when demand for products is falling, as during a recession, regardless of whether a city has passed a municipal living wage law.

But what if, holding overall demand for jobs constant, businesses decide to replace the low-wage workers they have with other workers they deem are more qualified for the higher pay? Even under such a *worst-case* scenario, there would be no net loss of job opportunities, since the laid off workers could still fill the jobs opened up by the workers who took their living wage jobs. This certainly would hold under the living wage laws we are examining, where, for better or worse, these laws affect only a tiny fraction of the available low-wage jobs. In Los Angeles County, for example, the living wage law will bring raises to 7–10,000 workers at most, while there are 2.4 million people earning less than the $7.25 living wage minimum.

Firms will not experience productivity-enhancing gains in morale through paying living wages, since all firms will be paying these wages.

Krugman makes this argument against us, but his reasoning is haphazard. First, Krugman misses the fact noted above that the living wage ordinances now on the books will affect only a small pocket of firms. Workers in these firms will indeed enjoy privileged conditions. Even by Krugman's logic, therefore, the raises these workers receive will create incentives for them to raise their productivity through, for example, reducing turnover and absenteeism.

But there is a more fundamental point. Krugman is claiming that workers respond positively to being treated well on the job only if they think they are being treated *better* than workers at other job sites. There may be an element of truth to this, but only to the extent that one accepts, with Krugman, a narrow, ego-centric view of what motivates people at work. Do workers respond positively to genuine acts of respect and solidarity—like paying decent wages and benefits and maintaining a healthy workplace—on their own terms, or do they dismiss such acts as long as their perception is that other workers at other jobs are also treated in the same favorable manner? Research to date cannot provide a definitive answer. At best then, Krugman is badly overreaching, especially given that, in any case, living wage workers *are* relatively better off than their counterparts at other firms.

Why not let the market rip, allowing income disparities to arise where they may, but then alleviate these disparities through government transfer payments?

In making such an argument, Krugman dismisses the distinction we draw between a dollar of income earned by a working person and a dollar received through a government program to support the poor. What came through clearly in the protracted debate in the United States over welfare reform was that, given the choice, the vast majority of people in this country would much prefer to work for a decent wage than to receive government transfer payments. Krugman would deny people their preference, since, in his view, the market could not rip with sufficient force when a living wage is legally mandated. But taxing market winners to cover transfer payments to market losers also distorts market outcomes. Krugman never explains why interfering with the market through government transfers is, overall, more just and efficient than allowing people to earn a living wage. In this context, we must keep in mind how, in the absence of a living wage minimum, government transfers to the poor benefit businesses. They do so because they allow businesses to pay sub-poverty wages while shifting on to the public the costs of alleviating the hardships of even those families that include full-time workers.

Krugman concludes, "The amorality of the market economy is part of its essence, and cannot be legislated away."

Economists from Adam Smith onward have recognized that market economies—dominated as they are by greed and competition—can survive over a sustained period of time only if they are buttressed by social institutions that also support our inclinations toward solidarity and reciprocity (Russia today being a good example of how well market economies perform absent such institutions). If we really took Krugman seriously here, his logic would mean not only abolishing municipal living wage ordinances but to similarly eliminate minimum wage, child labor, and even slave labor laws. What are these if not a series of attempts—successful in fact, as far as they have gone—at "legislating away" the market's inherent amorality? True, Krugman's logic would still provide government transfer payments to the losers in these amoral market situations. This means, for example, that slaves could still be guaranteed adequate sustenance through food stamps, if not from their owners.

When the national minimum wage was at its peak of $7.37 in 1968, it had become a reasonably effective vehicle for eliminating poverty among people who worked full-time while trying to raise a family. It is unfortunate that, over the past generation, the country has abandoned this achievement even though our economy is now 50 percent more productive than in 1968, and that economists such as Krugman so loosely invoke "economic laws" to justify our dramatic steps backward.

Part 2

IMPACTS ON BUSINESS

D o living wage laws, and related minimum wage initiatives, really benefit the people they are intended to help? The answer to this question is not obvious. Many people find this surprising and even disconcerting, given the strong moral resonance associated with the idea of living wages. The main reason the answer is not obvious is that, before we can say anything about how much workers will benefit from getting raises, we first need to know how businesses are likely to react to the labor-cost increases that these laws impose on them.

As I discuss in chapter 1, the issue comes down to whether businesses will respond to the cost increases by laying off workers, hiring fewer workers in the future, substituting workers with better credentials for their existing low-wage workforce, or perhaps even relocating away from areas that operate with living wage laws. Opponents of living wage laws have consistently claimed that this is exactly how businesses will respond. To the extent that the opponents are correct, the implication is that living wage measures will be ineffective at delivering gains to low-wage workers and their families—the intended beneficiaries of these measures—no matter how benign the intentions of living wage supporters.

The logic behind the opponents' view is straightforward. Living wage laws do impose cost increases on businesses, and the businesses will of course need to respond to the new economic landscape that living wage laws create. However, what the opponents do not generally consider is equally straightforward: whether businesses choose to lay off workers or relocate will depend on how large are the cost increases they will face and, in light of these cost increases, what other options businesses can reasonably pursue to absorb their increased costs.

Given the centrality of these questions, the starting point of our research has always been to estimate as carefully as possible the cost increases that living wage laws will impose on businesses. Once we have established what these cost increases are likely to be, our second step has been to consider the various ways that businesses could possibly respond to the new costs that they will face. Layoffs and relocations are indeed two possible options for business, but there may also be less costly and difficult adjustment paths for businesses. These other options include raising prices slightly to cover the new costs; improving productivity, again, by a small amount; or accepting a small profit reduction.

In this part, we present two of the many separate research studies that we have conducted to estimate business-cost increases resulting from living wage laws. Based on these estimates, we are then able to proceed with informed judgments as to how businesses are likely to adjust to these measures. Chapter 4 is from our work on the New Orleans minimum wage proposal in 1999, and chapter 5 focuses on the Santa Fe living wage ordinance in 2004. We also present evidence in this part on the benefits for business of higher minimum wages, including those derived from the increased buying power of residents of poor neighborhoods after they have received wage increases. We address this topic initially in chapter 4 on New Orleans, and then again somewhat more fully in chapter 6, which considers spending injections from minimum wage increases for the entire state of Arizona.

There are important similarities and differences between the New Orleans and Santa Fe studies that form the core of this part, both in terms of the histories of the two initiatives and with respect to our research work around these measures.

To begin with, both were initiatives aimed at creating wage floors above the federal minimum that would apply throughout an entire city. They were, in other words, two of the early area-wide measures, as opposed to the much more narrowly targeted contractor-only laws that remain prevalent as municipality-level mandates.

Both measures were also strongly endorsed, by the voters themselves in New Orleans with a 63 percent majority in February 2002 and by a seven-to-one vote by the City Council of Santa Fe, after an all-night public hearing on February 27, 2003. After being passed, both measures were then challenged in the courts by opponents. And in both legal cases, I served as the expert witness on the economic issues in behalf of the ordinances when the issues were under consideration at the trial-court levels. In both cases, my oral testimony was based on the written research work from which the next two chapters are excerpted, prepared for New Orleans with Stephanie Luce and Mark Brenner and for Santa Fe with Mark Brenner.

What were the differences between the two initiatives? To begin with, the New Orleans law was far less ambitious. It proposed a 19 percent increase in the citywide minimum wage, to $6.15 per hour. This figure would then be automatically adjusted so that it would remain $1.00 above the federal minimum wage, which was $5.15 per hour when the measure was proposed in 1999 (and remained at that level until July 2007). The Santa Fe measure proposed an initial 65 percent increase from the same $5.15 per hour federal minimum wage, to $8.50 per hour, starting in 2004. Subsequent increases, to $9.50 per hour in 2006 and then to $10.50 in 2008 were then built into this measure, although these were to be implemented only after the city council had examined the evidence as to how the preceding mandated increases had affected the city's job market.

In terms of the history of the two measures, the most important difference is in terms of their respective final outcomes. After having been endorsed by Judge Rosemary Ledet at the district court level in March 2002, the New Orleans law was subsequently overturned by the Louisiana Supreme Court in September of that year. The court ruled that the Louisiana State Legislature, not the voters or any other legal entity in the City of New Orleans, should be the final arbiters as to whether the city could establish a minimum wage standard above the federal or state level. As the final legal authority here, the Louisiana State Legislature, as opposed to the overwhelming majority of voters in New Orleans itself, held that the federal $5.15 per hour minimum wage was sufficiently high for the city's low-wage workers and their families.

In Santa Fe, the measure was upheld both in the district court in a decision by Judge Daniel Sanchez in June 2004 and then again by the New Mexico Court of Appeals in November 2005. The Santa Fe measure became law immediately after the June 2004 district court ruling, beginning with the $8.50 first-step minimum wage increase. The city then proceeded on schedule with the second-step raise to $9.50 in January 2006. This was done after a study conducted by the Bureau of Business and Economic Research Center at the University of New Mexico found that there had been no adverse impact on Santa Fe's job market while operating with the $8.50 minimum.

The University of New Mexico researchers' conclusions were not universally endorsed. In particular, Aaron Yelowitz of the University of Kentucky, in a 2005 paper released by the Employment Policies Institute, found that the unemployment rate for the city's least-educated workers rose dramatically in the first year under the $8.50 minimum wage standard. We review the relevant data and Yelowitz's econometric model in detail in chapter 13.

But the basic evidence is straightforward. In the 14-month period, from June 2004 to July 2005, after the $8.50 minimum wage was implemented in Santa Fe, overall employment in the city grew by 2.0 percent, a rate that was exactly equal to the employment growth rate for New Mexico overall, even though Santa Fe was the only area in the state operating with a minimum wage standard above the $5.15 federal minimum. Even more significant, employment growth for the leisure and hospitality industry in Santa Fe—primarily restaurants and hotels, the two industries that were most heavily impacted by the $8.50 minimum—was 3.2 percent. This is an employment growth rate substantially *faster* than either the rest of Santa Fe or New Mexico overall, despite the fact that, during precisely this time period, Santa Fe's restaurants and hotels were grappling with all their initial adjustments resulting from the $8.50 minimum wage.

In terms of our research on these two measures, there were important differences in the methodologies we employed to estimate the cost burdens that businesses would face. For the New Orleans study, our findings derive from our own extensive survey of New Orleans businesses themselves, led by Stephanie Luce. In this survey, we received responses from 444 firms in New Orleans, that, at the time, employed 68,751 workers, amounting to 23.4 percent of the city's entire labor force. Based on what the businesses themselves told us in this survey, we concluded that the average business in New Orleans would face cost increases of 0.9 percent of their overall operating costs. This figure included mandated wage increases, ripple effects, and increased payroll taxes. As always, the industries facing the largest cost increases were restaurants and hotels. From our survey data, we estimated cost increases relative to overall operating budgets of 2.2 and 1.7 percent, respectively, for the city's restaurants and hotels. We present these findings in detail in chapter 4.

In the Santa Fe case, we were not able to conduct our own business survey. We relied instead on publicly available data to derive the comparable cost estimates. In this case, we found that the representative (i.e., median) firm in Santa Fe would face a total cost increase equal to about 1.0 percent of its sales. For restaurants and hotels, we estimated a cost increase/sales ratio of about 3.3 percent.

In short, in comparing the New Orleans and Santa Fe studies, we generated basically the same findings in terms of this absolutely central piece of evidence—that is, how burdensome for businesses are the cost increases likely to be from the new minimum wage mandates in the two cities? We derived these similar findings despite the fact that we had used different research approaches in the two cases and despite the differences in the characteristics of the two cities and the measures being proposed in both places. Overall, the fact that our cost estimates in the two cities were so similar strongly supports the conclusion that our empirical findings are grounded in robust estimating methods.

As we discuss in chapter 5, we received further strong support for our research methods and findings in the course of conducting our Santa Fe study. The most important corroboration was with respect to our finding derived from publicly available data that restaurants and hotels would experience cost increases in the range of 3.3 percent of their sales. In the course of our research for the Santa Fe trial, we had access to the actual payroll and sales data of the four restaurants that were the plaintiffs in the case against the city. As we show in chapter 5, from these plaintiffs' own data, we derived an average cost increase from the $8.50 minimum wage that averaged 2.9 percent of these firms' sales. That is, our estimate from publicly available industry-wide data of a 3.3 percent cost increase/sales ratio was within 0.4 percentage points of the average figure that we obtained from the plaintiffs' own business records.

There is one final issue that we must mention with respect to the New Orleans case, in light of the subsequent calamity experienced by the city's poor residents in the aftermath of Hurricane Katrina, which struck the region in September 2005. The question we wish to raise is this: if the $6.15 minimum wage had become law in New Orleans, in line with the wishes of the overwhelming majority of the city's voters as opposed to the Louisiana State Legislature and Supreme Court, would the impact of Katrina have been less severe for the city's poor residents? In our full study for the New Orleans measure, we estimated that the annual gain in net income for low-wage workers and their families—that is, after taking account of changes in taxes and subsidies such as food stamps and the Earned Income Tax Credit—would have been about 4 percent. For a working mother and one child, this would mean a roughly $600 increase in net income, from about $13,300 to $13,900. This additional $600 per year would easily have allowed a single mother to make payments on a decent used car. It could have also allowed this small family to buy bus tickets from New Orleans to Baton Rouge, where they would have been out of Katrina's range, and to stay in a modest Baton Rouge hotel for a couple of weeks after the storm hit.[1] But, of course, in reality these options were not available to the poor working families in New Orleans because of the decision by Louisiana's Supreme Court to overrule the wishes of the overwhelming majority of city residents.

—R. P.

4   A $6.15 Minimum Wage for New Orleans

What It Would Have Meant for Businesses

ROBERT POLLIN, MARK BRENNER,
AND STEPHANIE LUCE

In February 2002, the citizens of New Orleans, Louisiana, endorsed with a 63 percent majority a ballot initiative that proposed to raise the minimum wage within the city to $1.00 above the federal minimum wage. The proposal means that all workers in New Orleans, with the exception of those in job categories that are explicitly exempted from the law, would have to be paid at least $6.15 per hour, 19.4 percent above the current national minimum wage of $5.15. The New Orleans law would also mean that workers within the city would get raises each time the federal minimum increased in order for New Orleans workers to maintain its $1.00 increment above the federal minimum.

In terms of its specifics, the New Orleans proposal is a hybrid between the municipal and statewide measures. This is because it is a municipal ordinance, but, corresponding to the various statewide measures, it covers all workers within the municipality, not only those employed by city contractors. The primary intended consequence of the proposal is straightforward: to raise living standards for as many as possible of the more than 40 percent of all households in the New Orleans area that are poor or near-poor. At most, however, the proposal is likely to reach no more than about half of the area's low-income households because only half of these households include members with jobs.

Among those who did have jobs in New Orleans and were paid below $6.15 at the time of our survey, the average hourly wage was $5.50. This means that the average hourly raise for such workers would be 65 cents, which amounts to an annual increase of about $1,100, given that, on average, low-wage workers in New Orleans were employed approximately 1,700 hours per year. For poor families in New Orleans that include employed workers, a $1,100 annual raise would produce a modest but still significant improvement in their living standard. We estimate that the pretax family income of such families would increase by roughly 12 percent. After allowing for changes in taxes as well as eligibility for food stamps and the Earned Income Tax Credit, the net gain for poor families would be between 3 and 4.5 percent.

But a crucial premise underlies these calculations as to the likely benefits of the proposal: that workers now employed in low-wage jobs in New Orleans will retain these same jobs after the minimum wage ordinance is implemented. Contrary to this premise, economists have long recognized that minimum wage mandates and similar labor market interventions can generate negative unintended consequences. Employment loss for low-wage workers is the unintended consequence that has been most widely recognized and debated in association with minimum wage proposals generally. But in the case of a municipal ordinance such as that proposed for New Orleans, an equally serious potential unintended consequence is businesses relocating out of the city to avoid the higher minimum wage requirements.

How significant are these negative unintended consequences of the New Orleans proposal likely to be? As a simple matter of accounting, it is clear that layoffs or business relocations are not the only possible ways New Orleans businesses could respond to an increased municipal minimum wage. Depending on their cost structures and production processes, firms could also absorb the increased costs through three other means: (1) raising prices; (2) raising productivity; and (3) redistributing income within the firm, either through wage compression or a fall in profit shares. The advantage of these three other adjustment mechanisms is that, within a reasonable range of small adjustments, firms could implement them more quickly and at a lower cost than either layoffs or relocations.[1] Beyond these various adjustment mechanisms, it is also likely that some New Orleans firms could benefit through an expenditure multiplier when the incomes of low-wage workers and their families rise by 3–4.5 percent due to the ordinance.

Our paper is an effort to establish what are the most likely effects of the New Orleans proposal. The cornerstone of this study is an extensive survey we conducted in 1999 of New Orleans businesses as to their employment levels, labor costs, and total operating budgets. There were approximately 12,700 business firms in New Orleans overall as of 1999, employing about 293,330 workers during our survey period of January–March 1999. In our survey, we received full responses from 444 firms that, together, employ 68,751 workers, amounting to 23.4 percent of the entire labor force of New Orleans. We generated estimates for the full city from these survey responses using standard statistical methodologies. Details on our survey methodology, data sources, and calculations are presented in Pollin, Brenner, and Luce (2002, app. 1).

In the next section of this chapter, we report the main results of our survey of New Orleans businesses. In the third section, we draw on these results and other data sources to consider the extent to which firms are likely to absorb these costs through some mix of the five possible responses—price and productivity increases, redistribution within the firm, layoffs, and relocations. In the fourth section, we then consider how large an expenditure multiplier is likely to result from this measure.

ESTIMATE OF COVERED WORKERS AND FIRMS

Mandated Effects

Of the 293,330 workers in the city, we estimate that 77,175 people, amounting to 26.3 percent of the total work force, earn below $6.15 per hour. However, 19,008 people were paid below the national minimum of $5.15 at the time of our survey, either through an exemption or noncompliance with the law. We assume these workers would not receive the higher municipal minimum wage.[2] In addition, we estimate that there are 11,117 public-sector workers in New Orleans presently earning $5.15–6.14, amounting to nearly 20 percent of the city's workforce within that pay scale. These workers would not be covered by the minimum wage proposal in its present form, which obviously limits the scope of the law considerably. The New Orleans proposal would, however, provide coverage for workers who receive part of their income in tips. The current federal minimum wage sets a minimum of $2.13 for people earning at least $30 per month in tips; the New Orleans proposal would raise the minimum for tipped workers to $3.08. Thus, excluding public-sector workers and including tipped workers earning below $3.08 among the covered segment of the New Orleans labor market, we arrive at our estimate that a total of 47,050 workers would be covered by the ordinance.

In table 4.1, we present figures as to the number of firms and workers covered as well as our estimates of the labor cost increases that would result from the minimum wage proposal. As the table shows, of the 47,050 total workers that would be covered by the law, 25,477 (54.1 percent) are full-time workers, 20,341 (43.2 percent) are part-timers, and 1,232 (2.6 percent) are tipped workers earning $2.13–3.08.

The average wage at present for the workers earning $5.15–6.14 is $5.50, so the average hourly increase would be 65 cents. On average, these workers are not full-time; they work 32.7 hours per week. Assuming these workers

Table 4.1. Wage increases and costs to New Orleans firms after raise to $6.15 minimum wage

Number of firms covered	12,682
Number of workers covered	
Full-time	25,477
Part-time	20,341
Tipped workers	1,232
Total	47,050
Mandated wage increases	
Wage-only workers	
Average hourly wage before ordinance	$5.50
Average yearly wage increase	$1,063
(65 cent hourly increase×32.7 hours/week×50 weeks/year)	
Tipped workers	
Average hourly wage before ordinance	$2.39
Average yearly wage increase	$804
(69 cent hourly increase×23.3 hours/week×50 weeks/year)	
Total mandated wage increase *(including 7.65% payroll tax)*	$53.5 million
Ripple-effect increases	
Total workers receiving ripple-effect raises	27,314
Total ripple-effect cost increases	$17.9 million
Total mandated and ripple-effect cost increases	$71.4 million
Cost increases relative to total operating budgets	
Mandated costs as percentage of operating budgets	0.7%
Total costs as percentage of operating budgets	0.9%

Sources: PERI New Orleans Employment and Wages Survey, 1999; Current Population Survey Outgoing Rotation Group 1997 files, Bureau of Labor Statistics, U.S. Department of Labor.

are employed 50 weeks per year, that means that they will get an annual raise of $1,063.[3] For tipped workers, the average hourly wage is presently $2.39, so the average wage increase would be 69 cents. These workers are employed an average of 23.3 hours per week. If we again assume they are working 50 weeks per year, this would bring their annual wage increase to $804. Adding these figures together, the total wage increase due to the minimum wage ordinance would be $49.7 million. In addition, the payroll tax that covered businesses will have to pay is 7.65 percent of this wage increase, or $4.4 million. This brings the total mandated costs for all 12,682 firms to $53.5 million, or $4,218 per firm.

Ripple Effects

Ripple effects are those wage increases that employers give to employees beyond what is legally mandated. Employers give such ripple-effect increases to maintain some measure of pay hierarchy between the lowest-paid workers receiving the mandated increase and those earning somewhat above the new minimum. For this New Orleans proposal, there are four categories of likely recipients of such wage increases: (1) employees who, prior to passage of the New Orleans law, were earning $5.15–6.15 and who receive wage increases that put them above $6.15; (2) employees earning more than $6.15 who, nevertheless, receive a raise when the minimum wage policy becomes law; 3) tipped workers earning above $2.13 but below $3.08 who receive a raise that will put them above $3.08; and 4) tipped workers earning above $3.08 but below $5.15. Recent research on the ripple effects arising from increases in federal and state minimum wages has consistently found these effects to be relatively weak. For example, we examined the combined state and federal minimum wage increase in California from $4.25 to $5.75 in 1996–1998, a 35 percent increase in the statewide minimum (Pollin and Brenner 2000). We found that workers earning between $4.25 and $4.99 in October 1995 (i.e., those within 75 cents of the minimum wage) received a median nominal wage increase of 51 percent by September 1998. The increase by September 1998 for those earning $5.00–5.75 in October 1995 was 25 percent less than that for the minimum wage category. Those earning $5.75–7.24 in September 1995 received wage increases roughly one-third that for the minimum wage category. These results are in line with other studies of the same California experience (Reich and Hall 2000) and similar experiences in other states (summarized in Card and Krueger 1995).

Because the ripple-effect raises are nonmandated, any estimate of their size is inherently more speculative than the figures we have calculated for the mandated increases to $6.15. Nevertheless, the basic ripple-effect patterns described in the literature provide guidance for calculating a rough approximation. Our approach to generating this approximation is to construct a sliding scale of wage increases for workers currently earning up to $7.14 per hour (i.e., $1.00 over the New Orleans mandated increase). The scale begins with a fifty-cent band between the current $5.15 minimum wage and $5.64. On average, those workers earned $5.33 in 1999, so raising them all to the $6.15 minimum wage will mean an average raise of 16 percent.

Based on this 16 percent raise for the lowest-paid wages-only workers, we then assumed a sliding scale of wage increases for workers in three other wage categories. We assumed wage increases of 8 percent for workers currently earning between $5.65 and 6.14; 4 percent for those earning $6.15–6.64; and, finally, 2 percent for those earning $6.65–7.14. As we show in table 4.1, these effects would cover 27,314 workers, a full 58 percent of the 47,050 who receive mandated raises. We calculate that the total set of ripple-effect labor cost increases will be $17.9 million, including 7.65 percent in payroll taxes on $16.6 million in wage increases.

Minimum Wage Costs Relative to Firms' Total Operating Costs

As table 4.1 shows, adding up mandated and ripple-effect costs brings our estimate of total costs to $71.4 million, or, on average, $5,630 for the 12,682 firms. Even more pertinent are the total minimum wage cost figures relative to the firms' overall operating costs. As we report at the bottom of table 4.1, the direct mandated costs of the minimum wage ordinance will amount, on average, to 0.7 percent of the covered firms' operating costs. If we add our estimated ripple-effect wage increases, this brings the average total costs of the minimum wage ordinance to 0.9 percent of firms' operating costs.[4]

This overall cost ratio is a crucial first benchmark for evaluating the impact of the ordinance on New Orleans firms. Clearly, however, we need to examine not just an average for cost impacts but the cost effects on different types of firms. We therefore now consider cost ratio figures according to firm size and industry.

Distinctions by Size

Table 4.2 shows our estimates of minimum wage cost/operating budget ratios by firm size. The clear pattern here is that the largest impact will be on medium-size firms (i.e., firms with 50–499 employees). For these firms, the minimum wage costs will entail roughly a 1 percent increase in their operating budgets. Smaller firms will be affected to a much lesser extent. For firms employing between 1 and 24 workers, the minimum wage bill will amount to 0.5 percent of their operating budget. The ratios are only slightly higher for firms that employ up to forty-nine workers. With the largest firms, employing more than five hundred workers, the ratio falls back to 0.5 percent. A widespread perception exists that changes in minimum wage laws have the greatest impact on the costs of small businesses. Our results in table 4.2 show that, at least in New Orleans, this is not the case.

Table 4.2. Impact of New Orleans minimum wage ordinance by firm size

Firm size	Total minimum wage costs relative to total operating costs
1–9 employees	0.5%
10–24 employees	0.5%
25–49 employees	0.6%
50–149 employees	1.0%
150–499 employees	0.9%
500+employees	0.5%

Source: PERI New Orleans Employment and Wages Survey, 1999.

These results for small businesses help explain the findings of a 1998 nationwide survey conducted at the Jerome Levy Economics Institute on the attitudes of small business owners to increases in the minimum wage (Levin-Waldman 1999).[5] The survey found that a large majority of small businesses did not make significant adjustments due to the 1997 national minimum wage increase and would not anticipate doing so if the national minimum wage went to $6.00 per hour. More specifically, only 6.6 percent of all small businesses changed their hiring or employment practices at all after the 1997 increase. Of these, only 10.8 percent indicated that they had laid off workers—in other words, a total of only 0.7 percent of small businesses in the sample laid off workers due to the 1997 minimum wage increase. This absence of any significant adjustments by small businesses in their employment practices after the 1997 minimum wage increase is certainly consistent with our New Orleans survey figures showing that small businesses would be affected by a less than disproportionate degree by the minimum wage measure.

Distinctions between Industries

Table 4.3 presents data on minimum wage costs relative to operating budgets based on two-digit Standard Industrial Classification (SIC) groupings. The table lists the industrial groups according to the minimum wage cost/operating budget ratio, starting with the industries with the highest ratios. In columns 3 and 4, the table then presents information on the size of the industry within the New Orleans economy. We measure industry size according to two dimensions: its share of total output and total employment. The table reports data only on industries in which either total output or employment exceeds 1 percent of the New Orleans total.

As table 4.3 shows, only the eating and drinking industry—restaurants, cafés, and bars—would experience a cost increase greater than 2 percent of its operating budget, and even here, the cost increase is just above 2 percent. The hotel industry would be the next most heavily affected, with cost increases at 1.7 percent of operating budgets. These two industries are responsible for about 6 percent of all production in New Orleans and almost 10 percent of all employment. Beyond these, three additional industries— business services, food stores, and wholesale trade—would face a cost increase greater than 1 percent of operating budgets. Together, these three industries account for another 8.2 percent of production and 11.4 percent of employment in New Orleans. Taking account of all the rest of businesses in New Orleans, our results show that industries accounting for 86 percent of production and 79 percent of employment in New Orleans would face cost increases of less than 1 percent due to the minimum wage ordinance.

Table 4.3. Impact of New Orleans minimum wage ordinance by industry

(1) Industry category	(2) Total minimum wage costs relative to total operating costs	(3) Share of total New Orleans output	(4) Share of total New Orleans employment
Eating and drinking	2.2%	2.8%	6.0%
Hotels and other lodging	1.7%	2.9%	3.9%
Business services	1.5%	2.6%	5.3%
Food stores	1.5%	0.9%	2.5%
Wholesale trade	1.5%	4.7%	3.6%
Personal services	0.9%	0.5%	1.4%
Other retail trade	0.8%	6.4%	14.4%
Educational services	0.8%	3.0%	5.6%
Transportation	0.7%	14.9%	7.4%
Manufacturing	0.5%	8.7%	3.8%
Health services	0.5%	6.2%	7.5%
Finance, insurance, and real estate	0.5%	12.3%	5.5%
Other services	0.4%	7.3%	11.0%
Construction	0.2%	4.4%	4.2%
Legal services	0.1%	3.7%	3.2%
Mining	0.0%	11.0%	2.8%

Sources: PERI New Orleans Employment and Wage Survey, 1999; IMPLAN Pro Software package, 1996; ES-202 data for Orleans County, Bureau of Labor Statistics, U.S. Department of Labor.

ALTERNATIVE ADJUSTMENT RESPONSES TO INCREASED LABOR COSTS

As we have said, New Orleans firms will respond to the cost increases imposed by the minimum wage ordinance through some combination of (1) raising prices, (2) raising productivity, (3) redistribution within the firm, (4) layoffs, and (5) relocations. At least initially, some combination of the price, productivity, and distributional adjustments is likely to be the primary channel through which New Orleans firms adjust to the ordinance because they can be accomplished more readily and at lower costs than either laying off workers or relocating. Once we have assessed how significant these adjustment processes are likely to be, we will then be in a better position to evaluate concerns about layoffs or business relocations stemming from the ordinance.

Price Effects

The adjustment process that would be least costly and disruptive for firms is to simply raise prices to reflect their increased costs. But whether firms can succeed in such a strategy depends on the competitive environment in which they operate and the price elasticity of demand for their products.

As part of their path-breaking work on minimum wages, Card and Krueger (1995) conclude after observing a variety of situations that price increases are a primary means through which firms absorb their increased costs resulting from a higher minimum wage. Indeed they conclude that the New Jersey fast-food outlets were able to raise their prices by about the same amount as their increased total costs, which amounted to about 3.4 percent. This conclusion is especially notable for our purposes because the average cost increase/operating budget ratio for the four fast-food restaurants in our New Orleans survey was 3.9 percent—thus corresponding closely to the price mark-ups observed by Card and Krueger for New Jersey.

But these results are based primarily on how increases in either a statewide or national minimum wage will affect fast-food restaurant prices only. How well can these results be generalized to the range of businesses in New Orleans that would be covered by a municipal minimum wage ordinance? Of course, all firms operating in New Orleans will face the same new minimum wage laws. But firms that compete with other firms in New Orleans will likely be better able to raise their prices because their competitors will have experienced similar mandatory cost increases. Businesses that compete in markets that extend beyond New Orleans will correspondingly have more difficulty marking up their prices.

In table 4.4, we categorize industries in New Orleans according to whether they compete primarily either with firms outside New Orleans, with firms inside New Orleans, or with some combination of competitors both inside and outside the city. The central issue in dividing up the industries is whether a major element of what a business sells in product markets is its location within New Orleans proper.[6] We discuss these divisions next, with detailed considerations relating to the hotel industry and food stores. The data presented for each industry are simply the same minimum wage/operating budget ratios reported in table 4.3.

Industries Competing outside New Orleans

These competing with firms outside New Orleans are going to be at a disadvantage relative to their competitors outside New Orleans because they alone will face an increase in their labor costs. Thus, if everything else remained equal in their industry, New Orleans firms would not be able to pass along their cost increases by raising their prices without risking a loss of their customer base to their out-of-town competitors. However, the cost increases faced by these industries are negligible, as we see in table 4.4—0.5 percent for manufacturing, 0.1 percent for legal services, and effectively no cost increase for mining. As such, we can assume that these firms will have to make

Table 4.4. Competitive environment for New Orleans industries

Industry and market environment	Minimum wage costs/ operating budgets
Competing outside city	
Manufacturing	0.5%
Legal services	0.1%
Mining	0.0%
Competing within city	
Eating and drinking	2.2%
Hotel and other lodging	1.7%
Personal services	0.9%
Transportation	0.7%
Construction	0.2%
Competing inside and outside city	
Business services	1.5%
Food stores	1.5%
Wholesale trade	1.5%
Other retail trade	0.8%
Educational services	0.8%
Finance, insurance, and real estate	0.5%
Health services	0.5%
Other services	0.4%

Source: PERI New Orleans Employment and Wages Survey, 1999.

essentially no adjustments in their prices and should therefore face no competitive disadvantage due to a New Orleans minimum wage ordinance.

Industries Competing within New Orleans

For firms competing mainly within New Orleans, it is likely that the situation will approximate that analyzed by Card and Krueger and others for the fast-food industry. That is, these firms should be able to raise their prices to reflect their higher costs, since all the firms in the market face similar cost increases. As shown in table 4.4, we have assigned five industries to this category—the eating and drinking industry, facing a 2.2 percent cost increase; hotels, with a 1.7 percent cost increase; and the personal services, transportation, and construction industries, all with cost increases below 1 percent. These numbers indicate that the hotel and restaurant industries would need to mark up their prices by about 2 percent to cover their additional costs, whereas personal service and perhaps transportation firms would seek price increases in the range of 1 percent. Given that the size of all these price mark-ups are still small, they are not likely to have a substantial impact on the demand for these firms' products, through, for example,

New Orleans residents eating in restaurants less frequently or visitors to the city staying with friends in private homes rather than hotels.

Some data on segmentation in the hotel industry in the New Orleans area will be useful in illustrating this point. We draw here on industry data compiled by HRG & Torto Wheaton Research (hereafter HRG) that distinguishes three distinct submarkets in the New Orleans area.[7] We compare two of these—the Central City submarket and the Metairie/Airport submarket. The Central City submarket consists of "hotels located in the Central Business District of downtown west of Iberville Street. Also included in this submarket are hotels near the Convention Center and in the Garden District." The second submarket, the Metairie/Airport submarket, consists of hotels located west of New Orleans along the Interstate 10 corridor. These hotels are outside of the city proper and therefore would not be covered by the minimum wage ordinance.[8]

The distinction between these two market segments are sharp. On average, for the full-service market, prices were 97.2 percent higher in the Central City hotels and the revenue per available room (i.e., the total revenues received by the hotel divided by the total number of its available rooms, including both vacant and occupied rooms) was 47 percent higher. For the limited-service hotels, prices and revenues were both slightly more than 50 percent higher in the Central City submarket.[9] It is clear, in other words, that hotel customers pay a very high premium for staying in the Central City area relative to the Metairie area. This suggests that the differences between the two markets would not change in any significant way if the Central City hotels raised their prices by 1–2 percent to cover their additional labor costs resulting from the minimum wage ordinance. Such a cost increase would mean that, for the full-service hotels, those in the Central City would now be about 98–99 percent, rather than 97 percent, more expensive than those in Metairie. For the limited-service hotels, the differential would rise to 53–54 percent rather than 52 percent.

In short, this evidence on prices and revenues per available room for New Orleans hotels supports the idea that a price increase for hotel rooms on the order of 1–2 percent for the Central City area should not have a significant influence on the competitiveness of these hotels in the regional hotel market. This in turn suggests that, at least for this one case of the hotel industry in New Orleans, small price increases are one viable means through which firms can adjust to the cost increases resulting from the minimum wage ordinance.[10]

Industries Competing Both Inside and Outside New Orleans

Industries competing with firms both inside and outside New Orleans are very heterogeneous, as, indeed, are many of the firm types within each industry category. For example, business services includes both advertising and building-maintenance firms; wholesale trade includes both durable and nondurable goods. For some of these businesses, such as janitorial firms or fresh-food wholesalers, proximity to their customers is important. As such, the main competitors for these firms are likely to be within New Orleans. By contrast, neither advertising firms nor wholesalers selling durable goods would be likely to face only local competitors. Given these differences, it is difficult to generalize as to how industries and firms in this category would react to a citywide minimum wage increase. Still, of the eight industries listed in this category in table 4.4, only three—business services, food stores, and wholesale trade—have minimum wage cost/operating budget ratios greater than 0.8 percent. Let us therefore consider these three industries in more detail.

BUSINESS SERVICES AND WHOLESALE TRADE The firms in both of these categories, such as nondurable goods or building maintenance, that compete in local markets should be able to mark up their prices without significantly affecting their customer base, as with the other industries operating in the local market. The more difficult problems emerge with the businesses facing competitors outside New Orleans, such as advertising firms or durable goods distributors. For these firms, much, if not all of the average 1.5 percent cost increase may well be difficult to pass along to customers. For these firms, the other adjustment mechanisms should be especially important.

FOOD STORES Food stores in New Orleans, as in other large cities, operate in very different markets, depending on whether they are located in poor or nonpoor neighborhoods. In nonpoor neighborhoods, the customers of these stores typically have cars and thus the ability to drive outside the city to avoid paying higher food prices. For stores operating in these markets in New Orleans, these stores may have some difficulty in maintaining their marked-up prices.

However, counteracting this factor is that, in most middle-class neighborhoods, price is rarely the sole determining factor around which food-shopping decisions are made. Convenience and quality are at least equally important factors in attracting middle-class food shoppers.[11] Heavily discounted food stores already exist on the outskirts of all major metropolitan areas. These discount stores have not driven customers away from the higher-quality but more expensive stores. Overall then, stores in these neighborhoods probably will be able to pass on to customers some share of their higher costs. They will then absorb the rest of their higher costs through some combination of the other adjustment mechanisms.

The situation will be different for food stores in poor neighborhoods. This is because customers in poor neighborhoods are not generally able to travel significant distances to find cheaper food prices. We therefore expect that, everything else equal, food stores in poor neighborhoods will be able to mark up their prices by an amount roughly comparable to the 1.5 percent increase in costs.[12]

This then raises other issues: How much would a 1.5 percent increase in food prices in poor neighborhoods affect the living standards of the poor? Would such an increase in food prices constitute another unintended consequence of a minimum wage policy? The answers depend, first of all, on what percentage of a family's food budget is covered by food stamps. If we assume that food stamps completely cover a family's food budget—regardless of any fluctuations in the market price of food—then the increase in food prices would have no effect on the family's standard of living.

But, in fact, food stamps will not cover a family's entire food budget. Probably about 70 percent of eligible families in Louisiana make use of the food stamp program.[13] For those that do use the program, coverage varies according to a family's needs. As a rough average, food stamps probably cover 50 percent of a poor family's food budget. If we also accept the official government estimate that spending on food constitutes about one-third of a poor family's overall budget, this implies that a 1.5 percent increase in food prices would mean an increase in the cost of living for poor people of between 0.25 (for those receiving food stamps) and 0.5 percent (those without food stamps).[14] How serious this problem would be depends, in turn, on whether the poor family includes a working member. For the roughly 50 percent of poor families in New Orleans that do include a working member, a 0.25–0.5 percent increase in living costs would be counterbalanced by the roughly 3–4 percent increase in disposable family income due to the minimum wage increase. Thus, even after allowing for a full mark-up of food prices commensurate with the minimum wage increases, and with no additional support through food stamps, the net effect of the minimum wage raise would still bring roughly a 3 percent average increase in disposable income.

That will not be the case for most of the poor families in which no member is employed, that is, depending on the threshold we choose, for about 50–60 percent of the poor households in New Orleans. If they also do not receive food stamps, they will face a 0.25–0.5 percent increase in their living costs that will not be counterbalanced by an increase in family income. Such families would be hurt by the minimum wage increase, although by only a small amount, if nothing else changes in their lives.

Productivity

New Orleans firms would probably experience at least modest increases in productivity through efficiency wage effects—increased worker effort;

lower turnover and absenteeism; and, following these, lower costs of recruitment, training, and supervision. The citywide minimum wage pay raise should encourage these effects through two channels; both the *absolute* pay raise itself, and the increase in pay *relative* to uncovered workers employed outside the city limits, should encourage increased job commitment.

This is likely to be especially important for the hotel and restaurant industries, which, as we have seen, would experience the highest relative cost increases through the New Orleans proposal. Research measuring turnover rates and the costs of turnover is limited. But the evidence available does strongly suggest that turnover rates are generally quite high in both industries, albeit with wide variations between firms. Our own employer survey of hotels and restaurants in Santa Monica, California, found that average turnover rates for both hotels and restaurants were in the range of 50 percent per year. The average costs of replacing workers ranged between about $500 and $700. Previous industry studies are broadly consistent with our finding that turnover costs are significant (e.g., Fernsten and Croffoot 1986; Worcester 1999). This is not to suggest that the efficiency wage gains are likely to match the covered firms' increased costs. However, the fact that, for most firms, these cost increases relative to total operating budgets themselves will be small suggests that the efficiency wage gains could absorb some significant fraction of the cost increases.

Redistribution

As we have mentioned, minimum wage increases could induce two types of downward redistribution: wage compression between lower and higher-paid workers, and a reduction in the profit share. We have already built into our overall estimates a considerable degree of wage compression through assuming a weak ripple effect. Any decline in the profit share will, of course, be resisted by business owners. But the extent of their resistance will be tempered by firms' capacity for productivity growth, since productivity growth allows for a rising absolute level of profit even when the profit share is declining. That is, productivity growth means that the firms' total income pie is capable of growing larger. When the income pie does grow larger, then business owners can retain a larger total amount of income even if their proportional slice of the income pie is smaller.

Consider, for example, the situation for the average firm in New Orleans, for which the minimum wage cost increase/operating budget ratio is roughly 1 percent. It is reasonable to assume that the average firm is also likely to improve its productivity each year by at least 1 percent, without even taking into account possible efficiency-wage-induced productivity gains. In this situation, the 1 percent productivity gain would mean that low-wage workers could get their raise, and all other operating costs could be covered equally, without anyone else at the firm experiencing a cut in the real level of their wages or profits. Of course, the benefits from the year's worth of productivity growth would accrue entirely to the low-wage workers. But by the same token, all gains from productivity growth in subsequent years could revert back to higher-paid workers and owners while low-wage workers would still be receiving the higher mandated minimum rate.

In fact, some variation on this scenario does appear to actually happen, as research shows that, in the initial period after a higher minimum wage is implemented, wage gaps do tend to return to their previous level (summarized in Spriggs and Klein 1994). Overall, then, because the average increase in firms' operating costs due to the New Orleans minimum wage ordinance would be only 1 percent, it is not hard to envision scenarios in which a redistribution of the firms' income could realistically cover a significant share of the wage gains for low-wage workers.

Employment Effects

The proposed increase in the New Orleans minimum wage relative to the national minimum, at 19.4 percent, is virtually identical to the 18.8 percent increase in New Jersey's statewide minimum in 1992. It is therefore reasonable to draw from studies of the New Jersey experience (most recently, Card and Krueger 2000; Neumark and Wascher 2000) that there is likely to be little, if any, employment losses in New Orleans resulting from the proposed citywide minimum wage increase. Indeed, if anything, we would expect the impact of the New Orleans increase to be significantly less than that observed by those studying New Jersey. This is because both of these studies examined fast-food restaurants only. For the fast-food industry in New Orleans, our survey results suggest that the minimum wage cost increase/operating budget ratio is just below 4 percent—about four times higher than the average ratio for all New Orleans firms.

The other possible effect on employment policies would be through labor substitution—firms replacing their existing minimum wage employees with workers having better credentials, something that could occur even in the absence of any net job losses. Because the jobs in New Orleans would pay higher than comparable positions outside the city limits, openings for the covered New Orleans jobs would probably attract workers with somewhat better credentials, on average, than those in the existing labor pool. In order to roughly gauge how extensive such labor substitution is likely to be, we first consider in table 4.5 the differences in personal characteristics for two groups of wage workers—those earning $5.15–5.64 and those earning $6.15–6.64

Table 4.5. Personal characteristics of low-wage workers in five Southern states, 1999

	Hourly wage categories (1999 dollars)		Difference between two wage categories
	(1) $5.15–5.64	(2) $6.15–6.54	(3) (column 2 – column 1)
Less than high school diploma	46.0%	30.2%	−15.8%
High school diploma or GED	31.5%	38.0%	+6.5%
Some college	20.7%	25.2%	+4.5%
Bachelor's degree or more	1.9%	6.6%	+4.7%
Under 20 years of age	32.2%	13.4%	−18.8%
Average age (years)	30.6	33.9	+3.3
Female	65.5%	61.5%	−4.0%
English as second language	13.9%	20.8%	+6.9%

Source: Current Population Survey Outgoing Rotation Group 1999 files, Bureau of Labor Statistics, U.S. Department of Labor.

Note: In addition to Louisiana, the southern states in the sample are Alabama, Arkansas, Georgia, and Texas.

in 1999. Our sample is drawn from a pooled sample of five southern states in the Current Population Survey, since both the New Orleans and Louisiana samples are themselves too small to provide reliable results.

It is important to emphasize that these data are useful only in establishing an extreme outer limit as to the likely degree of labor substitution. This is because, in considering these data, we are effectively asking: If covered New Orleans firms were newly hiring their entire low-wage work force and if they were advertising their job openings at a wage rate in the range of $6.15 rather than $5.15, how would the profile of the newly hired workers change?

As we see from table 4.5, the number of those without high school diplomas falls by 15.8 percentage points when we move from the $5.15 to the $6.15 wage category. Correspondingly, the number of those with high school diplomas, some college, and college degrees each rises by between 4.5 and 6.5 percentage points. Not surprisingly, the number of teenagers falls by 18.8 percentage points when we move from the lower- to the higher-wage category. The $6.15 wage category has fewer females but, surprisingly, more nonnative English speakers.

Having thus defined the outer limit of labor substitution effects through these data, the next step here is to recognize why any actual labor substitution effects are likely to be far more modest. This is first of all because, in reality, businesses are unlikely to newly hire their entire workforce after a higher municipal minimum wage is enacted, nor would they want to do so. Rather, as we have discussed, workers earning the higher minimum will be less inclined to leave their jobs, and their work effort should correspondingly rise. By the same token, businesses are not likely to terminate their existing workers, even if they have relatively poor formal credentials, as long as their performance is satisfactory. This is especially true because for virtually all jobs covered in the minimum wage range the qualities that distinguish one worker from another will not be based primarily on formal qualifications. More effective workers are, rather, those who simply exert more effort, and this employers can discern only through observation.

Recognizing these various factors, we would still expect some substitution to occur, both by educational credentials and age, although, again, the magnitude of such substitutions is likely to be modest.

Business Relocations

As we have seen, the cost increase due to the minimum wage ordinance for the average firm in New Orleans would be 0.9 percent of its operating budgets. It is reasonable to assume that for firms whose cost increase ratio is around this average or lower, the incentive to relocate would be weak. But even for many firms whose operating budget increases are somewhat larger, it would still not follow that relocation is a viable option. For example, as we have seen, restaurants and hotels are the two business types that would face the highest proportional cost increases, at 2.2 and 1.7 percent, respectively, of their operating budgets. But the customer base for these businesses is location-specific. This is why, for such firms, some combination of price mark-ups, productivity increases, and income share redistributions are far more efficient adjustment mechanisms than relocation.

Which firm types might have a stronger incentive to relocate? They would have two basic characteristics: their customer base would not be specifically tied to New Orleans, and they would face a significant increase in their operating costs through a rise in the city's minimum wage. To help identify how many such firms are in New Orleans, in table 4.6, we provide a distribution of all 12,682 private-sector firms according to their minimum wage cost/operating budget ratios. As we see, 26.5 percent of firms employ no low-wage workers. Another 71.8 percent, which do employ low-wage workers, average a cost increase of 0.7 percent of their operating budget. That leaves 209 firms, 1.7 percent of the total, that would have increased cost ratios of over 5 percent, the average cost increase ratio for these firms being 6.6 percent. Let us allow that all the firms with cost ratios of 5 percent or above would at least seriously consider relocating to avoid the increased

Table 4.6. New Orleans firms grouped by minimum wage cost/operating budget increases

Wage increase/ operating budget	Number of firms	Percentage of firms	Average increase in minimum wage cost/operating budget
0 percent	3,294	26.5%	0.0%
0–4.9 percent	8,936	71.8%	0.7%
5–9.9 percent	209	1.7%	6.6%
Industry profile of firms with cost ratios greater than 5 percent			
Industry	Number of firms	Percentage of firms	Average increase in minimum wage cost/operating budget
Other services	61	29.3%	5.1%
Wholesale trade	55	26.4%	8.8%
Other retail trade	47	22.5%	5.2%
Business services	46	21.8%	7.3%

Source: PERI New Orleans Employment and Wages Survey, 1999.

minimum wage costs. But whether such a move would be viable for any given firm depends on the nature of its business. As we see in the lower panel of table 4.6, these 209 firms are distributed fairly evenly across four industry categories, these being other services, wholesale trade, business services, and retail trade other than restaurants and hotels.

Of these, it should be most feasible for the wholesale trade firms to relocate, because their business is not tied to a specific location. At the same time, if proximity to customers is important to these firms, moving could then threaten their customer base. Moving would also add to their transportation costs. Retail businesses could move, but they may then risk losing customers whose purchasing habits are at least partially tied to convenience. Some business service firms, such as advertising agencies, could move without losing customers. But those with a high concentration of low-wage workers, such as security guard companies, would have to pay the higher minimum wage to workers whose jobs were located within New Orleans, regardless of where the firm's offices were located. In such cases, firms cannot avoid paying the higher New Orleans minimum wage by relocating. Finally, the category other services obviously encompasses a broad spectrum of firms, including those engaged in services such as repair shops, movie theaters, and parking lots. Here as well, some firms may be mobile, but others are not.

As an exercise, let us allow that 100 of the 209 firms whose minimum wage cost/operating budget ratios are 5 percent or above will actually relocate out of New Orleans. What would be the impact on the city and state's economy if these firms did depart?

First, we are assuming that these firms would leave New Orleans strictly to avoid paying the higher minimum wage. As such, we would expect that these firms would move just outside the city limits, so as to retain, if from a different specific location within the metropolitan area, their New Orleans–based operations and customer base. One crucial implication of this point is that no net employment losses would occur due to these firms' relocation. Workers would be able to retain their jobs without moving, which in turn would mean no change in the city's housing market.

The primary loss to the New Orleans economy would therefore be the loss of the city's authority to tax these firms. This authority basically amounts to a 5 percent sales and use tax. But because we are assuming that firms would move just outside the city limits, the state of Louisiana would not lose its 4 percent sales/use tax revenue. According to our rough estimates, the total loss of tax revenue to the city of New Orleans would be about $2 million if the one hundred firms did relocate.[15] This is a large absolute cost, and it may somewhat underestimate the total costs to the city of relocation because we have not attempted to incorporate any calculation as to how the departure of one hundred firms might also affect the business prospects of their neighboring firms. At the same time, to put this figure in perspective, it is equal to 0.4 percent of the city's $499.1 million approved budget for 1999.

BENEFITS TO BUSINESS: MULTIPLIER EFFECTS

The minimum wage ordinance in New Orleans will not produce only costs to businesses. It will also produce benefits via multiplier effects as low-income households spend their additional 3–4.5 percent of disposable income. At the same time, this multiplier effect is not equivalent to one induced by the federal government implementing expansionary macroeconomic policies, in which the injection of additional purchasing power results from increased federal borrowing or a fall in interest rates. For this case and similar measures, the increase in purchasing power for low-income households comes via a redistribution of income—primarily away from consumers in the city, when they pay slightly higher prices for some of their purchases, but also away from business owners and more highly paid employees, who would receive a somewhat smaller share of the overall income flowing to business firms to accommodate the minimum wage increases.

As such, the multiplier effects for the New Orleans measure would result primarily from changes in spending patterns within the city, even though spending overall in the city will not significantly change. In particular, retail firms that operate in lower-income neighborhoods in New Orleans should enjoy an increase in their business. Correspondingly, retail firms in the more affluent neighborhoods might experience a slight decrease in the growth of spending.[16] But precisely because so much more money is spent in the affluent neighborhoods, this slight decline in the growth of spending will not be noticed.

How significant will be the spending increase in the lower-income neighborhoods? We provide details on our estimation method in Pollin, Brenner, and Luce (2002, app. 2). Our major results are as follows.

Working from the overall figure for workers who would get either mandated or ripple-effect raises through the proposed ordinance, we have estimated the number of these workers who live in the lower-income neighborhoods in New Orleans.[17] These neighborhoods are in the Uptown, Midtown, and eastern Downtown sections of the city. They include, among others, the Central City/Magnolia area and the St. Thomas, Iberville, and Fischer projects. Overall, the populations in these neighborhoods make up 33.6 percent of the total population of New Orleans.

According to our estimates, about 40 percent of the workers getting minimum wage increases live in these neighborhoods. Overall, they would bring about $20 million in extra disposable income into their neighborhoods.[18] Of course, they would not spend all $20 million in the neighborhoods in which they live. According to our estimates, the amount they do spend would bring about an additional 2.7 percent in sales, on average, to the retail businesses in these neighborhoods.

Such a boost in sales for neighborhood retail businesses is a small but still significant benefit. It is an amount larger than the average growth rate of national Gross Domestic Product or the Louisiana Gross State Product for 1990–1999. That means that, with a 2.7 percent increase in sales, the retail businesses in lower-income neighborhoods would effectively jump more than 1 year ahead of a normal pace of sales growth. We finally note that this benefit to the retail stores might also reduce the pressure these businesses face to raise product prices commensurate with their minimum wage costs. This effect, in turn, could serve to diminish the small welfare losses of poor families that do not include employed workers, which we identified earlier—that is, the fact that these families will have to purchase food at slightly higher prices while not being able to offset these higher prices with the minimum wage increase.

CONCLUSION

Our results suggest that the New Orleans firms should be able to absorb most, if not all, of the increased costs of the proposed minimum wage ordinance through some combination of price and productivity increases or redistribution within the firm. This result flows most basically from the main finding of our survey research—that minimum wage cost increases will amount to about 0.9 percent of operating budgets for average firms in New Orleans and no more than 2.2 percent of operating budgets for the city's restaurant industry, which is the industry with the highest average cost increase. This also suggests that the incentive for covered firms to lay off low-wage employees or relocate outside the New Orleans city limits should be correspondingly weak. It is likely, however, that some displacement of the least-well-credentialed workers will occur as a result of the ordinance, although, again, this effect should also be relatively modest. Similarly, a relatively small number of New Orleans firms will likely relocate, generating a loss of municipal tax revenues on the order of 0.5 percent of the city's budget. Generally, however, the process through which New Orleans firms adjust to the minimum wage ordinance is likely to be relatively mild since the overall $71 million burden in increased wages and payroll taxes will be broadly diffused among the city's 12,700 firms as well as the city government.

5 The Santa Fe Citywide Living Wage Measure

The Impact on Business of the $8.50 Standard

ROBERT POLLIN AND MARK BRENNER

The Santa Fe City Council adopted its living wage ordinance in March 2003. The main provisions of the Santa Fe ordinance are as follows:

- *Wage level:* $8.50 starting January 1, 2004; $9.50 starting January 1, 2006; $10.50 starting January 1, 2008.
- *Employment threshold:* Twenty-five employees or more, on a head-count basis, evaluated every month.
- *Exemptions:* Excludes nonprofits whose primary source of funds is from Medicaid waivers.
- *Wage calculation:* "In computing the wage paid for purposes of determining compliance with the minimum wage, the value of health benefits and childcare shall be considered as an element of wages."[1]
- *Tip credit:* Unlimited tip and commission credit for employees customarily receiving $100 or more monthly in tips.
- *City service contractors:* Covers service contractors with twenty-five employees or more and $30,000 in contracts.
- *City employees:* Covers full-time permanent city employees.
- *Subsidy recipients:* Covers subsidies and economic development assistance of $25,000 or more.

In this assessment, we concentrate our attention on the effects of the initial establishment of a Santa Fe living wage mandate at $8.50 per hour. A more appropriate time to evaluate the likely effects of raising the living wage further, to $9.50 and $10.50, will be after the local economy has had some experience with the provision at the initial $8.50 minimum. (See chap. 13 for an evaluation of the first-year effects of the $8.50 measure on employment in Santa Fe.)

The next section of this chapter briefly reviews data sources and our statistical techniques. In the third section, we assess the costs of the ordinance for the covered businesses, including mandated wage increases, nonmandated ripple-effect wage increases, and local-supplier cost pass-throughs. The fourth section evaluates the likely ways that businesses will adjust to their increased costs. In terms of the adjustment mechanisms for businesses, we devote primary attention to the possibilities of covered businesses passing through their increased costs in the form of higher prices to consumers. We also consider the likelihood that turnover costs will fall after businesses give raises to their lowest-paid workers.

STATISTICAL METHODS AND SOURCES

There are two basic data sources for this study. The primary source is data collected and made publicly available by the U.S. federal government. In addition, we had access to the actual payroll data from the four business firms that brought their lawsuit against the city of Santa Fe. Combining information from these two distinct sources provided a unique range of perspectives on the questions we are addressing.[2]

It will be useful to highlight here some of the major issues in our use of these government data sources and in our statistical estimates.

1. *Year of estimation.* The evidence we provide in this study reflects as best we can conditions in Santa Fe for the year 2003. In some cases, we had to draw on data for previous years. For example, the figures we have for number of businesses in Santa Fe comes from a 2001 source. When we have had to use data for years prior to 2003, we have made adjustments to these data, as appropriate, to best reflect conditions in 2003. In the appendices to the original 2004 Report, we describe how we made these adjustments on the data for prior years.

2. *Data for City of Santa Fe.* The data are meant to reflect conditions in the City of Santa Fe as much as possible. As with the year of estimation, we were not always able to reach this level of specificity with the available government sources. For example, the data for workers in Santa Fe are for the metropolitan area (Metropolitan Statistical Area, MSA), not the city proper. Where possible, we again made adjustments in the

figures to reflect conditions in the city itself. Nevertheless, given that we are using data for the metropolitan area rather than the city itself, it is likely that, if anything, we have overestimated the effects of the ordinance. This is because, within the overall Santa Fe metropolitan area, employees outside the city itself tend to earn lower wages than those employed inside the city. The actual raises that go only to workers employed inside the city limits are therefore likely to be smaller than what would occur if lower-paid workers outside the city proper also received raises.

3. *Estimates of covered firms assumes twenty, not twenty-five, employees.* The Santa Fe ordinance applies only to firms that employ twenty-five or more workers. However, from our available data sources, we were unable to observe firms within this particular pool. This is because the publicly available data on which we relied gathers information on firms according to whether they have twenty or more, but not twenty-five or more, employees. All of our estimates are therefore based on firms having twenty or more, rather than twenty-five or more, employees. However, we are confident that this has not significantly altered any of the major findings we report here. For example, as we will see below, we estimate from our source that, as of 2001, there are 471 firms in Santa Fe with twenty or more employees, and it is from this baseline of firms that we derive our estimates. The University of New Mexico (UNM) initial baseline study, based on government data from 2002 that is not publicly available, reports that 423 businesses would be covered by the ordinance (Reynis 2004, 33). In other words, our estimate is quite close to the UNM figure, after allowing for the fact that our estimate is for 2001 and includes businesses with 20–24 employees, whereas the UNM figures are for 2002 and excludes businesses with 20–24 employees.

4. *Corroboration of main findings.* When a researcher develops evidence based on one set of data, it is important to corroborate these findings using data from other sources. This is not to suggest that the statistical findings from one source need to be precisely the same as those from other sources. The key goal is that the results from various sources be approximately accurate within the context of the question being explored. For example, if we estimate the total number of covered firms with twenty or more employees as 471, the UNM researchers' estimate that there are 423 covered firms with twenty-five or more employees shows approximate corroboration between the two sources. If the two estimates had been off by something on the order of 100–200 firms, that would suggest the presence of some flaws in one or both of the estimation procedures.

The results we report here are corroborated at several points:

- Our estimates both for number of firms covered and for the character-istics of the workers covered are very similar to those provided by the UNM research study.
- Our key findings—the estimates for the living wage cost increases/firm sales and of supplier costs/sales—are both corroborated by the payroll and sales data provided by three of the plaintiff firms.
- The same key estimate of cost increases from the living wage/sales are very much in line with previous estimates of similar ratios for different cities.

ESTIMATED COSTS OF LIVING WAGE ORDINANCE FOR BUSINESSES

We examine costs according to three categories: (1) mandated cost increases that would apply for firms with twenty or more employees, assuming they maintained their existing work force; (2) nonmandated ripple-effect costs; and (3) local supplier pass-throughs (i.e., the costs that some Santa Fe firms would face when their suppliers are other covered Santa Fe firms and these supplier firms pass along their increased costs in the form of higher prices).

Our basic approach to generating an estimate of the costs of the ordi-nance is straightforward, even while it entails a large number of detailed calculations. We first estimate the firms that would be covered by the or-dinance. We then generate a profile of workers employed by these covered firms and focus on the workers who are earning an hourly wage below the Santa Fe living wage minimum of $8.50.[3] From this, we are able to calcu-late the cost increases that covered firms would incur from the living wage ordinance, assuming they maintained their existing work force as is. We then add an estimate of nonmandated ripple-effect increases as well as local-supplier cost pass-throughs. We also calculate these total cost in-creases relative to the total sales (or gross receipts) of the covered firms. This cost increase/sales ratio enables us to address a basic question: How much is the living wage ordinance likely to impact the economic viability of the covered firms? From here, we can consider, in the next section, how firms are likely to adjust their operations to these increases in their costs.

We proceed by first examining data on mandated and ripple-effect wage increases and then estimate these cost increases relative to the sales (or gross receipts) of the covered firms. We present data on the costs/sales ratio first as an average for all industries and then as averages broken down by industry groupings. Only after we have estimated these cost/sales ratios by industry groupings can we be in a position to estimate the effects of local-supplier cost pass-throughs. The reason for this is straightforward: to measure the effects of local-supplier cost pass-throughs, we first need to know what the mandated and ripple-effect costs will be of the covered Santa Fe firms that are the suppliers for other Santa Fe firms.

Mandated Costs

Table 5.1 presents evidence on the number of firms and workers that we estimate would be covered by the Santa Fe ordinance, as it would apply under the $8.50 living wage mandate. According to table 5.1, there are 471 firms in the City of Santa Fe that employ twenty or more workers. These firms employ a total of 9,250 workers earning between $5.15 and $8.50 per hour; of these low-wage workers, 5,685 are full-time and 3,565 are part-time. The average workweek for these employees is 33.3 hours and the average number of weeks that they work in a year is 50. This amounts to an average total working year of 1,665 hours. If we convert all these workers to full-time, 40-hour per week equivalence, this would mean that the number of full-time-equivalent (FTE) workers earning below $8.50 per hour is 7,404.

Table 5.1. Mandated wage increases and costs to Santa Fe firms after raise to $8.50 living wage

Number of firms covered	
Total	471
Number of workers covered	
Total	9,250
Full-time	5,685
Part-time	3,565
Full-time equivalent workers	7,404
Wage workers	
Average hourly wage before ordinance	$6.91
Average hourly wage increase	$1.59
Average number of hours worked per week	33.3
Average weeks worked per year	50
Average yearly wage increase	$2,647
Total mandated costs	
Wage increase for year, all workers	$24.5 million
Payroll tax increase for year, all workers	$1.9 million
Total mandated cost increase	$26.4 million
Average cost increase per firm	$56,051

Sources: 2001 County and Business Patterns, U.S. Census Bureau; Current Population Survey Outgoing Rotation Group 2001–2003 files, Bureau of Labor Statistics, U.S. Department of Labor.

Note: See Pollin and Brenner, 2004 Report, app. 1 for details on calculations.

The next set of figures in table 5.1 shows the average wage for these below-$8.50 workers. We estimate their average wage at $6.91. Thus, to bring the average workers up to the $8.50 mandate, they would receive a raise of $1.59. It is worth emphasizing this finding: even though the current applicable minimum wage today in Santa Fe is the $5.15 national minimum, this does not mean that, once the Santa Fe ordinance is implemented, that affected workers will be receiving raises of $3.35 per hour (i.e., they are not all moving from the old effective $5.15 mandate to the $8.50 Santa Fe minimum). With the average worker receiving a $1.59 wage increase, and if we assume that these workers will maintain exactly their same working year of 1,665 hours, this means that the average yearly wage increase will be $2,647.

From these numbers, we are then able to estimate that the total wage increase for the 9,250 (7,404 FTE) workers in Santa Fe will be $24.5 million. To estimate the total direct costs of the ordinance for all the covered businesses, we then have to also take account of their increased payroll taxes. As we show in table 5.1, those will amount to $1.9 million, based on the $24.5 million in wage increases. As such, the total mandated cost increases for the 471 covered businesses in Santa Fe will be $26.4 million. This amounts to an average (mean) cost increase for the 471 covered firms of approximately $56,000.

Nonmandated Cost Increases: Ripple Effects

As described in chapter 4, businesses provide nonmandated ripple-effect raises to maintain some semblance of the wage hierarchy that prevailed prior to implementation of a new mandated minimum wage. With respect to the Santa Fe ordinance, there are two categories of likely recipients of such wage increases:

1. Employees who, prior to implementation of the Santa Fe living wage, were earning more than the federal minimum wage of $5.15 but less than the Santa Fe living wage of $8.50. After the living wage ordinance is implemented, some of these employees will receive wage increases that put them above the Santa Fe living wage minimum.
2. Employees who are now earning more than the Santa Fe living wage of $8.50 and who nevertheless receive a raise when the living wage policy becomes law.

The key question in determining the size of the ripple effect is to estimate how much of an increase in wage equality will occur in covered firms after the lowest-paid workers receive their mandated raises. The terms *wage compression* and *wage compaction* are used to describe the condition of wages becoming more equal, either within a given firm or more broadly, including throughout the economy as a whole. Recent research on the ripple effects arising due to increases in the federal minimum wage and statewide minimum wages has found that the increases tend to diminish fairly rapidly at higher wage rates, which means that wages will become more equal—that is, wage compression does indeed generally occur—within the affected firms.

It should be recognized that the plaintiff Pranzo has offered some comments about the size of the ripple effect. Pranzo states that, "Numerous discussions with my current employees and business peers indicate that employees currently making over $8.50 per hour expect an increase of $2.00 per hour. 4.5% is my best estimate but may be too low. I do not know how to predict the figure at the current time because no city has imposed such a large price increase on such a small population and there are no historical figures on which to extrapolate."[4]

Thus, Pranzo expects to experience a large ripple effect. At the same time, it acknowledges that is has little evidence on which to form this judgment. This seems to only increase the need for us to form some provisional estimates of ripple effects that are grounded in historical experience and the analysis of relevant data.

Ripple Effect Estimate

We present our estimate of the ripple effect in table 5.2. We generated these estimates as follows.

In the first row in the table, we show data on the highest-paid workers in Santa Fe who will be eligible to receive a mandated wage increase (i.e., those workers receiving mandated raises whose pay is closest to those likely to receive a nonmandated raise). We define this category of workers as those earning $7.75–8.49. Within this category, those earning $7.75 will be eligible for a 75-cent mandated wage increase, whereas those earning $8.49 will be eligible for only a 1-cent mandated raise. However, to build in a ripple effect for these workers, we assume that *all* workers in this wage category will receive a 75-cent wage increase, not just those who are earning $7.75 prior to implementation of the ordinance. Because the average worker in this wage category earns $8.12 before the ordinance, this means that the average wage increase we give to these workers brings them to a new average wage of $8.87—that is, a 9 percent raise over their previous average level of $8.12.

We then build again, as we did in chapter 4, from the findings that we report regarding the minimum wage increases in California in 1996–1998. In column 3 of table 5.2, we report figures for nonmandated wage increases

Table 5.2. Measuring the ripple effect: indirect wage costs to firms under mandated raise to $8.50 living wage

(1) Pre- ordinance wage range	(2) Average wage before raise	(3) Assumed average wage increase relative to $7.75–8.49 workers	(4) New average wage	(5) Average hours per week (50 weeks/ year assumed)	(6) Total workers in category	(7) Total wage increase above $8.50 (in millions)
$7.75–8.49	$8.12	100%	$8.87 +9.2%	35.9	2,303	$1.5
$8.50–9.24	$8.86	76%	$9.48 +7.0% *[7.0% is 76% of 9.2%]*	34.6	1,878	$2.1
$9.25–10.74	$9.96	33%	$10.26 +3.0% *[3.0% is 33% of 9.2%]*	37.5	3,968	$2.5
Total					8,149	$6.1

Sources: Current Population Survey Outgoing Rotation Group 2001–2003 files, Bureau of Labor Statistics, U.S. Department of Labor.

Note: See Pollin and Brenner, 2004 Report, app. 1 for details on calculations.

relative to the mandated increases based on this experience in California. The figures in column 3 show assumed wage increases for workers who earn between $7.75 and $10.75 as a percentage of the mandated wage increases that would bring all workers up to at least $8.50. Thus, we assume that workers in the first nonmandated wage range—those earning $8.50–9.24—will receive raises equal to 76 percent of those in the $7.75–8.49 category. This means that the $8.50–9.24 workers will receive an average raise of 7.0 percent for a new average wage of $9.48. We consider then workers in the next $1.50-wage range—those earning $9.25–10.74. We assume these workers receive a raise that is 33 percent as large as those in the $7.75–8.50 category, just as occurred in the California case. This means their pay, on average, rises by 3.0 percent to a new average wage of $10.26.

Based on these estimates, we are then able to calculate ripple-effect raises, assuming that these workers receiving ripple-effect raises will remain constant in number and that they maintain their same number of hours employed over a 50-week year. Adding the wage increases for each of the three wage categories, we see that the total ripple-effect wage increase based on this methodology is $6.1 million. These ripple-effect wage increases are received by a total of 8,149 workers.

Total Mandated and Ripple-Effect Costs

Table 5.3 presents our estimate of the total mandated and ripple-effect costs of the Santa Fe living wage ordinance for the 471 covered firms. In addition, we have included the payroll tax increases for the firms associated with these wage increases. As we have noted previously, we consider the question of local-supplier cost pass-throughs as a separate item below. But note also that local-supplier cost pass-throughs do not constitute a separate cost item for the covered businesses in Santa Fe as a whole. Rather, these local-supplier pass-throughs will net out when we consider Santa Fe businesses as a whole. To add them to the overall costs for Santa Fe businesses as a whole would therefore constitute double-counting.

In table 5.3, we can see that the mandated and ripple-effect cost categories total $33 million. Of this amount, 74.3 percent are the mandated wage increases, 18.5 percent are ripple-effect wage increases, and the remaining costs are payroll taxes on these mandated and nonmandated increases.

Total Mandated and Ripple-Effect Costs Relative to Sales

In table 5.4, we now consider these living wage cost increases as they would impact a representative (median) firm in our sample of 471 firms. The table shows the basic operating structure for this representative firm.

Table 5.3. Total mandated and ripple-effect costs of Santa Fe living wage ordinance (in millions)

Mandated costs	
Total wage increase	$24.5
Percentage of total increase	*74.3%*
Payroll taxes	$1.9
Percentage of total increase	*5.8%*
Total direct cost	$26.4
Percentage of total increase	*80.1%*
Ripple-effect costs	
Total ripple-effect increase	$6.1
Percentage of total increase	*18.5%*
Payroll taxes on ripple effect	$0.5
Percentage of total increase	*1.4%*
Total ripple cost	$6.6
Percentage of total increase	*19.9%*
Total costs	**$33.0**

Sources: Data are from tables 5.1 and 5.2.

Table 5.4. Cost increases relative to sales for representative (median) Santa Fe firm

Number of workers	46
Number of workers receiving direct wage increases	12
Number of workers receiving indirect wage increases	2
Cost of mandated wage increases	$34,370
Cost of ripple wage increases	$7,557
Mandated and ripple-effect cost increases	$41,927
Sales	$4,318,670
Cost increase relative to total sales	1.0%

Sources: 2001 County and Business Patterns, U.S. Census Bureau; Current Population Survey Outgoing Rotation Group 2001–2003 files, Bureau of Labor Statistics, U.S. Department of Labor; 1997 Economic Census for the county of Santa Fe, U.S. Census Bureau.

Note: See Pollin and Brenner, 2004 Report, app. 1 for details on calculations.

The firm employs forty-six workers, of whom twelve are earning below $8.50 and are eligible for a mandated wage increase. An additional two workers would also receive a nonmandated wage increase based on our methodology for calculating ripple effects.

Table 5.4 then presents the total cost figures (exclusive of local-supplier pass-throughs) due to the living wage. This total cost increase amounts to $41,927. We next present our estimate of total sales for this firm, which is $4,318,670. From these data, we can now calculate our key figure for evaluating the impact of the living wage on firms, which is the cost increase resulting from the living wage relative to total sales (gross receipts) for this representative Santa Fe firm. As we see, this estimate is 1.0 percent.[5]

Cost Increases by Industry Groupings

Table 5.5 presents data on living wage costs/sales by industry, following the industrial groupings of the North American Industrial Classification System (NAICS) coding system. The table lists the industrial groups according to the living wage costs/sales ratio, starting with the industries with the highest ratios. In columns 3 and 4, the table then presents information on the size of the industry within the Santa Fe economy. We measure industry size according to two dimensions: its share of the total employment for firms employing more than 20 workers and its share of total sales for these larger firms.

As table 5.5 shows, the accommodation and food services industry—which includes hotels, restaurants, bars, cafés, and caterers—is the only industry that, according to our estimate, will experience a cost increase in the range of 3–4 percent of sales. Only three other industries face cost increases greater than 2 percent—waste management, management of companies (including billing and record-keeping services and financial planners), and health care. Only two additional industries will experience cost increases greater than

Table 5.5. Impact of Santa Fe living wage ordinance by industry: mandated and ripple-effect cost increases

(1) Industry category	(2) Median living wage costs relative to total sales	(3) Share of total Santa Fe employment for large firms	(4) Share of total Santa Fe sales (gross receipts) for large firms
Accommodation & food services	3.32%	22.51%	7.67%
Administrative & support & waste management & remediation services	2.60%	4.68%	1.56%
Management of companies & enterprises	2.45%	0.38%	0.04%
Health care & social assistance	2.09%	14.68%	8.04%
Arts, entertainment, & recreation	1.59%	4.38%	3.12%
Other services (except public administration)	1.40%	4.31%	2.87%
Real estate & rental & leasing	0.73%	1.26%	1.22%
Transportation & warehousing	0.69%	0.75%	0.30%
Manufacturing	0.66%	2.34%	4.71%
Wholesale trade	0.61%	3.39%	11.33%
Information	0.55%	2.86%	3.39%
Construction	0.55%	6.06%	6.86%
Educational services	0.35%	4.85%	2.69%
Finance & insurance	0.26%	3.96%	9.06%
Retail trade	0.22%	20.40%	32.66%
Mining	0.08%	0.12%	0.17%
Professional, scientific, & technical services	0.04%	2.34%	2.01%
Utilities	0.01%	0.73%	2.30%

Sources: 2001 County and Business Patterns, U.S. Census Bureau; Current Population Survey Outgoing Rotation Group 2001–2003 files, Bureau of Labor Statistics, U.S. Department of Labor; 1997 Economic Census for the county of Santa Fe, U.S. Census Bureau.

Note: See Pollin and Brenner, 2004 Report, app. 1 for details on calculations.

1 percent of their sales. By our estimate, the large firms in the remaining twelve industries will face cost increases below 1 percent of their sales.

The accommodation and food services industry is clearly of major significance here, not simply because of the high costs it will experience. The other factor is its relative size in the Santa Fe economy. As we see in column 3, this industry is the largest single employer among large firms in Santa Fe, accounting for 22.5 percent of total employment. It is not the largest industry by sales; however, with 7.7 percent of total sales, it is the fourth largest industry by sales. The largest industry by sales/gross receipts is the retail trade, with nearly one-third of the Santa Fe economy's total sales. However, the impact of the living wage ordinance on the retail firms in Santa Fe is likely to be negligible because we estimate that the average cost increase in retail due to the living wage will be only 0.2 percent of sales. Overall, we find that industries accounting for 56 percent of employment and 83 percent of sales in Santa Fe will experience cost increases from the living wage of less than 2 percent.

Local-Supplier Cost Pass-Throughs

As we have discussed, some of the firms covered by the Santa Fe ordinance will be suppliers of other Santa Fe firms. For example, restaurants in Santa Fe will purchase products from food wholesalers that will themselves face increased costs due to the living wage ordinance. If we assume that local suppliers will pass through some portion of their increased costs to other Santa Fe firms, this will therefore produce increases in the overall costs of the living wage ordinance for the restaurants that absorb the pass-throughs.

Note that these supplier pass-throughs will not constitute an additional cost for Santa Fe business *as a whole*. Rather, some covered businesses are passing through their increased living wage costs to other covered businesses.[6] Nevertheless, local businesses that happen to rely heavily on local suppliers will feel a disproportionate effect from the living wage ordinance if their suppliers pass through their increased living wage–related costs. For individual industries, it is therefore useful to try to estimate how large these supplier pass-throughs are likely to be.

To estimate this, we have drawn on survey evidence from the federal government, which shows the input costs for various types of businesses and the breakdown of these input costs into their separate components. These government estimates of inputs have then been refined in what is known as a regional input-output model developed by researchers at the University of Minnesota. Their model, named IMPLAN, provides detailed estimates of business inputs within individual counties in the United States, including Santa Fe. We go through the details of our estimation of this effect in the appendix to this chapter.

Working from these data sources, we estimated local-supplier pass-throughs for the representative business in Santa Fe in the range of 0.1 percent of total sales. We estimate a slightly lower figure of 0.08 percent for the restaurants. But the basic point is clear. Once we take into account the effects of local-supplier cost pass-throughs, our estimate of the total cost/sales ratio for the average firm will rise from 1.0 to 1.1 percent. Similarly, for the accommodation and food services industry, our estimate of the total cost/sales ratio will rise from 3.32 to 3.40 percent.

Overall Assessment of Cost Increases Relative to Sales

Overall then, we find that for the average firm, the cost increase from the living wage—now including local-supplier pass-throughs—will be slightly more than 1 percent of total sales, somewhere in the range of 1.1 percent. For the restaurant industry, our estimate of the ratio of total costs/sales, including local-supplier cost pass-throughs, will be in the range of 3–4 percent.

Detailed Breakdown of Food Services Firms

Because of the importance of the restaurant industry for our analysis, we present in table 5.6 more detailed cost information on this industry. As we see, the table breaks down food services into six subcategories: full-service restaurants, limited-service restaurants, cafeterias, snack and nonalcoholic bars, food service contractors, and caterers. We can observe in this table the relative sizes of these various categories of food service firms in terms of the number of firms, their total employment, and the number of workers earning below $8.50 per hour. The table then provides the relevant figures for cost increases due to the living wage and total sales. In these calculations, we have incorporated the local-supplier cost pass-throughs in our total living wage cost estimates for restaurants. We then calculate the total cost increase/sales ratio for each of these subcategories of food service firms. As we see, by far the largest number of firms, employing the largest number of covered workers, are the full-service restaurants. The cost increase/sales ratio for these firms is at the broader industry average of 3.4 percent. The range for the industry varies between 2.7 percent for cafeterias and 5.6 percent for caterers.

Estimates of Cost Increase/Sales Ratios for Plaintiffs

As previously noted, the estimates that we have presented on costs and cost increases/sales are derived from government statistics. It is useful to

Table 5.6. Impact of Santa Fe living wage ordinance on food services (total costs in this table include local-supplier cost pass-throughs)

Type of food service	Number of firms	Total employment	Number of workers earning $5.15–8.50	Total costs	Total sales	Median cost increase as a percentage of sales
Full-service restaurants	55	2,725	993	$3,566,556	$104,864,658	3.4%
Limited-service restaurants	24	840	306	$1,102,637	$36,351,924	3.0%
Cafeterias	3	185	67	$243,527	$8,861,632	2.7%
Snack and nonalcoholic beverage bars	3	145	53	$188,909	$4,491,004	4.2%
Food service contractors	4	140	51	$182,935	$5,011,326	3.7%
Caterers	1	35	13	$45,380	$811,317	5.6%
Total	90	4,070	1,484	$5,329,943	$160,391,860	3.4%

Sources: 2001 County and Business Patterns, U.S. Census Bureau; Current Population Survey Outgoing Rotation Group 2001–2003 files, Bureau of Labor Statistics, U.S. Department of Labor; 1997 Economic Census for the county of Santa Fe, U.S. Census Bureau.
Note: See Pollin and Brenner, 2004 Report, app. 1 for details on calculations.

compare these estimates with the comparable figures provided by the plaintiffs themselves for their own operations.

In table 5.7, we report the relevant data as presented by the restaurant plaintiffs.[7] These figures were derived directly from the plaintiffs' actual payroll data and were presented publicly at the April 2004 trial in Santa Fe. As the table shows, the figures we have are for these firms' mandated cost increases only. As we can see, the mandated cost increases for the plaintiffs, based on their own payroll data, ranges between 1.0 and 4.2 percent of their sales (gross revenues).

Table 5.7. Estimated mandated cost increases/sales ratios for four plaintiff restaurants (estimates are based on restaurants' own payroll and sales data)

Restaurant-plaintiff	Mandated cost increases/sales
Pinon Grill	1.0%
Robbie Day	1.9%
Zuma	2.2%
Pranzo	4.2%

Source: State of New Mexico County of Santa Fe First Judicial District Court No. D0101-CV200300468, Hearing 4/15/04, vol. 8, 23–29.

As previously noted, we are unable to generate figures on ripple effects or local-supplier pass-throughs from the data provided by the plaintiffs. Nevertheless, it would be useful to obtain some sense of the full cost increase/sales ratios for these firms, that is, a ratio that includes both ripple effects and supplier pass-throughs. To generate such a rough estimate, we begin with the estimates of average ripple effects and local-supplier cost pass-throughs for all covered Santa Fe restaurants. We have reported in our previous discussion the figure for local supplier pass throughs at 0.08 percent of sales in the restaurant industry. The ripple-effect costs for the restaurant industry specifically, which we have not discussed earlier, are 0.56 percent of total restaurant sales.

If we assume the ripple effect and local-supplier pass-throughs for these firms are basically in line with the average figures we have generated, that means that these two cost items would amount to 0.64 of total sales. We then add these additional cost figures to the mandated cost ratios to obtain a rough estimate for these firms of their total cost increase/sales ratios. These ratios are as follows for the four plaintiffs:

- Pinon Grill: 1.6 percent
- Robbie Day: 2.5 percent
- Zuma: 2.8 percent
- Pranzo: 4.8 percent

If we take the medians and means of these four figures, we come up with a median total cost increase/sales ratio for the four plaintiffs of 2.6 percent and a mean of 2.9 percent. These figures are actually somewhat lower than the 3.3 percent estimate of the costs increase/sales ratio that we generated from government statistics for all covered Santa Fe restaurants. Nevertheless, it is remarkable that, working strictly from publicly available data, we were able to estimate a cost increase/sales ratio for covered firms in Santa Fe which, as an average, is within 0.4 percentage points of the figure we derived from the four restaurants' own payroll and sales data. Clearly, the evidence we derive from the plaintiffs' own payroll and sales records support the conclusion that our method of estimating living wage costs is highly reliable.

METHODS OF ADJUSTING TO THE LIVING
WAGE INCREASE BY SANTA FE FIRMS

A 23 percent average pay increase for more than 9,000 low-wage workers in Santa Fe, as well as additional raises for those workers receiving ripple-effect raises, will obviously bring about adjustments throughout the city's economy. What are these adjustments likely to be?

Two types of adjustment processes are most frequently the focus of discussions in considering the impact of raising minimum wages at the national, statewide, or municipal levels. The first is unemployment, or, more specifically, that businesses will lay off workers and will become more reluctant to hire new employees, thus creating job losses and fewer opportunities for the working poor. The second is business relocation; that is, to avoid paying the higher minimum wage, firms located in the city will move out and firms considering moving into the city will be discouraged from doing so. Such moves would also then create job losses and fewer opportunities for the working poor. Because the purpose of raising minimum wages is to improve living standards and create better employment opportunities for the working poor, a rise in unemployment or business flight from the city would obviously be unintended and undesirable consequences of passing such a measure into law.

However, laying off workers or relocating are not the only ways that businesses might adjust to a citywide minimum wage increase. In fact, there are three other ways that firms might respond to the Santa Fe living wage ordinance. They are that (1) businesses could raise prices; (2) firms could operate more productively; and (3) low-wage employees could receive a relatively greater share of firms' total wage, salary, and profit payments. At least initially, these three other adjustment paths are likely to be the primary channels through which Santa Fe firms adjust to the ordinance, since they can be accomplished more readily and at lower costs than either laying off workers or relocating. The adjustment process that would be least costly and disruptive for firms would be to simply raise prices to reflect their increased costs. Thus, if a restaurant faced a 4 percent cost increase relative to sales due to the living wage ordinance, if it was able to raise its prices by 4 percent without losing business, this means it would be able to fully pass through their increased living wage costs to their customers. In other words, their profits would not fall at all due to the living wage ordinance, and no other adjustments, such as unemployment or relocation, would be necessary to absorb their increased living wage costs.

But firms face competition. How much can we expect firms to be able to mark up their prices without losing customers to their competitors? This is the crucial question for understanding the adjustment process for firms, and it is therefore the one on which we concentrate most of our attention in this discussion.

Price Increases

As noted in chapter 4, Card and Krueger (1995) examined, among other questions, the effects on the fast-food industry in New Jersey when the state raised its minimum wage by 18.8 percent above the national minimum wage. They found that the New Jersey fast-food outlets were able to raise their prices by about the same amount as their total costs were increased, which amounted to about 3.4 percent.

Card and Krueger, along with other researchers, also compared this finding with experiences in the fast-food industries in other states after the national minimum wage was increased. Again, they found that, for the most part, prices at these restaurants were marked up roughly in correspondence with the increased total costs associated with the minimum wage increase. For example, a 2001 study by Daniel Aaronson of the Federal Reserve Bank of Chicago examines price pass-throughs in the restaurant industry after minimum wage increases in the United States and Canada between 1978 and 1995. After presenting a large and varied body of data, and pursuing alternative methods of testing the robustness of his statistical tests on the data, Aaronson concludes that "the majority of the evidence suggests that restaurant prices rise with increases in the wage bill that result from minimum wage legislation" (2001, 169).

Thus, these researchers provide strong evidence for the importance of the price mark-up as an adjustment mechanism in the fast-food industry. But the ability of businesses to mark up prices to reflect their higher costs depends on conditions in the markets in which they are selling their products. What can we say about businesses operating in Santa Fe?

There are two crucial questions to ask about the viability of price increases as a means for covered Santa Fe firms to cover their increased costs. They are:

1. *How much would they have to raise prices to cover their increased costs?* Based on the figures we have presented, a representative firm in the restaurant and hotel industry would have to raise prices about 3.3 percent to cover its increased costs relative to sales. A price increase of this amount would be the largest price increase needed among all the industries in Santa Fe, since the cost increase due to the living wage is correspondingly the highest. By contrast, retail firms would experience cost increases relative to sales of only 0.2 percent—thus, the price increase they would require to cover their increased costs would be negligible.

2. *How much would firms be able to raise their prices to cover these increased costs?* Answering this question, of course, depends first on the competitive environment of the markets within which these firms operate. It also depends on how sensitive consumers are to price increases. For example, consider an average restaurant. If the price of a meal was, say, $10.00 to begin with, would customers be discouraged

from buying this meal if, due to the living wage ordinance, its price were to rise by 4 percent—that is, to $10.40?

It therefore follows that, in examining the capacity of firms to raise prices to cover their increased costs, we should focus our attention on those industries in which price increases are highest, since that will be where the issues with competitors and customers will be most significant. In short, we should concentrate our attention on this issue primarily as it affects restaurants and hotels. Of course, it also happens that the plaintiffs in this case are all in the hotel and restaurant industry, making our focus on this industry even more pertinent.

Evaluating the competitive situation for the hotels and restaurants is complicated by the specific stipulations of the Santa Fe law, whereby only those firms with twenty-five or more employees are covered. Competing among themselves, the large hotels and restaurants will all face a comparable impact from the living wage ordinance. They could all choose on their own to raise prices to cover their increased costs, and it would not affect their relative competitive standing. However, these firms do not compete only among themselves. They may also compete with smaller firms in their industry that do not face the same mandated cost increases. The hotels, especially, also compete with venues outside the city, especially in attracting convention business. We therefore need to consider the effects of price increases within these specific contexts—the relative competitive situation with smaller firms and the relative competitive situation with other cities.

Basics of Price Competition in the Restaurant and Hotel Industry

As we have seen, the relevant average cost increase in this industry would be larger than in any other industry in Santa Fe. At the same time, the relevant price necessary to cover costs here, at 3.3 percent, is not high in absolute terms. For the four plaintiff firms, the average cost increase was slightly lower, at 2.9 percent, as derived from their own payroll and sales records. Even if we round up these estimates to assume a 4 percent cost increase relative to sales for the restaurants, this means that a restaurant with an average meal price of $10.00 would have to raise its price to $10.40 to fully cover the restaurant's cost increase. To help illustrate this point, it might be useful to run through a few more such examples. A restaurant with a $20.00 average-priced meal would need a price increase to $20.80. Similarly, the price of a $2.00 hamburger at a fast-food restaurant would have to rise to $2.08. And finally, considering the case for hotels, a $100 hotel room would have to rise to about $104 and a $200 room to $208.

How much would the large restaurants and hotels be hurt by having to charge this much more than their smaller competitors in Santa Fe?

Of course, the covered Santa Fe restaurants and hotels would face *some* degree of increased competitive pressure if they raised their prices even modestly relative to their competitors. The question is: How much more difficult would their competitive pressures be through price increases of this amount?

In fact, the available relevant literature suggests that such increased competitive pressures are not likely to be significant as long as the price increases remain within the broad general boundary that we have laid out—that is, an increase from $20.00 to $20.80 for a meal. This is because spending on hotels and restaurants are forms of discretionary consumption, especially as we ascend to higher-end market segments. As we move up from the lowest to highest segment of the overall market, consumers tend to be less price sensitive within a general price range. Within a given price range, they are largely interested in the quality they are purchasing, and the perceived quality differences between hotels and restaurants are more important in determining consumer demand than whether a meal will cost, say $20.00 or $20.80.

Consultants and researchers in the field of hotel management have long recognized this general situation. For example, a 1997 paper by Robert Lewis and Stowe Shoemaker in the *Cornell Hotel and Restaurant Administration Quarterly* explains how price can serve as a crucial indicator of *quality* to potential high-end hotel and restaurant clients. Such clients are not seeking low prices as a priority. They are rather seeking high-quality services and are willing to pay high prices in exchange for high quality. A hotel or restaurant that can maintain strong client demand with high prices is therefore signaling with its high prices that it is able to deliver on high quality. Correspondingly, for a hotel or restaurant in this market segment to cut prices would signal that it has failed to maintain the high level of quality that its potential clients are seeking.

Hotel clients in this market segment are therefore willing to accept a broad range of room prices, depending on how they perceive the quality of the service they are receiving in return. According to Lewis and Shoemaker's own research, the range of acceptable prices for hotels for business purposes varied by $54 around a midpoint price for rooms of a given quality. Lewis and Shoemaker also argue strongly against cost-driven pricing (i.e., letting costs rather than customer attitudes determine prices) for all hospitality services, including both hotels and restaurants. Citing leading management theorists Peter Drucker and Theodore Leavett, they argue that the error with cost-driven pricing is precisely that it does not attempt to gauge what the market will bear and, specifically, the fact that customers perceive prices as an important quality indicator.[8]

A similar finding focused on the restaurant business was obtained in an innovative 1994 study by Nicholas M. Kiefer, Thomas J. Kelly, and Kenneth Burdett, published in both the *Journal of Business and Economic Statistics* (1994b) and the *Cornell Hotel and Restaurant Administration Quarterly* (1994a). With the cooperation of a restaurant owner, these researchers set different prices within a given restaurant for a popular item on the menu, a fried haddock dinner. Specifically, they examined the effect on demand at the restaurant when they varied the price of the haddock dinner between $8.95 and $10.95 for different customers at the restaurant on a given night. Their major finding was that there was no effect on the demand for the haddock dinner regardless of the variation in the price within this range. They write, "The data clearly indicate that a substantial negative effect of price on the amount of fish fry ordered is quite unlikely in the range of prices we tested" (Kiefer, Kelly, and Burdett 1994a, 52).

More generally, they conclude that their findings are consistent with the view expressed by the National Restaurant Association itself in its publication *Price-Value Relationships at Restaurants* (1992). The National Restaurant Association suggests in this publication that "consumers view themselves as being more quality and value conscious as opposed to price conscious— they want quality and are willing to pay for it" (quoted in Kiefer, Kelly, and Burdett 1994a, 49).

This evidence from the trade industry literature is consistent with a broader range of evidence as well. One relevant case that we have studied is the hotel industry in Santa Monica, California (see Pollin and Brenner 2000). This Santa Monica experience provided an excellent basis for isolating the relationship between hotel room prices and demand because, by statute, the supply of rooms was basically fixed by the city's growth-restriction laws. Therefore, when room prices changed, those changes could reflect only changes in room demand, given that room supply could not change.

There were two important general findings from this study. First, considering the period 1987–1999, the average room price in Santa Monica rose from $86 to $179, an overall increase of 108.1 percent and an average annual increase of 9.0 percent. This is a 5.1 percent increase above the overall national inflation rate (measured by the Consumer Product Index, CPI) for these years. The second main finding was that despite these price increases, occupancy rates for Santa Monica hotels generally rose over this period as well. In 1987, average occupancy rates were 79 percent. In 1999, they were 81 percent. This positive correlation between prices and occupancy rates is still sharper when we focus only on the high-end hotels in Santa Monica. The point here is not that the clientele of the Santa Monica hotels were booking rooms at increasing rates *because* prices were rising. The evidence rather suggests that factors other than price—quality factors, including location—were dominant over price.

Let us emphasize here—this is not to suggest that hotels and restaurants in Santa Fe will enjoy an *enhanced* competitive position by raising their prices by 3–5 percent. But the literature on quality factors and the evidence from the Santa Monica hotels suggests that, within a given price range, relatively small price increases such as one from $20 to $21 for a meal, is not likely to change a firm's competitive position significantly for the worse. These findings seem to apply equally to the convention business and to the consumption patterns of private individuals and individual business firms. If the high-end hotels in Santa Fe are competing for convention business, the decisive factor is not likely to be a price difference of 3–5 percent relative to, say, hotels in Las Vegas or, for that matter, Santa Monica.[9]

Beyond even the higher-end market segments, the evidence from the Card and Krueger study of New Jersey fast-food restaurants suggests that, even with the fast-food restaurants, relatively small price changes do not lead to large changes in consumer demand. Card and Krueger deliberately studied fast-food restaurants along the border with Pennsylvania. The restaurants on the New Jersey side of the border raised their prices 3.4 percent to cover their increased costs, but in Pennsylvania, firms did not face any mandated wage increase at all.[10] Nevertheless, the New Jersey firms did not experience any significant change in consumer demand, despite having raised their prices 3.4 percent. In other words, fast-food restaurant clients along this border did not migrate to the Pennsylvania side of the border to avoid the price increases in New Jersey.

In fact, given the modest price increases, this seems to be the only likely outcome because an important reason for the popularity of fast-food restaurants is precisely that getting a meal at these restaurants is *fast*. According to a 1999 study of the sales growth in the fast-food industry, "People want quick and convenient meals; they do not want to spend a lot of time preparing meals, traveling to pick up meals, or waiting for meals in restaurants. As a result, consumers rely on fast food" (Jekanowski 1999, 11). In other words, modest price increases are unlikely to cause consumers to take the time to drive further away for a quick meal.

The Role of Ethical Consumers

Another factor that is likely to exert at least some influence on Santa Fe consumers is that, on implementation of the living wage ordinance, the large firms will become living wage businesses. When consumers recognize that this is why prices in the large restaurants and hotels are high relative to their smaller competitors, at least some of them may even deliberately seek out the living wage firms over the others. After all, a large majority of the Santa Fe City Council voted in favor of the living wage ordinance, and their voting decisions no doubt broadly reflect the ethical concerns of the Santa Fe population as a whole. It is also telling that, in a revised affidavit, Elizabeth Draiscol, president and general manager of the Zuma Corporation, states that "I have received telephone calls from members of the community telling me that they will no longer come to my restaurant because I oppose the ordinance."[11]

Such considerations by at least some portion of the Santa Fe population would be consistent with the widespread support for what has been termed ethical consumption practices. The best-known example of ethical consumption in the United States has been the antisweatshop movement and the effects this movement has had in targeting for public exposure firms such as Nike and Kathy Lee Gifford clothing. The antisweatshop movement has also forced the large-scale transformation of the worldwide production conditions for firms manufacturing college-logo apparel, such as T-shirts for the University of New Mexico. To date, more than one hundred colleges and universities follow codes of conduct in contracting out to private firms to produce their college-logo apparel. More broadly still, there is substantial polling evidence suggesting that high percentages of consumers support the principle of ethical consumption. For example, a 1999 survey of U.S. consumers directed by Kimberly Ann Elliott of the Institute for International Economics and Richard Freeman of the Harvard University Economics Department found that, *on average*, U.S. consumers were willing to pay 28 percent more on a $10 item and 15 percent more on a $100 item to ensure that the products they bought were made under "good working conditions" (see Elliott and Freeman 2003).

Given these various considerations, it seems plausible that the larger restaurants and hotels in Santa Fe might even benefit by advertising themselves as living wage firms. This is especially true, given that these firms are likely to have to raise their prices by only about 3–4 percent to cover their increased living wage costs. Price increases of this range are well inside of the 15–28 percent increment that the Elliot and Freeman poll suggests consumers are willing to pay to ensure good conditions for working people.

Raising Productivity

In previous chapters, we introduce the idea that firms may raise their productivity as the result of paying a higher wage. Research in recent years has shown that paying workers above-market-level wages for a given job can improve firm performance through several channels. These include lower costs for recruiting low-wage workers, lower turnover, and less absenteeism. Less turnover and absenteeism, in turn, mean that the firms' training and supervisory costs should also fall. Combining all these factors may then yield a workplace with better morale and higher productivity.[12]

But the view that large Santa Fe firms would gain in efficiency through paying a higher minimum wage raises an obvious question: If firms could benefit by paying a higher minimum wage, why haven't they already voluntarily been paying the higher wage? One answer, as already noted, is that some significant minority of firms *do* pay substantially higher wages than their competitors and still succeed in the market. But this is not the situation for the majority of firms. For this majority of cases, the savings the firms would generate through lowering turnover, absenteeism and associated recruitment, training, and supervisory costs will still be less than their direct cost increases resulting from paying higher wages. For our purposes therefore, we need to consider how significant these indirect cost savings might be among covered firms relative to the increased costs they would face due to a living wage ordinance.

Cost Savings through Reducing Turnover

In addition to the general research that relates productivity gains to higher wages, there is also an extensive literature in both academic and trade journals on the specific question of the costs of high turnover in the hotel and restaurant industry. This literature argues that high turnover rates for hotels and restaurants impose significant costs on these firms. For example, a 1998 study by the American Hotel Foundation shows that turnover ranges between 60 and 300 percent per year (Woods, Heck, and Sciarini 1998). For front-line-level employees, the average turnover rate was 92 percent. According to Jeffrey A. Fernsten and Steven A. Croffoot in *The Practice of Hospitality Management* (1986) the costs of turnover per employee in the hotel industry range between $176 and $4,220 (in 2005 dollars; between $150 and $3,600 in 1999 dollars). A 2001 study by Tony Simons and Timothy Hinkin, "The Effect of Employee Turnover on Hotel Profits," in the *Cornell Hotel and Restaurant Administration Quarterly*, sets the figure higher, at $5,860 (in 2005 dollars; $5,000 in 1999 dollars; Simons and Hinkins 2001, 68). For restaurants, a 1998 study by the National Restaurant Association also places average turnover costs at $5,991 per employee (in 2005 dollars; $5,000 in 1998 dollars; Worcester 1999).

A paper by Timothy Hinkin and J. Bruce Tracey in the *Cornell Hotel and Restaurant Administration Quarterly* (2000) divides these costs of turnover into five main categories: separation costs, recruiting and attracting costs, selection costs, hiring costs, and lost productivity costs. Within each of these categories, they provide further details as to how these costs are incurred. For example, the separation costs alone include the exit interviewer, the employee exit interview, the paperwork processing, and the severance pay. These costs of turnover entail loss of trained employees, the recruitment and training of new employees, and the general administrative overhead that surrounds these activities.

Turnover and Potential Cost Savings for Plaintiff Firms

In table 5.8, we show the basic calculations we made to estimate the turnover rates for the plaintiffs Zuma and Pranzo, based on their own payroll information. As table 5.8 shows, as of October 31, 2003, Zuma employed fifty-three people. But during this same payroll period, fifty-eight people were separated from the firm. Some of these separations were due to seasonal fluctuations in business activity, and we would not want to equate such seasonal fluctuations in employment levels with employee turnover. We therefore also report the employment rate at Zuma at its peak during this period, which was seventy-one employees in August. We then calculate a turnover rate for Zuma relative to this peak level of employment to be 82

Table 5.8. Estimated employee turnover rates for two plaintiffs

	Zuma *All employees* *Based on monthly payroll* *data from 1/1/03–10/31/03*	Pranzo *Non-managerial employees* *Based on 21 payrolls* *between 1/1/03–10/9/03*
Actual employment at end of payroll period	53	81
Number of employees separated during actual payroll period	58	81
Peak employment for payroll period	71	109 *[estimate based on Zuma ratio of October/peak employment]*
Turnover rate relative to peak employment for payroll period	82%	74% *[81/109]*
Estimated 12-month turnover rate	98% *[0.82×12/10 monthly payroll periods]*	92% *[0.74×26/21 payroll periods]*
Estimated number of separations based on 12-month turnover rate	70 *[71 peak employment×0.98]*	100 *[109 peak employment×0.92]*

Sources: Payroll data for Zuma and Pranzo.

percent turnover (i.e., 58 separations/71 peak employment). Finally, we project this rate of turnover for a full 12–month payroll period and estimate the number of separations that would occur assuming the 12–month turnover rate is equal to the actual 10–month rate we observe. As we can see, the estimated 12–month turnover rate is 98 percent, and the estimated number of separations is seventy.

Working from the rough industry estimate of the cost of turnover being $5,000 per employee separation, this would mean that, for the estimated full year, Zuma would be experiencing turnover costs of $350,000 ($70 \times \$5,000$). This figure is 4.6 times greater than the $76,830 we estimate as the amount that Zuma would pay through mandated living wage increases. Our estimate of the turnover costs for Pranzo is similar, as we see in the next column in table 5.8.[13]

These estimates of turnover costs—that turnover costs for Zuma and Pranzo are nearly five times greater than the mandated living wage cost increases—are obviously very high. But they still do not enable us to conclude that reducing turnover could by itself absorb the costs of a living wage ordinance. For one thing, we cannot assume that turnover would be entirely eliminated once the living wage ordinance is implemented. We also cannot assume that the $5,000 per employee estimate for turnover costs provided by the industry and academic sources are applicable to Zuma, Pranzo, or any other covered firm in Santa Fe. Moreover, there are no solid estimates in the literature to date as to how much turnover is likely to fall due to a given increase in pay for the low-wage employees.

To provide a deliberately low-end estimate as to what the opportunities may be for cost savings through reducing turnover, let us assume that: (1) the costs of turnover for Zuma and Pranzo are only 25 percent as large as the $5,000 figure estimated in the academic and trade literature (i.e., that these costs of turnover are, rather, on the order of $1,250 per employee) and (2) raising all employees at least to the Santa Fe minimum of $8.50 does lower turnover, but by only 25 percent at these two firms.

Based on these low-end assumptions, table 5.9 works through the steps to provide a new cost estimate for the two plaintiffs from turnover reduction. Working from these assumptions, we see that Zuma would save $21,250 from turnover reduction, which would amount to about 28 percent of its mandated living wage costs. Pranzo would save $31,250, which would be 29.2 percent of its mandated living wage costs. In other words, even operating with deliberately modest assumptions as to both the costs of turnover and the amount by which turnover is likely to fall, we still reach the conclusion that a fall in turnover resulting from providing living wage increases would generate cost savings equal to nearly 30 percent of the mandated costs of the ordinance for both Zuma and Pranzo.

Table 5.9. Estimate of potential savings from reducing turnover

	Zuma	Pranzo
Assumptions for estimate: 1. *Costs of turnover are $1,250/employee* 2. *Turnover rate falls by 25 percent after living wage ordinance is implemented*		
	All employees *Based on data payroll monthly from 1/1/03–10/31/03*	*Non-managerial employees* *Based on 21 payrolls between 1/1/03–10/9/03*
New annual turnover rate after rate falls by 25 percent	74% *[0.98×0.75]*	69% *[0.92×0.75]*
Fall in annual separations due to decline in turnover	17 *[New separation rate 74% × peak employment of 71 = 53 separations. Reduction = 70 − 53]*	25 *[New separation rate 69% × peak employment of 109 = 75 separations. Reduction = 100 − 75]*
Cost savings from reducing turnover/separations	$21,250 *[17× $1,250]*	$31,250 *[25× $1,250]*
Estimated mandated costs of living wage ordinance	$76,830	$107,170
Cost savings from reducing turnover/separations	27.7% *[$21,250/$76,830]*	29.2% *[$31,250/$107,170]*

Source: Authors' calculation based on data provided by plaintiffs.

Additional Channels for Productivity Gains

Cutting turnover costs is not the only channel through which higher wages might enhance the productivity of workers in covered firms. For example, these estimates do not attempt to measure the costs of absenteeism or supervision in low-pay/low-morale jobs or the corresponding gains that would accrue to firms if better pay encouraged more effort from workers. These benefits can be significant in various service-sector positions in which employees deal frequently with customers. Truman Bewley of Yale University emphasizes this point in *Why Wages Don't Fall during a Recession*, his major 1999 study of how employment relations can affect the economy's performance even at the macroeconomic level. For example, Bewley quotes the representative views of one manager of a nonunion hotel with sixty employees: "Morale is important for performance. Employees need to enjoy coming to work. They need to be treated as individuals, and their ideas must be noticed and appreciated. They must be encouraged to take the initiative to make customers happy. Employees have to be happy to present a positive image to guests" (1999, 50).

Adding the potential savings in supervisory costs, lowered absenteeism, and greater worker effort to the estimates we have derived on turnover costs, it seems reasonable that a modest estimate of the full productivity benefits of the higher living wage for some firms could be in the range of 40 percent of their total living wage costs. This rough estimate is based on first allowing for savings from lowered turnover at roughly 30 percent of the mandated living wage costs. We then allow for additional savings through lowered absenteeism and higher morale. Against these gains, we then add the additional ripple-effect cost increases and the local-supplier pass-throughs.

Combining Price and Productivity Effects

If we allow, based on our deliberately low-end assumptions, that improvements in productivity resulting from workers receiving living wage raises could save covered firms on the order of 30–40 percent of their total living wage costs, that would further imply that the need to raise prices to cover these increased costs would correspondingly diminish. If we again, for the sake of caution, take the lower-end figure and assume that productivity gains could cover only 30 percent of the living wage costs, that then means that prices would need to be marked up only to cover the remaining 70 percent of costs rather than the full 100 percent. Thus, considering our cost increases/sales ratios, the relevant price increases for the average restaurant would now fall from 3.3 to 2.3 percent.

Price, Productivity, and Alternative Business Adjustments

The general conclusion from the foregoing analysis strongly suggests that covered businesses in Santa Fe are likely to be able to cover their additional living wage costs through raising prices modestly and improving their firm's productivity, primarily through reducing turnover. This means that the Santa Fe living wage ordinance is very unlikely to induce firms to either lay off employees or relocate out of Santa Fe to avoid being covered by the ordinance. By extension, it also means that the Santa Fe living wage ordinance is not likely to have any significant impact on the capacity of Santa Fe hotels to attract tourists or conventions.

This general conclusion is fully consistent with the most recent academic literature on the effects of minimum wage increases on unemployment. The best-known work in this area has been that of Card and Krueger, especially their 1995 book, *Myth and Measurement: The New Economics of the Minimum Wage.* Card and Krueger have repeatedly found that changes in the minimum wage have not tended to raise unemployment by any discernable amount (and, indeed, have tended to be associated with slight *increases* in low-wage employment). However, the Card-Krueger research methods and results have been challenged by a number of authors, most notably David Neumark and William Wascher (e.g., 2000). But Neumark's most recent findings, although still at variance with those of Card and Krueger, also show either no significant employment effects at all resulting from a minimum wage increase or only small negative effects.

The differences between the Card-Krueger and Neumark-Wascher findings have been well summarized by Richard Freeman, who provides an apt summary of our discussion of employment effects in Santa Fe: "The debate is over whether modest minimum wage increases have 'no' employment effect, modest positive effects, or small negative effects. It is *not* about whether or not there are large negative effects" (1995, 833; emphasis in original).

APPENDIX: ESTIMATING LOCAL-SUPPLIER PASS-THROUGHS IN SANTA FE

IMPLAN is one of the leading regional economic analysis tools of its kind in the country, and is used extensively in academia, government, and the private sector.[14] We have drawn on the IMPLAN model to estimate how much of a cost increase various types of businesses in Santa Fe are likely to experience from their suppliers due to the living wage ordinance. We focus on the IMPLAN estimate of major supplier inputs for the restaurant industry in the City of Santa Fe. From these data on major supplier inputs, we are then able to illustrate how we provide an estimate of local-supplier cost pass-throughs flowing from the living wage ordinance.

We focus on the restaurant industry in part because of the relatively heavy impact it will bear from the living wage ordinance—a cost increase of over 3 percent relative to sales for a representative restaurant. But we also focus on restaurants here because, through data provided by three of the four plaintiffs that are themselves restaurants, we are able to check on the reliability of the IMPLAN model for our purposes here.

Thus, in table 5A.1, we reproduce the supplier cost information provided by Pranzo, Robbie Day, and Zuma, alongside estimates we have generated for a representative restaurant based on data from IMPLAN. Following the accounting approach presented by Pranzo, we have broken down supplier costs into two broad categories: (1) food and alcohol and (2) controllable expenses. As the table shows, for the three plaintiff firms the data are consistent as to the ratio of these supplier cost categories relative to these restaurants' sales. Food and alcohol ranges between 31.3 and 32.9 percent for the three plaintiff restaurants and controllable expenses range between 25.1 and 26.2 percent. In column 5 of table 5A.1, we then present our estimate, derived from IMPLAN, of these two supplier cost items as a percentage of sales for the representative restaurant. As the table shows, we estimate food and alcohol as 27.9 percent of sales and controllable expenses as 22.0 percent. In short, although the percentages from IMPLAN are lower than those of the plaintiff firms, they are lower by only a relatively small amount—the IMPLAN estimates, in other words, are broadly consistent with the figures provided by the plaintiffs on their supplier costs.

Based on this confirmation, we now proceed to use the detailed data from IMPLAN to estimate local-supplier pass-throughs. Table 5A.2 shows the method we used for generating local-supplier cost pass-through estimates. Again, we focus on the data for the restaurant industry, although we have conducted the same estimating exercise for all industries operating in Santa Fe and will report the overall estimate for all covered industries below.

Table 5A.1. Total supplier costs as a percentage of sales for plaintiffs and IMPLAN

(1)	(2) Pranzo	(3) Robbie Day	(4) Zuma (Zia Diner)	(5) IMPLAN
Food and alcohol	31.8%	31.3%	32.9%	27.9%
Controllable expenses	25.1%	26.2%	25.8%	22.0%

Sources: New Mexicans for Free Enterprise et al. vs. The City of Santa Fe documents: Plaintiff Zuma Second Supplementary Interrogatory & RFP, 128; Plaintiff Robbie Day financial statement including balance sheet statement of operations for 12 months ended December 31, 2003 (hand-delivered to city attorney Bruce Thompson March 3, 2004); Plaintiff Pranzo Supplemental to First Interrogatory & RFP, 274.

Conceptually, our estimation approach is quite simple, involving only two basic steps. First, we generate from IMPLAN figures for local-supplier costs for the covered restaurants in Santa Fe and then break down these costs according to the relative weights supplied by the various types of suppliers. Second, we estimate the ratios of the cost increases due to the living wage for these local suppliers relative to their sales. This cost increase/sales ratio for supplier firms is the same ratio that we have already reported in table 5.4 for a representative covered firm in Santa Fe as well as, in table 5.5, for covered firms broken down by industry categories. Thus, again, in table 5.4 we report that the cost increase/total sales ratio is 1.0 percent for a representative firm. This means that if this representative firm happened to be the supplier for the covered Santa Fe restaurants, then the representative firm would have to raise its prices by 1 percent to fully pass through its living wage costs to the restaurants. This is precisely what we mean by a full pass-through by local suppliers to the restaurants. To know how much that 1 percent local-supplier cost pass-through will be in terms of overall costs for the restaurant, we then simply look at the relative proportion of costs represented by a given local supplier. If, therefore, a local brewery supplies 10 percent of all supplies to a covered Santa Fe restaurant and if, due to the living wage ordinance, this brewery's costs rise by 1 percent relative to its sales, this implies that overall costs for the restaurant will rise by 0.1 percent—that is, $0.10 \times 0.01 = 0.001$, or 0.1 percent).

This estimation technique is clearly distinct from the approach taken by the three restaurant plaintiffs, as described in various interrogatories.[15] All three plaintiffs state in their interrogatories that they assume that labor costs for their local suppliers will rise to the same extent as their own labor costs. For example, the plaintiff Robbie Day writes:

> I will also see an increase in my indirect expenses because my suppliers will experience similar cost increases. I cannot predict with certainty the amount

Table 5A.2. Local-supplier cost pass-throughs as a percentage of restaurant/bar sales

(1)	(2) Food and alcohol inputs	(3) Controllable expenses	(4) All non-labor inputs (food and alcohol + controllables)
All supplier purchases before living wage	$43.4 million	$34.0 million	$77.4 million
Local supplier purchases before living wage	$4.2 million	$11.5 million	$15.7 million
Average supplier cost increase from living wage as percentage of supplier sales	0.89%	0.83%	0.85%
Increase in local supplier purchases due to living wage cost pass-throughs	$37,849 *(0.89 percent of $4.2 million)*	$95,738 *(0.83 percent of $11.5 million)*	$133,587 *(0.85 percent of $15.7 million)*
Total restaurant/bar sales	$160.4 million	$160.4 million	$160.4 million
Local supplier cost pass- throughs as percentage of restaurant/bar sales	0.02%	0.06%	0.08%

Sources: Current Population Survey Outgoing Rotation Group 2001–2003 files, Bureau of Labor Statistics, U.S. Department of Labor; 1997 Economic Census for the county of Santa Fe, U.S. Census Bureau; 2001 IMPLAN Pro Software, MIG, Inc.

Note: See Pollin and Brenner, 2004 Report, app. 1 and 2 for details on calculations.

of increase in these indirect expenses because that will depend on the increases in my suppliers' direct and indirect costs. *I assume that all of my Santa Fe suppliers will experience the same increase in labor costs of about 39.86%, 56%, and 75%.* However, we cannot predict the actual percentage increase of their total costs.[16]

But this assumption by Robbie Day that "all of my Santa Fe suppliers will experience the same increase in labor costs" takes no account of the fact that, for all other businesses in Santa Fe, the proportion of low-wage workers relative to total labor costs and total sales is far lower than those proportions are for restaurants. In addition, the plaintiffs present no evidence as to the relative weights of various types of local-supplier inputs relative to the overall cost structures of their restaurants.

To document our approach to estimating local-supplier cost pass-throughs, we proceed in column 2 of table 5A.2 with our estimate for food and alcohol supplies. We first report that all food and alcohol supplies for covered Santa Fe restaurants amounted to $43.4 million. Of that total, IM-PLAN reports that $4.2 million of food and alcohol purchases came from local suppliers. The next issue is, therefore, due to the living wage ordinance, how much will this $4.2 million of food and alcohol purchases need to increase for the local food and alcohol suppliers to fully pass through their own additional living wage costs? To answer this, we need to know the cost increases faced by these suppliers due to the living wage ordinance relative to their sales—that is, the same ratio that we have examined before both for a representative firm (table 5.4) and for representative firms by industry (table 5.5).

We see in table 5A.2 that, for food and alcohol suppliers to covered restaurants, the cost increase/sales ratio is 0.89 percent. In other words, assuming the sales of these suppliers remain constant, they would have to raise their prices by 0.89 percent in order for their increases in living wage costs to be matched by an equal increase in their sales revenue. Thus, as we see in table 5A.2, the spending by the covered restaurants on food and alcohol supplies will need to rise by $37,849 ($4.2 million×0.89 percent) for these suppliers to achieve a full pass-through on their living wage costs.

6 Spending Injections from the Arizona Minimum Wage Increase

How Businesses Benefit

ROBERT POLLIN AND JEANNETTE WICKS-LIM

In our 2006 full report, we examine in detail the costs Arizona businesses will face from raising the statewide minimum wage to $6.75 and how the businesses are likely to respond to these costs. But many businesses in the state will also benefit from the rise to the $6.75 minimum wage. The reason they will benefit is straightforward: when low-wage workers and their families have more money to spend, they will spend a good share of it in the lower-income communities in which they live.

Which businesses are likely to benefit and how much will they gain? As we document in our 2006 full report, raising the Arizona minimum wage to $6.75 ($3.75 for tipped workers) will provide mandated raises of about $190 million and ripple-effect increases of another $140 million—in total, roughly $330 million in wage increases for 350,000 workers. However, not all $330 million in wage gains will represent an increase in spending for Arizona businesses. There are two basic reasons for this.

1. As we have seen, the increases in *net* family incomes will be less than the wage gains because most low-wage workers will see their government subsidies go down and their taxes go up after they receive a raise. This is why, for example, among the families below the basic-needs threshold with at least one worker earning up to $8.00, workers' earnings rise by 8.4 percent but family disposable income increases by only 3.2 percent.

2. For the most part, the $330 million in wage gains will be paid for through small price increases by the affected businesses. This means

that the extra money received by low-income families is coming out of the pockets of everyone else who is spending money in Arizona: the benefits to low-income families is the result of an income transfer from the incomes of all consumers in the state. Considering this income transfer by itself, there should be no net benefit to businesses in Arizona from raising the minimum wage to $6.75, only a different set of people spending the $330 million worth of wage increases—lower-income consumers are in a position to spend more while higher-income consumers have slightly less to spend.

However, even recognizing that the gains from the low-income families come from the pockets of higher-income families, there are still two ways in which Arizona businesses will benefit from the minimum wage increase. We term these (1) an out-of-state spending injection and (2) a low-income-neighborhood spending injection.

OUT-OF-STATE SPENDING INJECTION

Some of the extra income going to low-income families in Arizona will come from the pockets of out-of-state consumers, in particular, out-of-state tourists spending money in Arizona restaurants, hotels, retail stores, and entertainment establishments. When these businesses raise their prices slightly to cover their higher labor costs, the effect of this is that extra money from out of state will be transferred into Arizona. This extra spending first goes to the low-wage workers in the tourist industry serving out-of-state tourists and, therefore, does not directly benefit the hotel and restaurant owners themselves or businesses in the state more generally. However, the low-wage workers in the tourist industry now have extra money to spend that came from outside of Arizona. When these workers spend their extra income, that is money that, if not for the minimum wage increase to $6.75, would not otherwise have been available to any consumers in the state. This is why we refer to this effect resulting from the minimum wage increase as an out-of-state spending injection.

How large is this out-of-state spending injection likely to be? We estimate that the annual net income increase to Arizona workers coming from out-of-state tourists will be $80 million.[1] But this $80 million in increased spending will, in turn, create further spending increases within the state—what economists call a multiplier effect. The multiplier effect will occur after low-income families spend their extra $80 million. The business owners and workers who receive this extra money will also then spend a major portion of it making purchases from other business owners and workers in Arizona.

Thus, the effects of the initial $80 million out-of-state injection multiplies throughout the Arizona economy. To be specific, this multiplier effect operates as follows: for every extra dollar spent by low-income families due to the out-of-state injection, the total increase in spending for Arizona's economy will be $1.43. In other words, the $80 million out-of-state spending injection will generate a total of $114 million in new spending in Arizona.

This $114 million figure for net new spending is, of course, tiny in comparison to the total sales figure in the state of $370 billion ($114 million is 0.03 percent of $370 billion). At the same time, as we estimate in our full study, the total costs to businesses from the minimum wage are $356 million (including now the public sector). From this perspective, the $114 million in new spending due to the out-of-state spending injection and the multiplier effects represents fully 32 percent of the increase in costs that businesses will face. Of course, there is no guarantee that the businesses that will be paying out $356 million in extra wages and payroll taxes due to the higher minimum wage will be the same ones who receive the extra $114 million in sales from the spending injection and multiplier. But there will certainly be some broad compensation operating through the effects of the out-of-state spending injection.

LOW-INCOME-NEIGHBORHOOD SPENDING INJECTION

The primary business beneficiaries from the minimum wage increase will be retail stores in poor neighborhoods. This is for the simple reason that low-wage workers and their families will spend most of their increase in disposable income in the neighborhoods in which they live. How significant will the spending increases be in low-income neighborhoods? To estimate this, we calculated how this effect is likely to operate within the 182 census tracts that constitute the low-income neighborhoods in the Phoenix metropolitan area. We present the basic data from this exercise in table 6.1.

As the table shows, we estimate that of the roughly 230,000 workers in the Phoenix area who will receive raises, 144,358, or 63 percent, are members of low-income families that live in one of the area's 182 low-income census tracts. The families of these workers will receive a total increase in disposable income of $148 million due to the minimum wage increase. This increase in disposable income amounts to about 2.2 percent of the total disposable income among families living in these neighborhoods.

For the purposes of our estimate, we make the reasonable assumption that, whatever the proportion of their total disposable income the affected families were spending in their own neighborhoods *before* the minimum

Table 6.1. Sales increases for retail firms in low-income Phoenix-area neighborhoods

Total number of workers in Phoenix MSA receiving raises	229,139
Number of workers living in low-income neighborhoods receiving raises	144,358 (63% of Phoenix workers receiving raises)
Total disposable income in low-income neighborhoods	$6.8 billion
Increased disposable income for low-wage workers and families living in low-income neighborhoods	$148.3 million
Percentage increase in disposable income	2.2%

Sources: Current Population Survey Outgoing Rotation Group and Annual Social and Economic Supplemental survey 2001–2005 files, Bureau of Labor Statistics, U.S. Department of Labor; 2000 Summary Tape File 3, U.S. Census Bureau; 2003 IMPLAN Pro Software, MIG, Inc.; 2004 Consumer Expenditure Survey, U.S. Census Bureau.

Note: See Pollin and Wicks-Lim (2006, app.1) for details on calculations.

wage rises, they will keep spending that same proportion of their disposable income in their neighborhoods *after* the minimum wage is raised to $6.75. As such, we estimate that spending in Phoenix's low-income neighborhoods will rise by about 2.2 percent after the minimum wage goes up to $6.75. We have not conducted the same focused data exercise for other communities in Arizona. However, broadly speaking, we expect that spending in the other low-income neighborhoods in the state will increase by approximately the same 2 percent.

Such a 2.2 percent boost in sales for retail businesses in Arizona low-income neighborhoods is a small, but still significant, benefit. For purposes of comparison, it is an amount that is approximately equal to two-thirds the average rate of annual income growth of the U.S. economy over the past full business cycle, 1991–2000; that is, it is equal to 8 months worth of average national income growth. If we assume that income growth in Arizona's low-income neighborhoods approximately mirror the average rate of income growth for the national economy, this means that the retail business in Arizona's low-income neighborhoods will effectively jump roughly 8 months ahead of a normal pace of sales growth.

Moreover, as with the income benefits to individuals and families, a 2.2 percent increase in sales for a business can be compounded to the degree that this additional income also increases the credit-worthiness of a business and of the community more generally. With increased access to credit, businesses are able to expand, increase amenities to customers, or smooth over periods when sales revenue may fluctuate. This should mean further benefits to the life of low-income neighborhoods throughout Arizona.

Part 3

BENEFITS TO WORKERS AND FAMILIES

If we can establish that living/minimum wage increases, at least at the levels at which they have passed in the United States over the past decade, will not cause large-scale employee layoffs and business relocations, we still have to face other major questions in evaluating the effects of these measures. That is, Who are the people who will benefit from these raises? What are their living situations? How much might their living standards improve, after taking into account the fact that, when their wages rise, their taxes will also increase while their eligibility for government subsidies, including food stamps and the Earned Income Tax Credit (EITC), will decline? And then there is the still more basic matter that frames all of these questions, which is, what is a living wage or a decent minimum wage standard in any given community? These are the issues we address in this part of the book.

We include in this part work from two separate and distinct studies. The first is the work that Mark Brenner, Stephanie Luce, Jeannette Wicks-Lim, and I (along with other collaborators) all did for the city of Santa Monica, California, in 2000, evaluating a proposal to raise the minimum wage to $10.75 per hour for all workers within a designated portion of the city known as its Coastal Zone. The Coastal Zone includes the city's major high-end hotels and a large numbers of similarly high-end restaurants. The second study, which Jeannette Wicks-Lim and I wrote, was for a proposal to raise the statewide minimum wage in Arizona to $6.75 in November 2006 from the then (and now, as I write) federal minimum of $5.15.

With the Santa Monica study, we begin chapter 7 by going through a set of steps to define what would constitute a reasonable living wage in this community. This discussion picks up from chapter 2, which presented some criteria for defining a living wage in the Boston area. Here we present a more detailed perspective that is of course, appropriate for Santa Monica. As we have seen in chapter 2, there is no straightforward way of identifying any single wage rate as the living wage in Boston, Santa Monica, or any other community. But the exercise enables us to establish a reasonable framework for how to proceed in detailed policy discussions.

Beyond this most basic issue of identifying what a living wage should be, questions arise as to whether these measures are well-targeted to actually help their intended beneficiaries (i.e., low-income workers and their families), as opposed to other types of people who are employed at low-paying jobs. Opponents frequently claim that a prime group of beneficiaries of such measures are middle-class teenagers, who work part-time at low-paying jobs to help finance their car upkeep, new iPods, and similar indulgences. A related claim is that a high proportion of the people holding low-wage jobs are young people on the initial rungs of career ladders that point inexorably upward. These people will experience wage increases regardless of the living wage standard as they move forward with their careers. Still another related claim is that a high proportion of the beneficiaries are second-earners in their families. The image here is of middle-class housewives who take low-wage jobs to supplement a family's living standard that is already reasonably comfortable.

A fourth issue is that, even to the extent that these measures do benefit low-income workers and their families, they do so in an inefficient way. This is because the truly needy already receive income support in the form of the EITC, food stamps, and related subsidies. Moreover, when living wage laws raise a family's earned income, it means that the government support for which such families are eligible correspondingly declines while their tax obligations rise. This means that some significant share of the benefits from living wage standards becomes a leakage—with government agencies, rather than low-wage workers and their families, becoming the beneficiaries of the law.

These are the questions that we try to sort out carefully in chapter 8 on Santa Monica and in chapter 9 on Arizona. Our findings here are based on two kinds of evidence. The first, standard data source is the federal government's statistics from the U.S. Labor Department's Current Population Survey (CPS). As with all other researchers in this area of work, we have relied on this survey extensively, both for the Santa Monica and Arizona studies.

At the same time, in the Santa Monica case in chapter 8, we believed that we needed to expand our perspective beyond what was attainable from the CPS. This is because, using just the CPS, we were unable to obtain a picture of workers employed within Santa Monica itself, but could only do so for workers within the greater Los Angeles area more generally. To be able to focus more sharply on the situation in Santa Monica proper, we therefore conducted our own survey of workers who were employed in Santa Monica itself. Thus, for the Santa Monica case, we present two separate sets of data and form an overall picture from the synthesis of the government's survey of the LA area and our own survey within Santa Monica proper.

As we see in both the Santa Monica and Arizona cases, the beneficiaries of the living/minimum wage measures are primarily the types of people the measures are intended to benefit. They mostly come from low-income families, with a very high proportion living in poverty or near-poverty. They are overwhelmingly adults and are well into their long-term employment trajectories. The jobs they held when the surveys were conducted are not, for the most part, initial steps on a career path that will bring large improvements in their living standards. A very high proportion of these workers are their families' primary bread-winners. And if they are not the main source of their family's income, they are contributing a significant share to the overall living standard. Finally, a disproportionate share of those eligible for living wage raises are African Americans, Hispanics, and women. It is significant that these general demographic patterns prevail in both Santa Monica and Arizona, despite the substantial differences in the proposed measures and the relevant communities—a $10.75 proposed minimum applying to a small subcommunity in Los Angeles heavily supported by affluent tourists versus a $6.75 minimum applying to an entire state of 5.9 million people.

Of course, there are government leakages. As we see in the Santa Monica case, a prototypical low-wage worker would receive a wage increase on the order of 40 percent from the raise to a $10.75 living wage standard. However, the net income gain for this family, after accounting for changes in their tax and subsidy status, as well as the money being contributed by other family members, is closer to 20 percent. This is still a significant gain for a low-income family, but obviously, only about half of the percentage increase in the wage itself. In addition, as we stress chapters 7 and 8, it matters that, through the living/minimum wage initiatives, the income increase coming to the families is earned income rather than money provided to them as a government subsidy. This is an important consideration, both in terms of workers' dignity as well as their level of commitment to their jobs (and, thereby, also their level of productivity on the job). These leakages to government should also be seen from the other angle. They mean that the economy is now operating with tax-paying workers and fewer families relying on government programs for support.

The Santa Monica measure was passed in a revised version—at a $10.50 rather than $10.75 wage standard in May 2001 by the city council after months of heated debate.[1] However, in November 2002, opponents of the measure managed to place a proposition before voters that would repeal the measure. After an extremely expensive campaign financed primarily by the major hotels that operate in the Santa Monica Coastal Zone, the repeal initiative was narrowly passed. Yet, despite the repeal, the city's living wage supporters have subsequently succeeded in obtaining much of what they had intended through the initial Coastal Zone initiative. By the end of 2006, many hotels in Santa Monica, representing half of all rooms in the city, had been unionized. In addition, the actual starting wage for hotel workers in Santa Monica rose by more than 50 percent, from $7.25 to $11.00, between 1996 and 2006.[2]

The Arizona measure was voted into law on November 7, 2006. On the same day as the Arizona law passed, voters in Colorado, Ohio, Missouri, Montana, and Nevada also passed similar laws. Because of these victories, by January 1, 2007, a majority of the states and the District of Columbia, covering nearly 70 percent of the U.S. population, was operating with a minimum wage standard above the federal minimum.[3]

—R. P.

7 What Is a Living Wage?

Considerations for Santa Monica,
California

ROBERT POLLIN

CONCEPTUAL DEFINITIONS OF LIVING WAGES

The living wage initiatives that have become law throughout the country are motivated by a common initial premise: that people who work for a living should not have to raise a family in poverty.[1] But the term *living wage* also suggests a more ambitious standard. In *A Living Wage: American Workers and the Making of a Consumer Society*, Lawrence Glickman writes that in the historical development of the living wage movement, supporters used the *living wage* concept to define a wage level that offers workers "the ability to support families, to maintain self-respect, and to have both the means and the leisure to participate in the civic life of the nation," (1997, 66). This Glickman definition of a living wage bears a close correspondence with the ideas of Amartya Sen on defining poverty relative to the achievement of what he calls "capabilities." These capabilities include such things as the ability to read and write, to lead a long and healthy life, to have freedom of movement, and to participate meaningfully in the civic life of the community. But how do we measure the ability to participate in community life? Sen acknowledges the difficulties with this issue, especially when considering the question according to the level of general affluence of the community in which a person lives. As Sen writes:

> The need to take part in the life of a community may induce demands for modern equipment (televisions, videocassette recorders, automobiles and so on) in a country where such facilities are more or less universal (unlike what

111

would be needed in less affluent countries), and this imposes a strain on the relatively poor person in a rich country even when that person is at a much higher level of income compared with people in less opulent countries. Indeed, the paradoxical phenomenon of hunger in rich countries—even in the United States—has something to do with the competing demands of these expenses. (2000, 89–90)

Quantifying the Concepts

Regardless of whether we define the term *living wage* narrowly, as adequate to provide a poverty-line living standard, or more generously, in line with both the historical meaning of the term and Sen's conception of attaining adequate capabilities, we still face problems in translating these concepts into concrete monetary amounts. What are the proper dollar values that we should assign to a poverty-level living standard or to a higher, but still relatively modest standard that would enable a person to participate meaningfully in his or her community life? These are the issues we pursued in evaluating the merits of the living wage proposal for Santa Monica.

In posing these basic questions for our present purposes, we leave aside for the moment some additional concerns that are also, always and everywhere, central for establishing viable living wage standards. These considerations include the relative merits of using government transfer programs, such as the Earned Income Tax Credit, as opposed to reasonable, mandated wage floors, as a means of guaranteeing decent minimum income levels for working families; and the negative unintended consequences, such as job losses for low-wage workers, that can occur from setting living wage standards that are above what existing market conditions can bear. These are issues that we take up elsewhere in this book and in previous work.

I proceed here by providing a range of dollar amounts consistent with both a poverty-line level of family income and a modest basic-needs level, as appropriate specifically to the Los Angeles area. Fortunately, reasonably solid research and data do exist to provide the foundation for such an exercise.

First, in terms of measuring poverty-line living standards, the U.S. Census Bureau, of course, has been producing such measures since 1963. But a broad range of researchers argue that the government's methodology—which has not been significantly altered since its introduction in 1963—is no longer adequate. I therefore attempted to develop some viable guidelines for establishing poverty thresholds for our purposes, drawing both from the Census Bureau estimates and the recent professional literature focused on developing improved methodologies.

In terms of measuring a basic-needs living standard, the California Budget Project (CBP) in Sacramento has done solid research in estimating this.

The CBP divided the State of California into eight regions, of which Los Angeles is one (and that with the largest population). The CBP then attempted to measure a "basic family budget" derived from observed costs of housing, food, health care, child care, transportation, clothing, basic telephone service, and a few other essentials. Unlike the Census Bureau's poverty thresholds, the standard of living that the CBP attempted to measure is, as they explain, is "more than a 'bare bones' existence, yet covers only basic expenses, allowing little room for 'extras' such as college savings or vacations" (California Budget Project 1999, 5). The CBP estimates should therefore serve as a good reference point in defining a more generous basic-needs living wage for workers in Santa Monica.

Measuring Poverty Thresholds

Since 1963, the U.S. Census Bureau has set detailed poverty thresholds for families of various sizes. For example, the poverty threshold in 1999 for a family of two was $10,869 and for a family of four with two children was $16,895. The family living at this threshold would subsist on what the Department of Agriculture terms the "thrifty food plan"—which is the amount of food needed for each family member to receive the basic caloric minimum.

The government's methodology then assumes that poor families spend approximately one-third of their budget on food. Thus, to generate the dollar figures for the poverty threshold, the government simply multiples the dollar value of the "thrifty food plan" by three.

In recent years, many researchers and government officials have questioned the adequacy of this method for establishing poverty thresholds. The most extensive scientific survey of these issues was that sponsored by the National Research Council (NRC; Citro and Michael 1995). According to the NRC study, establishing overall poverty thresholds on the basis of food costs alone presents many problems. For one thing, there are large variations in housing and medical care costs by region and population groups. In addition, food prices have fallen relative to housing costs. Child-care costs have also not been adequately accounted for. This has become increasingly important over time as labor force participation by mothers has risen.

The NRC study reports on six alternative methodologies to the current official method for measuring absolute poverty for a two adult–two child family.[2] The thresholds generated by these alternative methodologies are all higher than the official threshold, ranging between 23.7 and 53.2 percent above the official threshold. The average value of these alternative estimates is 41.7 percent higher than the official threshold. This standard for an alternative absolute poverty threshold will help establish our benchmark for a low-end living wage estimate.

Regional Living Costs

The alternative poverty thresholds reported by the NRC do not take into account regional differences in the cost of living. Considerable evidence suggests that living costs for low-wage workers in the Los Angeles area are significantly higher than those in other parts of the country. We consider two basic sources here: the American Chamber of Commerce Research Association (ACCRA) Cost of Living Index and the 1999 CBP figures.

COST OF LIVING ESTIMATES

The ACCRA data set provides the most detailed statistics on costs of living in approximately 300 cities within the United States.[3] According to ACCRA, overall living costs in Los Angeles were 26.4 percent above the national average for 1999. During the 1990s, this Los Angeles living cost differential averaged 23.3 percent above the national average for the decade as a whole. From this, it seems reasonable to conclude that for low-wage workers in Los Angeles, living costs are approximately 25 percent above the national average.

Los Angeles Living Costs and Poverty Thresholds

We are now in a position to establish a workable poverty-line living wage standard for Santa Monica workers. It follows from the two basic points that emerge from the material we have reviewed: (1) according to the average of the alternative measures of poverty reviewed by the NRC, the national poverty line for a family of four is about 40 percent above the official Census Bureau poverty line and (2) the cost of living in the Los Angeles area is about 25 percent above the national average.

These two figures suggest that an appropriate poverty-line estimate for the Los Angeles area should be about 65 percent above the official Census Bureau poverty line. To present this result cautiously, let us round down, assuming that an appropriate poverty threshold for Los Angeles would be about 60 percent above the official poverty line. Thus, when we report living wage figures and poverty estimates here, we report a 160 percent of official poverty threshold as our basic measure; we also report a 185 percent of official poverty threshold to measure a near-poor living standard. Along with these, we also report the official poverty threshold figures, but consider these as properly measuring a severe poverty standard.

Basic-Needs Budget

As already mentioned, the CBP attempts to measure a standard of living that is more than a " 'bare bones' existence, yet covers only basic expenses, allowing little room for 'extras' such as college savings or vacations." The CBP estimates typical costs of housing and utilities, child care, transportation, food, health coverage, payroll and income taxes, and miscellaneous expenses such as clothing, personal care, and basic telephone service. For example, for a single-parent family with two children, the study found the yearly budget includes (in 1999 dollars) $7,273 for housing and utilities, $11,701 for child care, $2,998 for transportation, $4,693 for food, $2,371 for health care, $3,873 for miscellaneous items, and $4,681 for taxes, for a total of $37,589.[4] The study assumes that the typical family rents housing, rather than owning a home, and that the rent it pays is at the lower 40th percentile of fair market value rents in the area, that is, that 40 percent of the rental housing in an area has lower fair market value rents and 60 percent has higher. The family does own a car, but drives an average of only 25 miles per day for commuting. Doubling the miles driven per month—still a modest estimate and one more likely to correspond to driving needs for workers in the Los Angeles area—would increase transportation costs by nearly $3,000.[5] No allowance is made for vacation travel or long commutes. The food budget is based on the Department of Agriculture "low-cost food plan" which is approximately 25 percent above its "thrifty food plan," used in measuring the official poverty threshold. The CBP assumes that a family includes two children, one below and the other above 6 years old. The study then estimates basic income budgets for three different family types: a single-parent family; a family with two parents, with one as the wage-earner and the other handling child care; and a family in which both parents earn wages.

Overall, the budget estimates generated by this approach correspond well to what we consider a basic-needs living standard, or something akin to a minimum amount needed to become capable, in Sen's sense, of participating meaningfully in community life.

Alternative Estimates of Living Wage Standards

In table 7.1, I present alternative estimates for both poverty-line and basic-needs income levels for workers in Santa Monica. As we see, the figures are presented for both a three-person, two-child family and a four-person, two-child family. For the four-person, two-child family, the basic-needs figures, derived from the CBP study, are presented in two ways,

Table 7.1. Living wage income and wage levels for Santa Monica workers (in 1999 dollars)

	Poverty-level income			Basic-needs income	
	Severe poverty (official poverty line)	Poor (160% of official poverty line)	Near-poor (185% of official poverty line)	One wage earner	Two wage earners
Three-person, two-child family					
Annual income	$13,423	$21,475	$24,831	$37,589	—
Hourly wage rate for full-time job	$6.45	$10.32	$11.94	$18.07	—
Four-person, two-child family					
Annual income	$16,895	$27,030	$31,254	$31,298	$45,683
Hourly wage rate for full-time job	$8.12	$13.00	$15.03	$15.05	$10.98 (both jobs)

Sources: Current Population Survey 1999; California Budget Project 1999.

assuming both one- and two wage-earners in the family. The increased income needs for the two-wage-earner family reflects the higher costs of child
care when both adult family members are working full-time outside the
home.

As we see from table 7.1, the alternative living wage rates range fairly
widely, depending on what we define as a living wage. Given our previous
discussion of the inadequacies of the official poverty thresholds, especially
as a standard relevant for the Los Angeles area, it is reasonable to exclude
these official threshold levels—what we term the severe-poverty income
thresholds—as a level that we should define as corresponding with a living
wage. This still leaves, for 1999, wage rates between $10.32 and $18.07 as
the range of values associated with different living wage standards for a
three-person family with one working adult. For a four-person family, the
corresponding wage rate is $13.00–$15.05 with one wage-earner in the
family. When both adults in a four-person family work, the average wage
for both workers needs to be $10.98 for the family to reach the basic-needs
threshold.

It is clear from these figures that no single dollar amount can be associated with a living wage threshold. Nevertheless, the figures in the table provide a sense of what an appropriate wage level would be in 1999, assuming
that workers hold full-time jobs and that they are supporting between one
and two additional family members on their wages.

In fact, it may be unrealistic to assume that low-wage workers hold full-
time jobs over the course of a year. If they do not, their wage rate would

clearly have to be higher to earn an income level corresponding with either a poverty-line or basic-needs living standard. At the same time, it may not be the case that workers are trying to support additional family members on their wages, in which case a lower dollar amount would be adequate to supply a living wage.

Such additional considerations need to be weighed carefully in constructing an adequate threshold for a living wage (we have attempted to do so in Pollin and Brenner 2000). But this exercise itself strongly suggests that the California minimum wage, which was at $5.75 when we did our research and is $7.50 as of 2007, remains far below even the low-end estimate of a living wage for a worker living in the Los Angeles area. Indeed, the living wage level rate of $10.50 plus health benefits that passed in Santa Monica in 2001 (only to be repealed in November 2002) is itself only at the low end of a proper living wage standard. It is therefore clear from this small exercise alone that, in the Los Angeles area as well as throughout the country, living wage proponents have a large task ahead of them in establishing wage norms that provide all workers with the capabilities to support families, maintain self-respect, and participate meaningfully in the civic life of the community.

8 How Santa Monica Workers Would Have Benefited from a $10.75 Living Wage

Robert Pollin, Mark Brenner, Stephanie Luce, and Jeannette Wicks-Lim

WHO ARE THE LOW-WAGE WORKERS IN SANTA MONICA?

We rely on two basic data series here in considering conditions for low-wage workers and their families in the Los Angeles/Santa Monica area: the Current Population Survey (CPS) of the U.S. Department of Labor and our own survey of workers employed in the Santa Monica Coastal Zone.[1]

These two data sources complement one another. The strength of the government data set is that it is derived from a large random sample of Los Angeles residents. It therefore offers a broad and reliable picture of the people who are employed in low-wage jobs in the Los Angeles area. However, the government statistics cannot provide us with a detailed picture of the workers who would be affected by a living wage proposal in Santa Monica. That is why it was important that we also conduct our own survey of these workers. Because of the conditions under which our Santa Monica survey were undertaken, it would not have been possible for us to create a random sample of workers for our interview pool. Nevertheless, we made every effort to produce a representative sample of workers in the Coastal Zone.[2]

All the data presented in this chapter are expressed in 1999 dollars. We have not adjusted the figures upward to reflect the effects of subsequent inflation on the cost of living. If we had made these adjustments, we also would have had to change the $10.75 living wage figure, itself, that was under debate in Santa Monica at that time. This would have only added confusion to our current presentation.

118

Evidence from Los Angeles Current Population Survey Data

Our research considers workers in Los Angeles ranging from the California minimum wage rate of $5.75 up to the proposed Santa Monica living wage rate of $10.75. We do not present systematic evidence on workers earning below $5.75. These workers are exempted from U.S. and California minimum wage coverage and would presumably also be exempted from a Santa Monica living wage ordinance. Nevertheless, we occasionally refer to data about these workers when pertinent for our main areas of concern.

Basic Demographics

NUMBER OF WORKERS   To begin, as we see in table 8.1, there are a total of nearly 1.3 million workers in our three wage categories that range between $5.75 and $10.75. These workers constitute 34.4 percent of the total Los Angeles workforce. As we see, the breakdown is 14.8 percent for $5.75–7.40; 10.2 percent for $7.41–9.10; and 9.4 percent for $9.11–10.75. People earning below $5.75 constitute another 392,000 workers, or 10.4 percent of the total Los Angeles workforce. Overall, then, 44.8 percent of all workers in the Los Angeles region earn below $10.75. Our analysis focuses on the 33.4 percent between $5.75 and $10.75.

AGE OF WORKERS AND JOB TENURE   The average age of workers earning between $5.75 and $10.75 is 35.4 years old, and their average estimated labor force tenure is 18 years. For the most part, therefore, the jobs that these workers now hold reflect their long-term occupational trajectory. They are

Table 8.1. Basic demographics of Los Angeles low-wage workforce

	Totals	Hourly wage rate categories		
	$5.75–10.75	$5.75–7.40	$7.41–9.10	$9.11–10.75
Number of workers	1,290,024	555,624	383,249	351,151
Percentage of workforce	34.4%	14.8%	10.2%	9.4%
Average age	35.4	34.8	34.6	37.1
Estimated labor force tenure (years)	18.0	18.1	17.3	18.7
Percentage teenagers	4.2%	5.9%	3.2%	2.7%
Percentage non-White (including Hispanic)	77.8%	83.9%	79.0%	66.8%
Percentage Hispanic	59.5%	68.9%	60.3%	43.9%
Percentage female	46.3%	48.4%	44.7%	44.9%

Source: Current Population Survey 1999.

not on a career ladder that will be moving them to a significantly better job situation.

Only 4.2 percent of the workers in our sample are teenagers. This figure is lower than is generally observed in measuring the low-wage labor market, including, as we will see, our own survey of Coastal Zone workers. The reason this figure is low is that our sample from the Los Angeles CPS survey excluded people who worked fewer than 250 hours per year (i.e., less than 12 percent of a full-time working year), an adjustment we made to increase the overall reliability of our sample.[3]

RACE AND GENDER Finally, we see in table 8.1 that low-wage workers are predominantly non-White and Hispanic. Overall, 77.8 percent of all workers earning $5.75–10.75 are non-White or Hispanic, and 59.5 percent are Hispanic. We also see that slightly fewer than half of all low-wage workers are female.

Wages and Earnings

The top panel of table 8.2 provides a more detailed picture of the earnings and living situations for low-wage workers in Los Angeles. We see, first of all, the average wage rates in our three wage categories, which are $6.55, $8.26, and $10.08. We also see that in none of the three categories do workers hold a job full-time for the entire working year. Rather, they average about 38 hours per week at work and about 46–48 weeks on the job. Such arrangements lead to an overall working year ranging between 1,764 and 1,861 hours. If we say that a full-time working year amounts to 2,080 hours (i.e., 52 weeks at 40 hours per week), low-wage workers in Los Angeles are averaging about 14 percent less than full-time at their jobs. Combining these wage rates and working year figures then generates the average yearly earnings for workers in the three categories: $11,969, $14,757, and $18,735.[4]

To provide some perspective on these earnings levels, it is helpful to compare them to the figures discussed in chapter 7 on living wage income thresholds. Some of the pertinent comparative statistics are brought together in figure 8.1. For workers in the lowest $5.75–7.40 category, their average annual earnings of $11,969 is 11 percent below even the official poverty threshold for a family of three of $13,423, what we term a severe-poverty threshold. From a different angle, the lowest-wage workers' average earnings are barely more than 30 percent of the basic-needs income level of $37,589 for a family of three. The situation is obviously more favorable for workers earning $7.41–$9.10, but not dramatically so. Thus, the families in which these workers live would be in considerable deprivation if they depended, as their primary income source, on the wages earned by the workers in the sample.

Table 8.2. Los Angeles survey data: earnings and family living standards of workers covered by Santa Monica proposal

	Hourly wage rate categories		
	$5.75–7.40	$7.41–9.10	$9.11–10.75
A. Average wages and annual earnings of low-wage Los Angeles workers			
Average wage (in 1999 dollars)	$6.55	$8.26	$10.08
Average hours per week	38.1	38.1	38.7
Average weeks per year	47.3	46.3	48.1
Total hours per year worked	1,802	1,764	1,861
Average annual earnings (in 1999 dollars)	$11,969	$14,757	$18,735
B. Family structures and earnings of Los Angeles low-wage workers			
Average family size	3.8	3.8	3.6
Average number of wage-earners per family	2.1	2.0	2.0
Average dependency ratio (family size/number of wage-earners)	2.1	2.1	2.0
Total family earnings (in 1999 dollars)	$26,335	$27,432	$35,560
Percentage of total family earnings contributed by worker in sample	48.0%	53.0%	52.6%
C. Total family income of Los Angeles low-wage families			
Total family income (in 1999 dollars)	$28,735	$30,691	$37,287
Percentage of total family income contributed by worker in sample	41.4%	49.0%	49.9%
D. Poverty status of Los Angeles low-wage families			
Families in severe poverty (below official poverty line)	16.0%	14.1%	2.6%
Families in poverty (below 160% of official poverty line)	34.2%	26.1%	16.6%
Near-poor families (below 185% of official poverty line)	51.7%	38.4%	26.8%
Below basic-needs threshold	86.0%	72.9%	79.1%

Source: Current Population Survey 1999.

Note: Basic-needs figures apply only to those family types for which the California Budget Project calculated thresholds.

FAMILY STRUCTURES AND INCOMES   What is the family status of workers in each of these three earnings levels? Table 8.2, section B, offers some evidence on this. First of all, the average family size is 3.8 people among workers in the lower two wage categories, and 3.6 people in the $9.41–10.75 category. These families have between 2.0 and 2.1 wage earners in their families. This, in turn, implies that the average worker in our sample is supporting him- or herself and nearly one additional family member. As we see, the de-

Figure 8.1. Living wage thresholds and earnings levels for Los Angeles low-wage workers (1999 dollars)

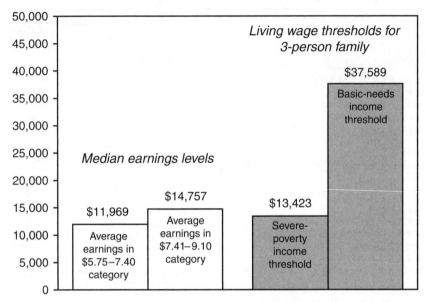

Sources: See tables 7.1 and 8.2.

pendency ratio (which is simply the ratio of family size/number of wage-earners in a family) has a range of 2.0–2.1 for our three wage categories.

How much of these families' total earnings are supplied by the workers in our sample? We see that total family earnings (median values) range between $26,335 and $35,560. The workers in all three categories of our sample are providing roughly 50 percent of their families' earnings.[5]

ADDITIONAL SOURCES OF FAMILY INCOME   The figures on earnings from wages do not, however, provide a complete picture of the living standards of low-wage workers. Such families also receive income from a wide array of additional sources, including unemployment insurance, the Earned Income Tax Credit, workman's compensation, and retirement benefits.[6] In table 8.2, section C, we present data on total family income and the percentage of total income contributed by the workers in our sample. As we see, the total income levels are about 10 percent higher than total family earnings, with family incomes ranging between $28,735 and $37,287. Thus, the workers in our sample contribute 41–50 percent of their families' total income.

AVERAGE FAMILY INCOMES AND LIVING WAGE THRESHOLDS   Having now collected all sources of income for these families, we again turn to our

Figure 8.2. Incomes of Los Angeles low-wage families relative to living wage income thresholds (1999 dollars)

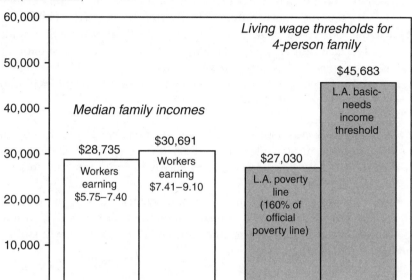

Sources: See tables 7.1 and 8.2.

various living wage standards to assess these families' living standards. Given that the average size of families in our two lower wage categories is 3.8 people, we should therefore compare these families' total income against our living wage standards for a family of four. We bring some of the pertinent figures together in figure 8.2. As we see, the family incomes for our two lower wage categories—$28,735 and $30,691—are somewhat above our poverty-line income level for a family of four, which is $27,030. These low-wage family income levels are also about 35 percent below the basic-needs family income level of $45,683 for a four-person family.[7]

POVERTY AND BASIC-NEEDS STATUS   In addition to examining statistics on representative families, we obtain a fuller picture of living conditions for the low-wage families by looking at the percentages living below our Los Angeles poverty and basic-needs thresholds. These figures are presented in table 8.2, section D. Focusing first on the families of workers in the $5.75–7.40 category, we see that over half of these families are either poor or near-poor, according to our 160 percent and 185 percent of official poverty standards. More than one-third are living below the Los Angeles poverty line of 160 percent of official poverty, and 16 percent live in severe poverty (i.e., below the official threshold). A full 86 percent of these families are living below the California Budget Project's basic-needs threshold. Not surprisingly, conditions are somewhat better for the families of workers earning $7.41–9.10, but not dramatically so. Nearly 40 percent of these families are below either our 160 percent or 185 percent of official poverty thresholds, and nearly 73 percent are below the basic-needs threshold. The situation is not as severe for families with workers earning $9.11–10.75. But here as well, over 25 percent are below our two poverty thresholds, and 79 percent are below the basic-needs threshold.

NONMONETARY TRANSFERS AND HEALTH COVERAGE The figures on family income do not include nonmonetary transfers, including items such as food stamps, subsidized housing, and energy assistance. It also does not include health insurance coverage. The amounts being received by the families with low-wage workers through nonmonetary transfers is relatively small—for example, only 6.1 percent of families with workers earning $5.75–7.40 receive food stamps, and those percentages are lower still for families in higher wage categories.

In terms of health coverage, more than half of the workers in the $5.75–7.40 category have no coverage and about one-third in the higher wage categories also have no coverage. For the lowest wage category, only about one-third have coverage that includes their families and fewer than 40 percent have coverage provided by their employer. As usual, these figures are somewhat better for those in the higher wage categories, but not dramatically so.

Summary of the Los Angeles Survey Evidence

The overall picture of low-wage workers in the Los Angeles area is clear. For the most part, these are people well into their working lives. They are not teenagers, and they are not moving to a career trajectory different than their present one. Their overall earnings are less than what might be suggested even by their low hourly wage rates. This is because, on average, they work only 85 percent of a full working year. The majority live with their families and are a major contributor—although not the only provider—of the families' overall income.

Adding up all the income sources for the families of low-wage workers, we still find that, for those workers whose wages are in the two lower categories, nearly half are living in poverty or are near-poor. Most of these families are well below the basic-needs living standard, as defined by the California Budget Project. And, finally, these workers have very poor health insurance coverage, especially in terms of what is being provided for them by their employers.

Worker Survey for Santa Monica

We now turn to the data we generated through our own survey of work-ers in Santa Monica. We focused our efforts on sampling low-wage workers employed at potentially affected firms within Santa Monica's Coastal Zone. With these workers, we have used standard nonrandom sampling tech-niques to generate a reliable representative sample. We surveyed a total of 202 workers during April and May of 2000. Of the 202 workers, sixty-one were employed in hotels, fifty-three in restaurants, thirty-nine in retail, and forty-nine in a variety of other worksites.[8]

Basic Demographics

Table 8.3, section A, presents the basic demographic evidence on the work-ers in our sample. To begin, we see that of the 202 workers surveyed, the ma-jority are in our two lower wage categories—34 percent earn $5.75–7.40 and 38 percent earn $7.41–9.10. These figures incorporate income received from tips and commissions into workers' hourly earnings totals.

From our figures on average round-trip commuting time, we see, as noted earlier, that most of our surveyed Coastal Zone workers do not themselves live either in or close to Santa Monica. Rather, they are traveling roughly 1.5 hours per day to get to their Coastal Zone jobs, 53 percent of them by car (42 percent traveling alone and 11 percent in carpools). As we show ear-lier, daily commutes of this distance place a substantial financial burden on low-wage workers and their families.

The average age of those in our survey is 32.6 years. This is lower than for the full Los Angeles Survey, in which the average age was 35.4. The most significant difference between the two samples is that the Santa Monica sur-vey includes a substantially higher proportion of teenagers, 14.4 percent in total. (As we noted before, the proportion for teenagers from our Los An-geles sample was 4.2 percent, but a more accurate figure that would include all working teenagers would be 6.8 percent.) The largest concentration of teenagers in the Santa Monica sample is in the $5.75–7.40 wage category, where they make up 29 percent of the total. Over half of the teenagers in the sample are working at retail outlets. Given the large number of retail outlets in the Coastal Zone, it is not surprising that the Santa Monica sur-vey includes a higher proportion of teenagers than a random sample of workers in all businesses throughout the Los Angeles area.

Although the percentage of teenagers in our sample is high relative to the Los Angeles survey, it is still the case that 85.6 percent of the workers in our survey are adults who have labor market tenure of an average of 17 years. As such, the jobs held by the large majority of low-wage Santa Monica

Table 8.3. Santa Monica survey data: earnings and family living standards of workers covered by Santa Monica proposal

	Totals	Hourly wage rate categories		
	$5.75–10.75	$5.75–7.40	$7.41–9.10	$9.11–10.75	+$10.75
A. Basic demographics of low-wage workers in Santa Monica				
Number of workers	202	69	78	23	32
Percentage of total	100.0%	34.2%	38.6%	11.4%	15.8%
Average round-trip commute (minutes)	87.3	95.0	90.3	85.4	60.7
Average age	32.6	28.1	35.1	33.9	35.0
Percentage teenagers	14.4%	29.0%	9.0%	8.7%	0.0%
Estimated labor force tenure (years)	17.0	12.6	19.4	18.9	18.7
Percentage female	39.1%	34.8%	48.7%	34.8%	28.1%
Percentage Hispanic	76.7%	78.3%	76.9%	87.0%	65.6%
Percentage non-White (excluding Hispanic)	14.9%	20.3%	16.7%	8.7%	3.2%
B. Wages and annual earnings of workers in Santa Monica worker sample				
Median hourly wage (1999 dollars)		$6.25	$8.00	$9.94	
Median annual earnings (1999 dollars)		$10,426	$16,170	$17,746	
C. Family structures and incomes of Santa Monica worker sample				
Average family size	3.5	3.7	3.5	3.4	
Average number of wage earners per family-	1.9	2.2	1.7	1.8	
Average dependency ratio (family size/number of wage-earners)	1.8	1.7	2.1	1.9	
Family income (1999 dollars)	$23,500	$19,000	$20,000	$25,000	
Percentage of total family income contributed by worker in survey		66.2%	88.3%	56.8%	

Source: PERI Survey of Santa Monica Coastal Zone Workers 2000.

workers, as with the larger Los Angeles sample, reflect these workers' long-term occupational trajectory.

In terms of other basic demographic data, table 8.3 also shows that over 75 percent of the workers surveyed are Hispanic and that roughly 40 percent are female.

Wages and Earnings

Here we focus on workers earning $5.75–10.75 per hour, including tips and commissions. We divide these workers into our three basic wage categories. The figures on wages and incomes are presented in table 8.3, section B. As we see, the representative (median) wages in the three categories are $6.25, $8.00, and $9.94.

Table 8.3, section B, then shows the annual earnings figures for our three groups: $10,426, $16,170, and $17,746. These figures are somewhat different than those generated by the Los Angeles CPS survey. But especially as regards the two lower wage categories, these differences are not substantial. As such, the general convergence between the earnings figures in the two samples supports the conclusion that our Santa Monica sample figures are reliable. Considered more generally, given the two separate samples, the evidence is strong that we have constructed an accurate picture of the earnings situation for low-wage workers employed in the Santa Monica Coastal Zone.

Family Structures and Incomes

In Table 8.3, section C, we see data on family size and household arrangements for workers in our sample. Again, there are small differences here relative to the Los Angeles survey but nothing dramatic. Average family sizes are a bit smaller than in the Los Angeles sample (3.5 vs. 3.8 people), but the number of working members is slightly less (1.9 vs. 2.1 earners). Adding these factors up, the dependency ratio in the Santa Monica sample is basically the same as in Los Angeles. For all workers in our sample, the average dependency ratio is 1.8, meaning that each worker supports 1.8 people through his or her earnings. This figure then ranges from 1.7 for the $5.75–7.40 workers to 2.1 for the $7.41–9.40 workers.

We last consider in table 8.3 the figures for overall family incomes and the share of that income contributed by the workers in our sample. We see that family incomes range between $19,000 and $25,000. The workers' contribution to this overall family income is substantially over 50 percent for all three wage categories.

Overall, we see that there are significant disparities between the Los Angeles CPS and Santa Monica surveys. In particular, the family income figures from the Santa Monica survey are about one-third lower than those we reported for Los Angeles. This disparity is much larger than differences in individual worker earnings between the two samples, which, as also shown in the tables, were negligible between the two surveys. Still, this income differential is broadly consistent with the fact that the average family size for workers in the Santa Monica survey was about 10 percent smaller than those in our Los Angeles sample.[9] Another factor in this disparity may be that workers in the Santa Monica sample may have been less scrupulous in reporting sources of unearned income than those in the official U.S. government sample from which the Los Angeles figures are drawn. Even after we recognize these sources of disparity between our two sets of income figures, we nevertheless reach the same basic conclusion about the living standard of families in the Santa Monica sample that we did with the Los Angeles sample—the majority of families of low-wage Santa Monica workers are living in conditions of poverty or near-poverty, and their overall income levels do not bring them close to a basic-needs living standard.

LIVING WAGE PROGRAMS AND FAMILY LIVING STANDARDS

How would a living wage ordinance affect the living standards of the covered workers and their families in Santa Monica? We have seen that the majority of low-wage workers live in families in which they are not the only income earner. This means that we have to show how much a family's overall income changes after accounting for all the family's income sources. Moreover, the family's overall size and combined earnings level, rather than just the covered worker's wage income, will establish the family's tax obligations and eligibility for government subsidies.

To provide a sense of how the living wage proposals would affect the average families in our survey, we construct two prototypical family types from the data we have just reviewed.[10] Table 8.4 shows the two family profiles. In Family 1, the worker in the family, who corresponds roughly to the average worker in our Santa Monica worker survey, earns $8.00 per hour, has no private health insurance, and lives with one additional adult and one child. This worker contributes 70 percent to the family's total earnings. The Family 2 worker, corresponding more closely to the average worker in the Los Angeles–CPS survey, earns $8.30 per hour, does carry private health in-

Table 8.4. Prototypical low-wage families drawn from Los Angeles and Santa Monica worker surveys

	Family 1	Family 2
Family income		
Wages of surveyed worker	$8.00	$8.30
Annual hours of work	1,700	1,800
Worker's yearly earnings	$13,600	$14,940
Total family earnings	$19,430	$29,880
Worker's share of family earnings	70%	50%
Family members	2 adults, 1 child	2 adults, 2 children
Surveyed worker's benefits		
Health coverage	No	Yes
Paid days off	8	8

surance, and lives with three other people, including two children. The Family 2 worker contributes 50 percent to the family's overall earnings. Making these distinctions between the two families enables us to observe how a given living wage ordinance will have a variable effect, depending on the family situation of the covered worker.[11]

We consider the impact on these two families when the low-wage worker in our sample receives a raise to $10.75 per hour, with table 8.5 presenting the situation for Family 1 and table 8.6 showing results for Family 2. In both cases, we assume that the covered worker is the only member of the family receiving a raise. All other family earnings remain fixed. We also assume that the covered worker continues to be employed at the same job working the same number of hours annually.

Considering first table 8.5, we see in row (1) the effect on the $8.00 worker's gross annual earnings of getting a raise to the proposed $10.75 living wage standard. This amounts to an increase in gross earnings of 34.4 percent. We next show the impact of this increase on the rise in the family's gross income, which is 24.1 percent.

Rows (3)–(5) then show various tax obligations and how they change, according to the amount of the family's income increase. These various tax adjustments enable us to calculate the after-tax earned income, which we show in row (7). Here we see the family's after-tax earned income rises by 20.8 percent as a result of the wage increase to $10.75.

Table 8.5. Prototypical family 1: impact of living wage increase on living standard

	Wage = $8.00/hour	Wage = $10.75/hour
Family income		
1. Worker annual earnings	$13,600	$18,275
percentage increase from $8.00	—	+34.4%
2. Gross family earnings	$19,430	$24,105
percentage increase from $8.00	—	+24.1%
3. Federal income tax	$596	$1,301
4. FICA tax	$1,486	$1,844
5. California state income tax	0	0
6. State disability insurance	$155	$193
7. After-tax earned income	$17,193	$20,767
[rows 2–(3+4+5+6)]		
percentage increase from $8.00	—	+20.8%
8. Earned Income Tax Credit	$1,199	$448
9. Disposable income [rows 7+8]	**$18,392**	**$21,215**
percentage increase from $8.00	—	*+15.3%*
Surveyed worker's benefits		
10. Paid days off	8	15
11. Private health insurance	0	$2,375

Table 8.6. Prototypical family 2: impact of living wage increase on living standard

	Wage = $8.30/hour	Wage = $10.75/hour
Family income		
1. Worker annual earnings	$14,940	$19,350
percentage increase from $8.30	—	+29.5%
2. Gross family earnings	$29,880	$34,290
percentage increase from $8.30	—	+14.8%
3. Federal income tax	$1,751	$2,411
4. FICA tax	$2,286	$2,623
5. California state income tax	0	0
6. State disability insurance	$239	$274
7. After-tax earned income [rows 2–(3+4+5+6)]	$25,604	$28,982
percentage increase from $8.30	—	+13.2%
8. Earned Income Tax Credit	$148	0
9. Disposable income [rows 7+8]	**$25,752**	**$28,982**
percentage increase from $8.30	—	*+12.5%*
Surveyed worker's benefits		
10. Paid days off	8	15
11. Private health insurance	prior coverage	prior coverage

In row (8), we present the subsidy the family would receive through the federal Earned Income Tax Credit (EITC) program, which provides a cash payment to working families whose total earned income falls below a given threshold level. According to the profile we assigned to Family 1, the EITC payment is $1,199 with the $8.00 wage, but drops to $448 after the raise to $10.75. Because this family's earned income is over the official poverty line of $13,423 (in 1999 dollars) for a family of three, it does not qualify for food stamps at any wage level.

In row (9), we present figures for disposable income, after accounting for all tax and subsidy adjustments. We see that disposable income increases by 15.3 percent with the $10.75 raise. Finally, we see the worker's additional benefits in the bottom row: seven additional paid days off and $2,375 in health insurance.[12]

Table 8.6 then repeats the same exercise for our prototypical Family 2. Of course, the increases are smaller under this scenario. Still, even for this higher-income family, a raise to $10.75 yields a 12.5 percent gain in disposable family income, even given that the family falls out of eligibility for the EITC income supplement.

It will be useful, finally, to observe how the living wage raise will change the living standards of our two prototypical families relative to our poverty and basic-needs threshold levels. The relevant figures for Family 1 are shown in figure 8.3 and those for Family 2 in figure 8.4.

Figure 8.3. Family 1: Change in living standard under the $10.75 ordinance (family income and threshold levels are *prior* to taxes and subsidies; figures are in 1999 dollars)

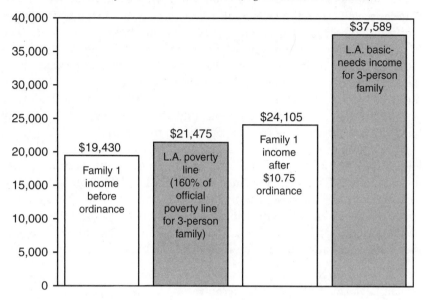

Sources: See tables 7.1 and 8.5.

Figure 8.4. Family 2: Change in living standard under $10.75 ordinance (family income and threshold levels are *prior* to taxes and subsidies; figures are in 1999 dollars)

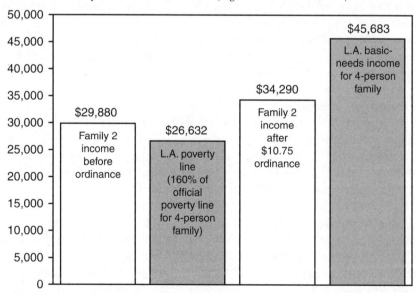

Sources: See tables 7.1 and 8.6.

Before the implementation of a living wage ordinance, as we see in figure 8.3, Family 1's income is about $2,000 below what we have termed the Los Angeles poverty line of $21,475 (all income figures in the figure are pretax and transfer because that is how the poverty thresholds are defined). The $10.75 ordinance raises the family's income to $24,105. This 24 percent increase in family income means that Family 1 now lives 12.2 percent above the Los Angeles poverty line. Even after the implementation of a $10.75 ordinance, Family 1 remains well below the $37,589 basic-needs standard. But raising the family's income significantly above the Los Angeles poverty line would no doubt bring tangible benefits to the family.

Now considering Family 2 in figure 8.4, their pre–living wage income level of $29,880 is 12 percent above the Los Angeles four-person poverty line of $26,632. The $10.75 ordinance raises the family's income 15 percent to $34,290. After the raise, Family 2's income is 29 percent above the Los Angeles poverty line. As with Family 1, they remain well below the basic-needs standard of $45,683 for a four-person family. Nevertheless, again, the living wage raise will provide some significant benefits to Family 2.

Benefit Leakages/Savings for Government

As we have seen, the net income gains that Families 1 and 2 obtain from a living wage ordinance are lower than the direct wage increases alone might suggest. This is because when pretax income rises for these families, as with most other families, their tax obligations also increase and their eligibility for government subsidies diminish. These net income reductions are often termed leakages of benefits away from the intended program recipients (i.e., the low-wage workers and their families). In table 8.7, we show the extent of this effect using the relevant figures from tables 8.5 and 8.6.

As we see from the first three rows of table 8.7, the families are able to retain only 60–73 percent of the wage increases they would receive through a $10.75 ordinance. The remaining portion of their raise is absorbed through higher income and payroll taxes and a decline in the families' eligibility for the federal EITC. The families' California disability insurance payments also increase slightly. Overall, as we see in the last row of the table, the total government savings (leakages) amounts to $1,852 for Family 1 and $1,180 for Family 2.

As it happens, even before receiving living wage raises, our two prototypical families would be at income levels too high to qualify for food stamps, Medi-Cal, or Los Angeles County indigent health care. Had we considered cases of workers at lower initial family-income levels, the net gain to the family through a $10.75 ordinance would have been larger, but the leakages would also have been greater.

Table 8.7. Leakages between pretax and disposable income gains from the $10.75 ordinance

	Family 1	Family 2
Family Disposable Income Gain		
1. Pretax income increase	$4,675	$4,410
2. Disposable income increase	$2,823	$3,230
3. *Net benefit ratio [rows (2)/(1)]*	60.4%	73.2%
Federal Government Saving		
4. Higher income taxes	$705	$660
5. Higher payroll taxes	$358	$337
6. Earned Income Tax Credit declines	$751	$148
State Government Saving		
7. Higher disability insurance	$38	$35
Total Government Savings		
[rows (4)+(5)+(6)+(7)]	$1,852	$1,180

From the perspective of government budgeting, of course, these leakages appear as savings—a reduction in the fiscal obligations to low-income families. However, the primary beneficiary here would be the federal Treasury, not the City of Santa Monica or even the State of California.

9   How Workers and Their Families Will Benefit from the Arizona Minimum Wage Increase

Robert Pollin and Jeannette Wicks-Lim

WHO ARE THE LOW-WAGE WORKERS IN ARIZONA?

We consider here the characteristics of the roughly 350,000 workers in Arizona—13 percent of the state's total employed workforce—who would receive either mandated raises or ripple-effect wage increases after the state raises its minimum wage to $6.75 per hour on January 1, 2007. We consider three basic features of these workers' lives: their individual characteristics, their family characteristics, and the poverty status of the workers and their families. We also provide the same set of information for the roughly 230,000 workers in Phoenix, 63,000 in Tucson, and 20,000 in Yuma[1] who would receive raises through the $6.75 minimum wage proposal.

Individual Characteristics

As we see from table 9.1, section A, these workers constitute nearly 13 percent of the total Arizona workforce. Of these, 77 percent are adults (ages 20 or over); 50 percent are non-White (including Hispanics) and 42 percent are Hispanic; and 57 percent are female. Their average age is 28 years old, and they have been in the labor force for over 12 years. In other words, the jobs that these workers hold now reflect their long-term occupational trajectory. They are not on a career ladder that will be moving them to a significantly better job situation. Put another way, the overwhelming majority are not middle-class teenagers earning some extra spending money.

Table 9.1. Individual characteristics and family living standards of workers covered by Arizona minimum wage increase, 2005

	Arizona	Phoenix	Tucson	Yuma
A. Individual characteristics of low-wage workers in Arizona				
Number of workers	345,565	229,139	62,880	19,777
Percentage of workforce	12.8%	12.5%	15.1%	31.2%
Average age	28	27	24	30
Labor force tenure (years)	12	11	7	14
Percentage teenagers (15–19)	22.6%	24.5%	26.9%	14.3%
Percentage non-White (including Hispanics)	49.7%	48.4%	47.4%	79.8%
Percentage Hispanic	42.1%	41.3%	31.1%	79.8%
Percentage female	56.5%	53.1%	58.4%	53.9%
B. Family structure, earnings, and incomes of representative low-wage workers in Arizona				
Representative family size	3.0	3.0	3.0	4.0
Number of wage earners for representative family	2.0	2.0	2.0	2.0
Total family earnings	$26,323	$30,356	$21,865	$23,709
Percentage of total family earnings contributed by worker	41.9%	39.3%	48.1%	31.0%
Total family income	$31,097	$33,093	$31,463	$33,219
Percentage of total family income contributed by worker	35.7%	32.3%	37.2%	25.7%
C. Poverty status of low-wage workers in Arizona				
Families in severe poverty (percentage below official poverty line)	22.3%	18.9%	22.3%	26.0%
Families in poverty (percentage below 150% of official poverty line)	43.0%	39.3%	41.3%	53.9%
Families in near-poverty (percentage below 175% of official poverty line)	49.4%	48.2%	46.0%	64.2%
Families below basic-needs threshold (percentage below threshold)	73.3%	73.3%	66.8%	[a]

Sources: Current Population Survey Outgoing Rotation Group and Annual Social and Economic Supplemental survey 2001–2005 files, Bureau of Labor Statistics, U.S. Department of Labor.

[a]Percentage below basic-needs threshold for Yuma is not reported because of its small sample size.

Considering the results for these metropolitan areas, the profile of workers in Phoenix closely resembles that for the state overall. This is not surprising because two-thirds of all the low-wage workers in the state are in Phoenix. In Tucson, with 18 percent of the state's low-wage workers, the major departure from the state's overall profile is that the percentage of Latino workers, at 31.1 percent, is well below the statewide average. The story is roughly the reverse for Yuma, where 5.7 percent of the state's low-wage workers live. Here, as table 8.1 shows, nearly 80 percent of the low-wage workers are Hispanic. Moreover, the Yuma workers tend to be older and to have more work experience. Their average age is 30, and they have been in the workforce for more than 14 years.

Family Structure and Income Levels

Figures on family status and income of workers who would be covered by the minimum wage are presented in table 9.1, section B. Here we present data on representative low-wage workers and their families in Arizona.[2] Let us consider such a representative worker, who would receive mandated or ripple-effect raises from the increase to a $6.75 Arizona minimum wage. He or she lives in a family that includes approximately two other people, of whom one of the other people is likely to also be working. These statewide figures also apply to Phoenix and Tucson. In Yuma, families are larger, with 4.0 people on average, but the number of workers in the family is still 2.0. Broadly speaking, the figures on family size have an important implication: as we have seen, approximately 350,000 workers will receive either mandated or ripple-effect raises due to the minimum wage increase. But the benefits of this increase will apply to all family members—that is, to 1.1 million people. Considering the family as a whole, then, nearly 20 percent of the 5.9 million people living in Arizona will receive some direct income through raising the state's minimum wage to $6.75.

In terms of earnings, for the state overall, we see that the workers in our sample who get a minimum wage increase live in families with overall earnings of about $26,323.

The representative low-wage worker's earnings amount to roughly 42 percent of the family's total earnings. This figure is higher in Tucson, at 48 percent, and slightly lower in Phoenix, at 39.3 percent. The earnings figure for our representative worker is substantially lower in Yuma, at 31.0 percent, where there are more likely to be more than two earners within the family.[3] Regardless of this variation, the basic picture holds throughout the state—the representative low-wage workers in our sample are not bringing home the majority of their family's total earnings. At the same time, by contributing somewhere between 30 and 50 percent of earnings in most family situations, their contributions are clearly crucial to the family's overall well-being.

We next consider data on workers' contributions to their family's overall *income,* as opposed to earnings. The income figures are necessarily higher than those for family earnings. This is because the income figures include sources of money other than earnings to support the family—including welfare, interest, dividends, alimony and child support, Social Security, and unemployment insurance. The family's median income is about $31,000. This statewide figure is also very similar to that for Phoenix, Tucson, and Yuma. For the state overall, representative low-wage workers are contributing about 36 percent to their family's total income. So again, the representative workers in our sample are not the primary source of their family's income. But they are a very large income source in families in which overall incomes are generally low.

Poverty Status

In table 9.1, section C, we obtain a further sense of the situation of the families in which low-wage workers live by comparing their income levels to some basic living standard benchmarks. The four benchmarks we use are derived in the same way as those we described in chapter 8 on Santa Monica, California: severe poverty, the official federal poverty line; poverty, corresponding in the Arizona context to 150 percent of the official poverty line; near-poverty, corresponding to 175 percent of the official line; and a more expansive basic-needs threshold.

For the basic-needs threshold for Arizona overall, as well as the three cities of Phoenix, Tucson, and Yuma, we drew on the definitions provided by the Economic Policy Institute (EPI).[4] In Phoenix in 2005, for example, the EPI estimates the following as constituting a basic family budget for a family with one parent and one child (in 2004 dollars): $817 per month for housing, $265 per month for food, $363 per month for child care, $255 per month for transportation, $249 per month for health care, $292 per month for other necessities, and $266 per month for taxes. This amounts to a total of $2,467 per month, or roughly $30,000 per year. Their estimate of a basic family budget would then obviously rise for a larger family. For a family with two parents and three children, the basic family budget level for Phoenix is a little more than $52,000. The comparable figures for both Tucson and Yuma are somewhat lower; for example, the basic family budget for a family with one parent and one child in both Tucson and Yuma is about $26,000. Drawing from this general methodology, we then estimate the percentage of families with low-wage workers that fall below the basic family budget threshold.

As we see in table 9.1, section C, 22 percent of the families with low-wage workers in Arizona now live below the official government poverty line, which we conclude should properly be termed a severe-poverty threshold. Moreover, 43 percent of low-wage workers and their families in Arizona live below what is a more reasonable poverty line, and 49 percent are near-poor. Finally, we see in table 9.1 that fully 73 percent live below the basic family budget line.[5]

IMPACT OF MINIMUM WAGE INCREASE ON VARIOUS LOW-INCOME FAMILIES

How will raising the Arizona minimum wage affect the living standards of the workers receiving raises and their families? We have seen that the majority of low-wage workers in Arizona live in families in which they are not the family's only income source (and indeed are frequently not the primary income source). This means that we have to show how much overall family income changes after accounting for all income sources for the family. Moreover, the family's overall size and combined earnings level, rather than just the covered worker's wage income, will establish the family's tax obligations and eligibility for government subsidies—the most important of these being the Earned Income Tax Credit (EITC) and food stamps.

In table 9.2, we present data on what the overall change in disposable income—the most direct measure of a family's living standard—will be due to the minimum wage increase.[6] We present these calculations for all families that include tipped workers earning between $2.13 and $3.74 and untipped workers now earning between $5.15 and $8.00. Workers now earning between $7.25 and $8.00 are likely to receive only a modest ripple-effect raise, on the order of 5 percent. As such, the gains for their families in disposable income will be much smaller than for families with workers in the $5.15–6.75 wage range; these workers who receive raises will get an average increase of about 13 percent. In table 9.2, section A, we show the effects on all families that now fall below what we have termed the poverty threshold (150 percent of the government's official poverty line). This includes the families of 43 percent of all workers that will receive raises through the minimum wage measure. In table 9.2, section B, we show the same calculations for all families falling below what we have termed the basic-needs threshold, which include the families of the 73 percent of workers that will benefit from the minimum wage increase.[7]

Our calculations take into account all income sources within the affected families—that is, the change in earnings from all the workers who would receive either mandated or ripple-effect raises resulting from the minimum

Table 9.2. Changes in living standards for low-wage workers and their families after Arizona $6.75 minimum wage raise
Data are for workers earning up to $8.00 per hour before minimum wage increase.

A. Affected workers in poor families *(families at 150% of official poverty line or below; 43% of all affected workers)*

	Minimum wage at $5.15	Minimum wage at $6.75	Percentage Increase/ Decrease
1. Worker annual earnings	$10,676	$11,541 (+866)	8.1%
2. Total family income before taxes and subsidies[a]	$15,688	$16,569	5.6%
3. Food stamps	$958	$837	−12.6%
4. Medicaid/SCHIP	$757	$757	0.0%
5. Earned Income Tax Credit	$1,584	$1,567	−1.0%
6. Child Tax Credit	$624	$714	14.5%
7. Federal tax	$111	$200	80.2%
8. State tax	$69	$94	36.5%
9. FICA	$1,070	$1,137	6.3%
Disposable income [rows (2+3+4+5+6)-(7+8+9)]	$18,361	$19,012 (+652)	3.5%

B. Affected workers in families below basic-needs thresholds *(73% of all affected workers with at least one child under 12 years old)*

	Minimum wage at $5.15	Minimum wage at $6.75	Percentage Increase/ Decrease
1. Worker annual earnings	$11,045	$11,969 (+924)	8.4%
2. Total family income before taxes and subsidies[a]	$18,412	$19,389	5.3%
3. Food stamps	$889	$762	−14.2%
4. Medicaid/SCHIP	$762	$733	−3.8%
5. Earned Income Tax Credit	$2,380	$2,337	−1.8%
6. Child Tax Credit	$873	$1,000	14.5%
7. Federal tax	$18	$116	528.4%
8. State tax	$88	$116	31.5%
9. FICA	$1,227	$1,302	6.1%
Disposable income [rows (2+3+4+5+6)-(7+8+9)]	$21,981	$22,687 (+706)	3.2%

Sources: Current Population Survey Annual Social and Economic Supplemental survey 2005 files, Bureau of Labor Statistics, U.S. Department of Labor.

Note: See Pollin and Wicks-Lim (2006, app. 4).

[a]Total family income includes other subsidy income not examined separately here (e.g., Supplementary Security Income).

wage increase and the effect of these earnings increases on overall pretax family income. We then also calculate the effects of changes in income tax and social security (Federal Insurance Contribution Act, FICA) taxes, as well as changes in eligibility for the EITC and food stamp subsidies.[8]

Considering all families in poverty in table 9.1, section A, we see that the average worker in such families will receive an $866, or 8.1 percent, wage increase—from $10,676 to $11,541 per year. This wage increase then leads to a 5.6 percent gain in the family's overall income before changes in taxes and subsidies. However, the family will now have to pay $91 more in taxes (including federal, state, FICA, and the Child Tax Credit). The family's support from both the EITC and food stamps will also fall by $138. Overall then, the family's disposable income rises by $652, a 3.5 percent gain. In table 9.2, section B, which considers workers in families that now fall below the basic-needs threshold, we see that the overall disposable income rises by $706, from $21,981 to $22,687, a 3.2 percent increase.

The roughly $650–700 gain that these families receive is clearly not going to bring about a dramatic improvement in their living standards. Nevertheless, such increases can bring modest but still significant improvements in a variety of ways, as previous studies of the impact of living wage laws have shown. For example, having the extra $650–700 per year should enable the family to reduce its debt, take a vacation, or reduce work hours; it could also help toward purchasing a car. At the same time, in the context of the contemporary economy where, as we have seen earlier, the real purchasing power of the minimum wage has fallen precipitously over the last 35 years, previous studies have shown that workers who did not receive increases in the minimum wage appear to have experienced a worsening of their living standard.[9] The increase in the Arizona minimum wage will therefore at least serve as a counterweight to the tendency that otherwise appears prevalent for low-wage workers and their families in the United States today, which is a long-term deterioration of their living conditions.

It is also significant that this improvement in living conditions for low-income families in Arizona is occurring through an increase in the family's earned income rather than raising their benefits from EITC, food stamps, or some other government-assistance program.[10] Surveys of low-wage workers suggest that to receive a dollar of government assistance is by no means the same in terms of dignity and commitment to work as receiving a dollar of earned income. For example, the sociologist Kathryn Edin and anthropologist Laura Lein interviewed nearly four hundred welfare and low-income single mothers in cities of four states during the late 1980s and early 1990s and found that, "Self-reliance through work remained most mothers' long-term goal. The vast majority said that they wanted to pay all their bills with what they earned. Full financial independence, allowing them to forgo any outside help, was the only strategy that, in these mothers' eyes, involved no loss of self-respect" (1997, 144).

Part 4

RETROSPECTIVE ANALYSIS

The contemporary living wage movement has a relatively short history in the United States. As such, the initial debates that began in the mid-1990s as to what the effects of these measures would be were necessarily guided by prospective analyses of various sorts. These include our own prospective studies that we presented in parts 2 and 3, as well as other similar works, including the 1998 book *The Living Wage: Building a Fair Economy*. However, as living wage ordinances passed into law and were implemented, it then became possible to examine not simply what was likely to happen as a result of these measures but what actually did happen. The work by Mark Brenner and Stephanie Luce that we present in chapter 10 is one of a small but growing set of retrospective studies on living wage ordinances—studies that examine what did in fact happen in the years after these measures were adopted.[1]

The Brenner and Luce study focuses on the experiences in three New England cities—Boston, Massachusetts, and Hartford and New Haven, Connecticut. In all three cases, the living wage ordinances in place were contractors-only measures. That is, the living wage standard applies only to private businesses that hold service contracts with these municipal governments. As noted in the book's introduction, this is by far the most common type of living wage initiative among the roughly 140 measures in place in U.S. cities today. The strength of these measures is that they do set a minimum wage standard that at least approximates what we may reasonably term a living wage pay rate in various communities. Thus, the $9.11 living wage minimum as of 2001 in Boston was 35 percent higher than the statewide Massachusetts minimum wage of $6.75. The weakness of these measures is that their coverage is very narrow. As Brenner and Luce report, approximately 2,000 workers were covered by the Boston measure. This is in contrast to the 750,000 workers in Massachusetts overall who were earning less than $9.11 in 2001. Fewer workers still were covered in Hartford and New Haven.

Despite this modest coverage, the contractors-only living wage laws still provide important laboratories for examining the key questions that would apply to more expansive initiatives as well (in addition to, of course, providing improved living standards for the modest numbers of people getting raises). Brenner and Luce focus on three sets of issues, the impacts on (1) city contracting patterns, (2) affected businesses, and (3) affected workers.

In terms of contracting patterns, Brenner and Luce examine how these may have changed once firms were faced with the obligation to incorporate living wage standards into their contractual commitments. Critics of living wage measures have argued that because of this increased cost mandate, fewer firms would be willing to bid on city contracts. This would then weaken competition for these contracts, which in turn would raise the costs for the city of providing services to their residents. Such increases in contract costs would, in turn, require either cutbacks in the services the city provides or increased taxes on residents to cover the higher contract costs.

However, the evidence compiled by Brenner and Luce shows that, in fact, there was no systematic change in the competition for contracts. In Boston, the number of firms bidding on contracts was unchanged. In New Haven, the number of bidders fell, but in Hartford the number actually increased. Many firms reported that the living wage provision served to "level the playing field" among bidders, enabling firms to compete for contracts on the basis of quality as opposed to the lowest possible wage rates. In addition, Brenner and Luce show that, overall, the winning bids on these contracts were not generally higher than what they had been before the living wage laws were in place. Evidently, living wage mandates were only one of many factors—and probably not a major factor in most cases—that influenced the firms' strategies in competing for what are, after all, desirable city contracts. In studying the impact on firms, Brenner and Luce provide an in-depth examination of seventy-two service contractors covered by Boston's living wage law, including a large number of nonprofit firms. Brenner and Luce show that these firms did not respond to their living wage mandate by laying off workers. In fact, after the living wage law took effect, the covered businesses actually increased their number of employees working on city contracts. The main adjustment that the firms made in response to the living wage mandate was to accept a lower rate of profit on these contracts (for nonprofit firms, this translates to a lower amount of net revenue per contract after subtracting their costs). This finding suggests that firms were earning substantial profits from these contracts before the living wage law was implemented.

In considering the impact on workers, Brenner and Luce surveyed nearly one hundred employees working on contracts covered by Boston's living wage law. Their survey found that the workers receiving raises were, for the most part, well into their working lives. They were predominantly women and people of color. A high proportion of them were living in poverty before the living wage law was implemented. The incidence of poverty did decline among these workers after the living wage law took effect, though in most cases the improvement in their living standard was modest.

Overall, the findings from the Brenner and Luce retrospective study correspond closely with the results we obtained in our prospective research. As such, both sets of findings provide corroboration for the validity of our research methods and the reliability of the conclusions emerging from both our prospective and retrospective studies. In broadest terms, through both sets of research we find that the benefits of living wage measures are real, if modest, for low-wage workers and their families. Meanwhile, the business firms that are mandated to comply with these laws do not have to make major adjustments in their modes of operation to absorb these increased costs. They do, of course, make adjustments, but these are generally modest. Moreover, the evidence on bidding patterns for city contracts suggests that living wage laws can actually improve the business environment through increasing competition. This results through enabling businesses to compete on the basis of quality as opposed to focusing on maintaining their employees at the lowest possible wage rates.

—R. P.

10 *Living Wage Laws in Practice*

Retrospective Studies on Boston,
Hartford, and New Haven

Mark Brenner and Stephanie Luce

INTRODUCTION AND SUMMARY

This chapter investigates the impacts of living wage laws in New Haven, Boston, and Hartford—early adopters in one region of the country—in 2001, several years after those laws went into effect. The ordinances in these cities reflect national trends and thus include common elements, but they also differ in the types of services they cover and the provisions they mandate. They therefore provide a good platform for investigating the impacts of living wage laws on city contracts, the firms they cover, and low-wage workers—the ultimate beneficiaries of the laws.

Our findings are largely based on three sources of information, each of which takes advantage of the fact that we could observe what actually did happen after the living wage ordinances in these cities had been put into effect. In considering the effects of the living wage laws on contract bidding patterns, the first source is a sample of city contracts and contract bids for all three cities before and after the enactment of their living wage ordinances. Our surveys of employers and workers covered by Boston's living wage law provide the other two sources. With respect to the effects of these measures on workers and business operations, we focused our attention on Boston because its living wage mandate covers numerous contracts and subcontracts, creating the best conditions for such surveys. Our employer survey included 140 vendors holding 212 service contracts covered by Boston's law in the fall 2001. Our worker survey included almost one hundred workers covered by Boston's living wage law between November 2001 and May 2002.

Our study finds that these laws have led to concrete improvements in the lives of workers without significantly harming firms covered by their mandates or consistently raising costs for cities. However, living wage laws in these three cities often do not lift covered workers up to a more ambitious, if still modest, standard of living such as the Economic Policy Institute's "basic family budget." Such mandates can also serve as springboards to more ambitious efforts to improve the living standards of low-wage workers.

BACKGROUND ON BOSTON, HARTFORD, AND NEW HAVEN ORDINANCES

The living wage ordinances in New Haven, Boston, and Hartford were all adopted during the first wave of living wage legislation in the 1990s, and they include most of the key features of these early measures. City councils approved all three, and all apply to city service contracts above a certain dollar value, for example. However, our three ordinances also differ from one another in several important respects. We document these differences in tables 10.1 and 10.2.

Like many living wage laws, the New Haven ordinance, enacted in July 1997, covers contracts of a certain value, in this case at least $25,000. Also like many ordinances, the New Haven law applies only to firms that provide certain services. These include the preparation and distribution of food on city property, security guard services, transportation among city facilities, custodial work, cleaning, nontechnical repairs, and clerical and office work. The ordinance further applies to firms that manage those activities. The New Haven ordinance requires these employers to follow federal, state, and local affirmative action laws, to inform low-wage workers about the federal earned income tax credit (EITC), and to give priority in hiring to laid-off city employees and workers referred by a community hiring hall.

New Haven initially designed its wage floor to enable a single wage earner with a family of four to reach the federal poverty threshold. However, the city raised the threshold to 105 percent of the federal poverty level in July 1998, 110 percent in 1999, 115 percent in 2000, and 120 percent in 2001, which meant that the living wage climbed from $7.43 to $9.75 per hour over this 4-year period (a Living Wage Task Force must determine any future adjustments, but this group did not convene in 2002 and 2003). Over the entire period, the New Haven living wage floor stood roughly 50 percent higher than the state minimum wage.[1]

The Boston ordinance—adopted in September 1998 as a revision of an earlier law—covers firms with service contracts of at least $100,000 and subcontracts of at least $25,000. Reflecting a more recent trend, Boston's

Table 10.1. Main provisions of the living wage ordinances in New Haven, Boston, and Hartford

	New Haven	Boston	Hartford
Adopted by:	City council	City council	City council
Adopted in:	July 1997	September 1998	October 1999
Law covers:	City service contracts	City service contracts	City service contracts and economic development assistance
Covers all service contracts?	No	Yes	No
Covers nonprofits?	No	Yes	No
Covers subcontractors?	Yes	Yes	Yes
Contract value threshold:	$25,000	$100,000 ($25,000 for subcontracts)	$50,000
Employment threshold:	None	25 employees (100 employees for nonprofits)	None
Does wage level rise?	Adjusted annually for first 4 years	Indexed to inflation	Indexed to inflation
Higher wage required if no health benefits?	No	No	Yes
Nonwage provisions:	Employers must follow affirmative action laws Employers must give employees information on the Earned Income Tax Credit Employers are encouraged to hire through a community hiring hall	Employers must give employees information on the Earned Income Tax Credit Employers are encouraged to hire through a community hiring hall	Employer must be neutral in any attempt by employees to organize a union

Note: Details for Boston reflect the ordinance as it was before it was expanded in September 2001.

law applies not only to private, for-profit service contractors working in areas such as security guard services or janitorial services but also to nonprofits providing human services, such as special education, assisted living, and child care. The law exempts firms with fewer than twenty-five full-time-

Table 10.2. Minimum wage and living wage levels in New Haven, Boston, and Hartford

		1997–1998	1998–1999	1999–2000	2000–2001	2001–2002
New Haven	Living wage	$7.43	$8.03	$8.61	$9.14	$9.75
	Minimum wage	$4.77	$5.18	$5.65	$6.15	$6.40
	Difference	+56%	+55%	+52%	+49%	+52%
Boston	Living wage			$8.23	$8.71	$9.11
	Minimum wage			$5.25	$6.00	$6.75
	Difference			+57%	+45%	+35%
Hartford (with health benefits)	Living wage				$8.77	$8.97
	Minimum wage				$6.15	$6.40
	Difference				+43%	+40%
Hartford (without health benefits)	Living wage				$10.51	$10.71
	Minimum wage				$6.15	$6.40
	Difference				+71%	+67%

Note: Minimum wages represent the legal rate at the start of each fiscal year (July 1). Massachusetts and Connecticut generally change their minimum wage on January 1, although Connecticut did raise its minimum wage from $4.77 to $5.18 on September 1, 1997. Minimum wage rates thus rose to those listed for the following fiscal year in the second half of several fiscal years.

equivalent (FTE) employees and all nonprofits with fewer than one hundred employees. Nearly two-thirds of covered contracts in Boston apply to human services, distinguishing Boston even from other cities that have extended coverage to nonprofits. This is due to the fact that city employees in Boston continue to perform many services that private contractors provide elsewhere.

The law set an initial floor of $8.23 in July 1998. The living wage rises each July 1 to reflect either inflation as measured by the regional Consumer Price Index (CPI) or 110 percent of the state or federal minimum wage, whichever is higher. The wage floor has remained at least 35 percent above the state minimum wage. Apart from wage mandates, the Boston law also requires that employers notify employees of the EITC and encourages firms with contracts worth more than $100,000 to hire through city job-training centers.[2]

Boston dramatically expanded its living wage ordinance in September 2001, raising the wage floor to $10.25 per hour, lowering contract thresholds to $25,000, and lowering the FTE threshold to twenty-five employees for nonprofits. However, because these changes did not go into widespread use until July 2002 and because they apply only as contracts expire and are renewed, we restricted our analysis to contracts covered under the initial provisions.

The Hartford ordinance—passed in October 1999—covers service contracts of $50,000 or more and also extends to subcontractors. Much like the New Haven ordinance, it does not cover all service contracts. The law applies to firms providing food and security services on city property and to firms providing custodial services and nontechnical maintenance, clerical and nonsupervisory office work, and transportation and parking services. However, unlike the ordinances in Boston and New Haven, the Hartford living wage law also applies to any development project greater than $100,000 that is subsidized by city, state, or federal funds, tax abatements, grants, or pension funds. The ordinance also extends coverage to any real estate development costing more than $25,000 on city-owned land of which the city is the landlord.

The Hartford law sets the living wage at 110 percent of the federal poverty level for a family of four if the employer provides health benefits. Like a growing number of living wage laws across the country, the Hartford ordinance requires a firm to pay a higher rate if it does not offer health benefits. In these cases, the difference between the two wage rates reflects the average cost of comprehensive health insurance for a family of four, as determined by the city's director of human relations. The living wage rate for workers with health insurance was about 40 percent above the state minimum wage in the first two years, whereas for workers without insurance it was as much as 71 percent higher.

Like some 25 percent of ordinances nationwide, the Hartford law includes nonwage provisions relating to labor relations. Specifically, it includes a labor peace clause requiring firms engaged in city-financed development projects to sign an agreement with any labor union seeking to represent their employees. In essence, employers agree not to interfere with union organizing and unions agree to a no-strike clause for the duration of the contract.

The Impact of Living Wage Laws on City Contracting

For many firms, labor costs account for a significant portion of their overall costs. If living wage laws force companies to raise wages for a sizable portion of their workforce, then the price of their services—and therefore contract costs paid by cities—might rise. In addition, if living wage laws raise the cost of doing business with cities, they might also discourage some firms from bidding on service contracts, undermining competition and opening the door to even higher prices from remaining bidders. Although these are indeed possible outcomes from living wage implementation, have they in fact occurred?

Examining the evidence from other cities as well as New Haven, Boston, and Hartford, we found a modest overall impact on contract costs and bidding, and a somewhat mixed picture both within and between cities. For example, contract costs actually fell in two of our three cities after living wage implementation, and contract costs rose in one city.[3] The impact of a living wage law on individual contracts often varied widely, reflecting the type of services they cover and the way cities conduct the bidding. We further found that competitive bidding remains strong under living wage ordinances and that such laws may even boost the number of bidders on city contracts. On balance, these experiences imply that a living wage law is only one of many factors influencing the cost and competitiveness of city procurement.

The Record in Other Cities

Living wage laws have been in place in many cities around the country for quite some time. What impact have those cities experienced? Fortunately, a growing body of evidence is beginning to shed light on that question. For example, two studies examined the Baltimore living wage law, implemented in 1995. One study, conducted after the first year of implementation, reported that the total cost of nineteen contracts had risen only 0.25 percent since the law took effect. The other, conducted 3 years later, found that the cost of twenty-six contracts had risen just 1.2 percent. In both cases the rate of inflation was higher, so real costs actually fell.

Both studies also found that the impact on individual contracts varied substantially. For example, the contract for the Baltimore bus services—by far the largest—rose by just 2 percent. The cost of a small janitorial contract, in contrast, rose by 47 percent, whereas the cost of a contract for summer food services fell by 12 percent.[4]

Another review of twenty living wage laws across the country found that city officials in almost every location reported higher contract costs, with the absolute amount varying, but in no case amounting to more than 0.1 percent of the overall budget. As with the Baltimore experience, some city officials reported considerable variation in the costs of individual contracts. For example, the cost of a janitorial contract rose 22 percent in Warren, Michigan, whereas the cost of the contract between the City of San Jose and its convention center increased by only 1.5 percent. Whereas City officials in San Francisco and Hayward, California, noted that the living wage ordinance had negligible effects on contract costs, in Corvallis, Oregon, an analysis in June 2001 found that the total cost of thirty-one contracts covered by a living wage ordinance had risen 13 percent—much faster than the inflation rate of 3.5 percent.[5]

Some cities have taken active steps to mitigate the costs of their living wage laws. For example, in a 1-year report filed in February 2000, Pasadena City Manager Cynthia Kurtz found that the cost of five contracts rose by $168,000 (the report did not specify the total contract cost; Kurtz 2000). However, according to Steve Mermell, who oversees Pasadena's living wage law, the city had actually budgeted $340,000 to cover an expected cost increase.[6] Officials negotiated with their contractors to split the higher costs, agreeing in exchange to extend existing contracts rather than put them out for competitive bid.

In a similar case, Multnomah County, Oregon, reported a 5 percent rise in total contract costs for covered services after implementing its living wage policy. However, costs would have risen 27 percent under the old contracts; the county saved funds by consolidating janitorial services at the Department of Corrections, the courthouse, and the county jail into a single contract. This appears to be an example of "relational contracting"— wherein the parties recognize "that for all intents and purposes they depend on one another" and "that it's in their self-interest to establish a long-term cooperative relationship" (Sclar 2000, 123).[7]

Evidence also shows that living wage ordinances can boost the satisfaction of the municipalities with service contracts. In Multnomah County, the contractor's performance rating rose from 2 out of 5 before the living wage to 4 out of 5 six months after it took effect. These gains may reflect a drop in annual turnover among janitors, which fell from 60 to 25 percent over the same period.

Some of these studies reveal contradictory effects of living wage laws on bidding patterns. For example, one of the two Baltimore studies found that the total number of bids the city received fell from ninety-three before the law took effect to seventy-six afterward (the number of bidders rose on three contracts and fell on eight). An official in Ypsilanti Township, Michigan, in contrast, reported that major contracts attracted "more bidders than ever before, at even better rates," after the living wage took effect, forcing them to "be tighter and provide less of a profit margin." City officials in Alexandria, Virginia, noted a similar boost to competitive bidding after the city adopted its living wage law (Elmore 2003, 10).

In Corvallis, Oregon, several firms indicated that they would not bid on city business because of the living wage, yet every vendor the city contacted submitted a bid "and the bids have continued to be competitive," according to the city finance director (Brewer 2001, 2). In Hayward, California, the acting finance director reported that all contracts remained competitively bid and that "productivity and service quality have not been adversely affected" (Finance Director's Office 2000, 3).

How We Approached Our Three Cities

To further investigate the impacts of living wage laws on contract costs and competitive bidding, we compared experiences in New Haven, Boston, and Hartford before and after they implemented their ordinances. Because the scope of the law in each city varies and because the cities differ in the amount of contracting they pursue, we found dramatic differences in the number of covered contracts among the three. We can see this in table 10.3, section A.

For example, because the Boston law does not restrict its coverage to specific services, the city reported 219 covered contracts in September 2001. Some 53 of these contracts were effectively exempt, leaving 166 with a total value of close to $137 million.[8] Although this large number of contracts would be ideal for analyzing the effects of the city's living wage law, the cost of obtaining copies of each contract proved prohibitive. Thus, we restricted our study to high-impact contractors—those reporting at least five employees earning between $8.71 (the living wage floor in fiscal year 2000–2001) and $12 per hour. To identify high-impact contractors, we relied on quarterly reports that covered vendors must file with the Living Wage Division of the Office of Jobs and Community Services. Those reports include the number of employees falling within several wage ranges.

That strategy made the results from the three cities more comparable because both New Haven and Hartford restrict their living wage laws to low-wage sectors such as janitorial and security guard services, as we see in table 10.3, section B. The contracts we excluded from our Boston analysis, moreover, cover professional services such as legal, engineering, and architectural services, which are unlikely to have experienced significant cost increases as a result of the living wage law. Overall we found that twenty-five contract holders in Boston met our criteria—eighteen of them nonprofits.

We asked city departments to provide copies of the contracts we intended to analyze, and only one (Elderly Services) failed to comply with our request. Even so, we could not match many of these contracts with equivalent services performed before the living wage law took effect. To compensate, we added several special-education contracts from the Boston Public Schools to our analysis because that sector experienced the heaviest impact from the living wage law. (The law forced nearly 60 percent of special-education contractors to raise wages, as we show later.) In all, we obtained information on twenty-eight contracts in Boston, twenty-two of which applied to special education, with a total value of $41 million. Those contracts represented some 30 percent of the total value of all covered service contracts at that time.[9]

In marked contrast to Boston, the New Haven law affected some fifteen service contracts at the time of our data collection. However, the city had funded only eight of these both before and after the law took effect. Because

Table 10.3. Contracts covered by living wage laws in Boston, Hartford, and New Haven

A. Contract coverage as of June 2001

City	Covered contracts	Total contract value
Boston[a]		
Total	219	$201.8 million
Covered	166	$136.8 million
Exempt	53	$65.0 million
Hartford	2	$1.2 million
New Haven	7	$596,574

B. Services covered by living wage laws in Boston, Hartford, and New Haven

City	Service
Boston	Adult education
	Architectural and engineering services
	Assisted living[b]
	Consulting services
	Childcare services[b]
	Cleaning services[b]
	Community learning center services[b]
	Computer services and support
	Educational consulting
	General repair services
	Janitorial services[b]
	Legal services
	Security guard services[b]
	Special education[b]
	Supportive housing[b]
	Temporary office assistance[b]
	X-ray services[b]
Hartford	Security guard services
	Temporary office assistance
New Haven	Busing services
	Food services
	Janitorial services
	Security guard services

Source: Authors' calculations based on data obtained from the three cities.

[a]Boston data are through September 2001.

[b]High-impact services; these are services for which at least one contractor reports a concentration of low-wage workers. The study focuses on those services.

the city merged two of these contracts in fiscal year 2001–2002, we focused on seven contracts with a value of nearly $600,000. In Hartford, the living wage law had affected only two contracts worth $1.2 million when we collected our data, although the city reported that the law will eventually affect eight contracts. Both the contracts covered services because no economic development projects had yet come under the law's purview. That experience is not uncommon; many cities whose living wage law covers economic development aid actually apply the law to few, if any, projects.[10]

The Impact of Living Wage Laws on Bidding Patterns

How have living wage laws affected competitive bidding in our three cities? In Boston and Hartford the number of bids either stayed the same or grew after the living wage law took effect, whereas in New Haven the number of bids declined by three. Overall, as we see in table 10.4, we found that the total bids for all three cities declined by only one after living wage implementation.

Within each city we saw a wide variation among individual contracts. More than one-third of all contracts saw no change in the number of bidders, nearly one-third saw increases, and nearly 30 percent saw bids decline. Declines in the number of bidders were most prevalent in Boston, occurring for three of five types of services.[11] Given that less than one-third of contracts saw declines in the number of bidders after living wage implementation, forces *other* than the living wage law seem to be exerting at least as strong an effect on the number of firms willing to compete for contracts. In line with experiences in Baltimore and other cities, we did find that bidding patterns varied systematically across a few sectors. One example is janitorial services. The number of bidders declined for four of seven janitorial and cleaning contracts after the living wage took effect. That total includes two contracts in New Haven, where winning bids usually come from small, individually owned and managed janitorial companies, and two in Boston, where large, commercial building services firms tend to compete for the city's janitorial contracts.

Two out of three security guard contracts, in contrast, saw an increase in the number of bidders, as did one of two temporary office assistance contracts. In these cases, the living wage floor may have actually improved bidding by reducing the ability of vendors to undercut their competition. As New Haven Controller Mark Pietrosimone noted, the living wage ordinance "puts all vendors on equal footing . . . [and] it has leveled off undercutting," forcing contractors to compete with one another along dimensions other than wages and benefits, such as service quality.[12] Experience in Hartford sheds light on why and how that occurs.

Expanding the Bidding Pool: Security Guard Contracting in Hartford

In September 1999, a month after passing its living wage law, Hartford solicited bids for a new city contract for security guard services. The contract

Table 10.4. Total number of bids before and after implementation of the living wage

City and Service	Before	After	Difference
Boston *(high-impact firms only)*			
X-ray services, Suffolk County Jail	3	1	−2
Temporary office help, Dept. of Neighborhood Development	5	9	4
Janitorial services, Police Dept.	9	7	−2
Security services, Library	3	4	1
Cleaning services, Property Management Office	6	5	−1
Boston subtotal	26	26	0
Hartford			
Temporary office help, citywide	3	3	0
Security services, citywide	7	9	2
Hartford subtotal	10	12	2
New Haven			
Security services, Main Library	5	5	0
Janitorial services, Health Office	5	4	−1
Janitorial services, Police Station	9	5	−4
Janitorial services, Main Library	4	4	0
Janitorial services, Branch Libraries	3	4	1
Janitorial services, Senior Center	3	3	0
Food preparation services, Child Development	1	2	1
Bus services, Parks Dept.	1	1	0
Bus services, Child Development	1	1	0
New Haven subtotal	32	29	−3
Total for all cities	68	67	−1

Source: Authors' analysis of data obtained from the three cities.

was scheduled to begin on January 1, 2000, and run through December 31, 2001. The initial request solicited proposals for some 54,000 hours of security guard services over the 2-year period, and firms submitted their bids in the form of an hourly rate the city would pay for each hour of services actually performed. Two companies bid on the contract, including Command Security, which had won the last contract for these services.

That number of bids was much lower than in past years: seven companies had bid during the 1997 round, and five had done so during the 1993 round. (The contract was not competitively bid in 1995; the city extended the Effective Security 1993 contract for 2 years.) Most firms decided not to compete with Command Security (the incumbent contractor) in 1999, perhaps because the Hartford-based company was guaranteed special consideration under a provision giving preference to local businesses. That provision had been decisive when the city awarded Command Security the contract in 1997.

Upon review, city officials realized that the contract was subject to the new living wage ordinance but that they had not informed contractors. The officials determined that the contract should be rebid, and this time included information on the living wage in all materials they sent to prospective bidders. In this second round, the city received nine bids, including new bids from the two companies that had bid during the first round. The Hartford living wage law seems to have sparked a dramatic increase in the number of bidders. Table 10.5 provides the basic evidence on bidding patterns.

The living wage ordinance was not the only factor underlying the quadrupling of bidders. One second-round bidder, Argus Security Group, pointed out that the City of Hartford did a better job of advertising the request for proposals in the second round. Pat Paboway, Argus representative, said that the firm would have probably entered the first-round bidding had it been aware of the opportunity.[13]

Still, a closer look at the record shows that the living wage may also have leveled the playing field, encouraging more companies to bid. An analysis by the city 2 years after implementing the living wage found that, under the prior contract, Command Security had employed ten security guards earning $6.77 and two guards earning $6.60 per hour. The former group did not receive health benefits and the latter did, but in both cases the guards were earning only about $1.00 above the state minimum wage of $5.65.

Table 10.5. Bids for Hartford security guard contracts

| | | 1999 | |
Bidder	1997	Round 1	Round 2
Command Security Corp.	$9.75	$10.07	$14.96
Metro Loss Prevention	$9.87		
Elite Security	$9.90		
Tri-City Security Services	$10.38		$18.85
Burns International Security	$10.49		$19.35
Pinkerton Security Services	$11.50	$10.56	$15.65
Wackenhut Corp.	$13.34		
Lance Investigations			$14.58
Argus Security Group			$14.61
Jo-Ryu Security			$17.77
Novas Security			$18.55
Al Washington and Associates			$18.62

Source: Authors' analysis of data obtained from the City of Hartford.

Note: Bids for Hartford's security guard contract are made on the basis of an hourly billable rate charged to the city. The values are reported as they were submitted in each year; that is, we have not adjusted them for inflation.

According to the Bureau of Labor Statistics, those wages were nearly 30 percent below the average hourly wage for security guards in the Hartford area at the time ($9.45) and 20 percent below the median ($8.38).

An analysis of Command Security's contract reveals that wage costs accounted for more than two-thirds of the hourly bid price prior to the living wage. (The company charged the city $9.75 per hour, but the highest-paid guards were earning $6.77.) This suggests that firms paying higher wages were at a disadvantage when competing with Command Security in the city security guard market when the only floor was the statewide minimum of $5.65. By setting a wage floor well above the state minimum wage, the Hartford ordinance substantially enlarged the market for security guard services.

Rod Murdoch of Tri-City Security Services confirmed that his company decided to enter the Hartford security guard market because "the playing field had been leveled." Tri-City, he said, often receives opportunities to work in "low-ball" niches, where the guards make little money and the company's margins are thin. However, he said, Tri-City prefers to work in " 'middle niches,' where the guards are making more in the range of $9 to $10 and the company's margins aren't so thin." He also maintained that Tri-City prefers to work with the private sector because the public sector often has more contract requirements but, in his opinion, is unwilling to pay for them. "We'll provide a guard with certain credentials," he said, "but you must be willing to pay for it."[14]

Donald Coursey of Al Washington and Associates concurred that he considers the municipal contracting market problematic, "because cities are usually obliged to take the lowest bid, which means that there is an incentive to low-ball, and it's hard to compete against that. It means you end up paying people minimum wage, which is very unstable, because people can make that money anywhere, and they may just disappear tomorrow, and the city is calling up saying, 'Where is my guard?' and you are hamstrung, and in the process your reputation gets ruined." He added, "Most companies with any business sense would concentrate on a higher-wage niche, because there is more stability involved, and it gives you better control of the business, and allows you to preserve your reputation." Coursey held that any firm with a long-term approach to working in the security guard industry would avoid the low-wage end of the market.[15]

Mark Cratin of Lance Investigations similarly reported that his company usually avoids low-wage guard work, instead seeking out contracts in which guards can earn at least $10 per hour. He argued that the low-bid method is inefficient; his firm sat out the 1999 bidding on the Hartford security guard contract for precisely that reason.[16] These results reinforce the argument that cities can exert a major impact on the market in which they procure services.

The Impact on Contract Costs in Our Three Cities

How have living wage laws affected city contract costs? Table 10.6, section A, reports the evidence. In Boston, we found that the total annual cost of the twenty-eight contracts we analyzed fell markedly in real terms—from $20 million to $17 million, or 17 percent—after the city implemented its living wage ordinance. A 19 percent drop in the twenty-two special-education contracts drove this decline; however, the six other contracts also declined by 3 percent. New Haven similarly registered a 12 percent decline in annual contract costs after implementing its living wage law. The overall cost of the two Hartford contracts, in contrast, rose sharply—by 33 percent.[17]

To better understand these results, we examined average cost changes across all the contracts in our study, as presented in table 10.6, section B. This more detailed view initially seems to show that living wage laws boosted the average cost of a service contract in these three cities. As we see in the column of unweighted changes in contract costs—that is, each contract is counted equally in establishing an average value, regardless of the size of each contract—in Boston, special-education contracts rose an average of 3 percent and the other contracts rose an average of 7 percent. In New Haven, the average contract rose 0.3 percent, whereas in Hartford it rose 29 percent.

However, we find a different story when we factor in the size of the contracts, weighting them according to their total dollar values. Adjusting for contract size is important when we want to get a sense of whether a city will experience overall cost increases due to the living wage. In this case, we find that the Boston special-education contracts declined an average of 9 percent, whereas the non–special-education contracts rose 16 percent. The New Haven contracts declined by an average of 11 percent, whereas the Hartford contracts rose an average of 33 percent. Except for non–special-education contracts in Boston—which reflect a substantial increase in the cost of temporary office services—these results mirror the total average annual changes reported in table 10.6, section A.

What forces underlie the remarkably different cost outcomes between Boston and New Haven, on the one hand, and Hartford on the other? The most obvious influence is the different nature of services contracted out in Boston. A much higher proportion of the Boston contracts apply to human services such as special education, for which reimbursement rates are set by state and federal agencies. These contracts are not competitively bid, and their fixed reimbursement rates do not allow contractors to pass on higher labor costs to the city.

Table 10.6. Change in contract costs due to living wage laws

A. Annual contract costs before and after living wage implementation (in 2001 dollars)

City	Before	After	Difference
Boston *(high-impact firms only)*			
Special education	$18.4 million	$15.1 million	−18%
(number of contracts=22)			
Non–special education	$1.4 million	$1.4 million	−3%
(number of contracts=6)			
Total	$19.8 million	$16.5 million	−17%
(number of contracts=28)			
Hartford	$465,338	$617,416	33%
(number of contracts=2)			
New Haven	$692,697	$611,411	−12%
(number of contracts=9)			

B. Average annual change in contract costs under the living wage

City	Unweighted	Weighted
Boston *(high-impact firms only)*		
Special education	3%	−9%
(number of contracts=22)		
Non–special education	7%	16%
(number of contracts=6)		
Total	3%	−7%
(number of contracts=28)		
Hartford	29%	33%
(number of contracts=2)		
New Haven	0.3%	−11%
(number of contracts=9)		

Source: Authors' calculations based on data collected from the three cities.

However, contract costs also declined in Boston even for some competitively bid services such as x-ray and janitorial services. The major difference among the three cities seems to be that Hartford bid both of its contracts on a unit-cost basis. Under that approach, cities ask vendors to submit the rate they will charge for each hour of work they perform rather than submitting a bid for the total value of the work. This approach encourages firms to apply cost-plus markups and thus appears ill-suited to holding down total contract costs. Indeed, we find that most contracts bid on a unit-cost basis in Boston and New Haven display a similar pattern. Because of the systematic impact unit-cost bidding appears to exert on contract costs, their dynamics merit more attention.

How Unit Costs Change under Living Wage Laws

Behind the changes in contract costs reported in table 10.6, we find a clear pattern of cost increases for security guard services and temporary office assistance in all three cities. Officials rely on unit-cost bidding for these services because they can rarely anticipate their exact need for them in advance. That approach opens the door for significant cost increases under a living wage law.

For example, the winning bidder for security guard services in Hartford raised the average markup—the difference between what the city paid and the amount the vendor paid its workers—from $3.12 to $4.36 after living wage implementation. Some of this undoubtedly reflected higher payroll taxes and worker's compensation payments stemming from the living wage. The company may also have passed on raises for employees not working on city contracts or raises for employees earning above the living wage. Mandated wage increases for part of a company's workforce are expected to create pressure to raise wages for workers not covered by the mandate. But, as the next section of this chapter shows, nonmandated wage increases under living wage ordinances are actually relatively modest. This implies that the firm may have padded its bid not only to recuperate the indirect costs of the living wage but also to maintain or boost its profit margin on each hour worked.[18]

Higher contract costs after living wage laws take effect are more common in cities where unit-price bidding is more prevalent. Indeed, contractors bidding on unit prices often appear to pass higher labor costs back to the city more than dollar for dollar, as with security guard services in Hartford. Although that case represents the extreme among our cities, almost all contracts bid on a unit-cost basis experienced the problem.[19]

The Hartford case also shows that efforts to consolidate services can hold down markups and unit prices even under unit-cost bidding. For example, the real unit cost for security guard services in Hartford grew by 43 percent. In contrast, six of the twelve unit prices for temporary office assistance bid both before and after the living wage fell, and only two rose by more than 15 percent. Although these results may partly reflect the market for temporary office services in Hartford, they may also reflect a conscious strategy by bidders to hold down the unit prices of some services while raising them for others in an effort to win the contract for consolidated services. Evidence from Boston and New Haven also suggests that in cases in which they consolidated services, even those bid on a unit-cost basis, the cities were able to prevent higher labor costs from translating into higher prices. In sum, when cities bundle service contracts—such as by awarding a single contract for cleaning all libraries rather than a separate contract for each building—

firms appear to lower the amount of overhead they add to their bids.[20] Our results suggest that consolidating service contracts can cut cost pass-through by contractors as much as 20 percent.[21]

Do Living Wage Laws Force Cities to Curtail Services?

Concern often arises that cities will curtail services if living wage mandates force contract costs to rise. However, higher contract costs have not prompted our three cities to cut public services. The contract for security guard services at the Boston Public Library is a good example. Unit prices rose nearly 39 percent in real terms after living wage implementation, but the city actually expanded the number of guard hours at the library and total contract costs rose by nearly 60 percent. Diane Collins, who oversees the contract, believes that higher wages actually spurred positive changes that helped sustain the level of services. She agreed that "The guards seem a little happier than the batch that was here before. Plus, they seem to be here longer. Before the living wage, you'd see new faces all the time. With higher wages, the guards seem to take the work more seriously and provide better service."[22]

Joanne Keville-Mulkern, contracting specialist for the Boston Public Schools (BPS), reported that the living wage ordinance has not forced the city to curtail services for which BPS contracts, nor have human service agencies proved less willing to bid on city contracts. She did, however, express the concern, shared by many of the Boston nonprofit contractors, that if living wage mandates generate significant costs, providers will have no way to pass those costs through to the city because federal and state agencies set their reimbursement rates.[23] Although this dilemma was not a real issue under the original law, nonprofits were concerned that the September 2001 expansion may lead to hardship.

Overall, staff members responsible for implementing the living wage law in the three cities confirmed our findings that its impact on costs and competitive bidding has been modest. In New Haven, where the ordinance mandates that the city evaluate its impact each year, staff members found only a 6 percent increase in the cost of busing for field trips. They also noted that the workforce for several contracts was unionized, so workers already received wages higher than the living wage threshold. When discussing the Boston law with the Providence City Council, Mimi Turchinetz, director of Boston's Living Wage Division, attested, "We have not seen a decrease in competition for these contracts. We also have not seen increased costs to maintain city contracts. Vendors and the city have successfully absorbed the cost of the living wage ordinance. There has been no adverse financial impact on the city. The living wage ordinance has been good for Boston."[24]

THE IMPACT OF LIVING WAGE LAWS ON FIRMS

Most studies of living wage laws—both proposed and enacted—find that they affect a very small number of firms. Such studies also find that the overall costs to firms covered by such mandates are low, averaging 1–2 percent of total operating costs or sales.[25] However, these estimates are averages for all firms covered by living wage laws. The costs to firms in low-wage industries such as food service, janitorial services, parking lot maintenance, and security services are often much higher. How do firms—particularly these low-wage firms—adjust to higher costs?

Some economists maintain that firms respond by laying off workers and that living wage laws thus worsen prospects for low-wage workers. Recent research on the minimum wage, however, shows that average firm employment does not drop after the minimum wage rises, even in high-impact industries such as fast food, and that the employment prospects of individual low-wage workers do not worsen (e.g., Katz and Krueger 1992; Spriggs 1993; Card and Krueger 1994, 1995, 2000; Zavodny 2000). Some analysts have even found a positive relationship between minimum wages and the number of jobs available to low-wage workers (e.g., Bhaksar, Manning, and To 2002; Manning 2003). Other studies suggest that lower turnover—and hence lower recruitment and training costs—may offset higher labor costs for firms (e.g., Akerlof and Yellen 1986; Stiglitz 1987).[26]

Recent empirical evidence suggests that firms have indeed relied on adjustment mechanisms other than layoffs—particularly raising prices—in the face of higher minimum wages (see Card and Krueger 1995, chap. 2; Aaronson 2001). In light of this evidence, studies of proposed living wage ordinances have predicted that firms can absorb higher costs—even on the order of 10 percent—through some combination of price increases, higher productivity, and lower profits.

Have firms actually taken such steps in the face of living wage mandates? To investigate that question—and to better understand the kinds of firms affected by a living wage law—we conducted an in-depth telephone survey of the 140 vendors holding 212 service contracts covered by the Boston law in fall 2001.[27] Among our three cities, Boston offers the best conditions for such an analysis because its living wage mandate covers numerous contracts and subcontracts, including those of nonprofits, which often pay low wages.

We conducted our survey 3 years after Boston implemented its living wage ordinance, when the living wage was $9.11. (As mentioned, Boston dramatically expanded its living wage ordinance in September 2001, raising the wage floor to $10.25 per hour, lowering the contract threshold for coverage to $25,000, and lowering the threshold for the number of FTE employees to twenty-five for nonprofits. However, these changes did not go into widespread use until July 2002, so we evaluated only contractors covered under the earlier terms of the law.)

After developing an overall profile of firms covered by the law, we investigated whether firms responded to higher labor costs by reducing the overall number of jobs, or increasing the number of part-time jobs, as predicted by standard models of the labor market. In contrast to such theoretical predictions, we found that firms forced to raise wages actually significantly expanded the number of staff assigned to their city contracts and did not turn to part-time instead of full-time jobs to absorb higher labor costs. We also found little evidence that firms raised prices—to the city or other customers—to accommodate higher labor costs. Nor did they take other steps, such as cutting turnover, raising productivity, or substituting higher-skilled workers or equipment for their low-wage workforce. The one clear move a significant number of affected firms pursued was to accept lower profits.

How We Conducted Our Survey

We initiated our survey by mailing a copy of a questionnaire to a contact person at each firm, along with a cover letter and a letter from the head of Boston's Living Wage Division.[28] We then called the contact person to determine who could best respond to the survey and to establish a date and time for the interview. Overall, human resource directors were most likely to answer our questionnaire, but several individuals within a given firm often provided responses to different parts of the survey. For example, the finance director often answered questions on revenues and expenditures, and the human resource director responded to workforce-related questions.

We continued to contact each firm until we obtained an interview—which typically lasted 20–30 minutes—or until the firm declined to participate. Our survey produced seventy-two valid interviews, a 51 percent response rate. Participating firms held $101 million in city service contracts, or some 40 percent of the value of all contracts covered under the living wage law. Our respondents closely mirror the profile of all covered firms, although our sample includes a smaller percentage from the repair and construction sector than in the overall profile (that sector accounts for 24 percent of all covered firms but only 18 percent of our sample).[29]

Because, unlike most cities, the Boston living wage law includes nonprofits, a full 63 percent of the contracts covered by the ordinance involved human services. Those contracts accounted for 44 percent of the total value of all covered contracts.[30] In most other cities, private, for-profit services such as janitorial and security guard services account for a much larger share of covered services.

This has two important implications for our study. On the one hand, a large number of low-wage workers probably received raises as a result of the Boston living wage law because human service employees are among the most poorly remunerated in the services sector.[31] However, the high concentration of nonprofits also makes it more difficult to anticipate the behavior of firms because nonprofits may well respond differently than for-profit firms to higher wage mandates. Although few analysts have investigated how nonprofit human service agencies respond to mandates such as living wage laws, those that have done so suggest that nonprofits—in particular, those in the hospital industry—may try to maintain employment levels even in situations in which their for-profit counterparts would not.[32]

A Profile of the Boston Covered Firms

Because we know comparatively little about the firms covered by living wage ordinances, we first used the results of our survey to create an overall profile of the firms covered by the Boston law. As we report in table 10.7, we found that those firms are relatively large, averaging 203 employees. Some 63 percent reported more than 50 employees, and over one-quarter reported more than 250. Some 80 percent of these employees are nonmanagerial, and 16 percent work part time.

The firms in our survey are substantial enterprises, averaging $105 million per year in revenue. (Four-fifths reported revenues greater than $1 million; nearly two-thirds had revenues greater than $5 million; and close to one-third reported revenues in excess of $15 million.)

Despite their significant revenues, we found that many firms covered by Boston's living wage ordinance pay comparatively low wages. Nearly 20 percent of employees in covered firms earned less than $11.75 per hour (about $24,000 per year for a full-time employee) and one-third earned less than $14.25 per hour (about $30,000 per year for a full-time employee). For comparison, one recent study estimated that in 2001 a one-parent, two-child family in Boston needed at least $38,000 to maintain a basic living standard, which meant that a wage earner working full-time needed to make $13.60 per hour (Boushey et al. 2001).[33] These firms may compensate their workforce in other ways; 94 percent offered both individual and family health plans, for example. However, as we discuss in the next section of this chapter, many workers cannot necessarily afford these plans.

Despite the fact that a substantial percentage of employees received low wages, we found that the impact of the living wage law on firms' costs was

Table 10.7. Characteristics of firms covered by the Boston living wage law, 2001

Employment, hours, and wages *(number of firms = 72)*	
Employees	203
Part-time employees	16%
Nonmanagerial employees	80%
Employees earning < $14.25	33%
Employees earning < $11.75	18%
Monthly turnover among nonmanagerial employees[a]	3.4%
Unscheduled absenteeism (days per employee per year)[b]	4.6
Revenues and costs *(number of firms = 51)*	
Average revenue per firm	$105 million
Firms with revenue less than $500,000	10%
Firms with revenue less than $1 million	14%
Firms with revenue greater than $5 million	61%
Firms with revenue greater than $15 million	29%
Labor costs as a share of total costs	63%
Other firm attributes *(number of firms = 72)*	
Firms that are nonprofits	47%
Firms offering benefits	94%
Firms that are franchises or branches	38%
Firms reporting some unionized employees	13%

Source: Authors' survey of covered firms.

[a]Only 67 firms reported valid data on turnover.

[b]Only 44 firms reported valid data on absenteeism.

relatively modest. That is because low-wage labor accounted for a relatively small share of these firms' total costs. For example, workers earning less than $11.75 accounted for 9 percent of the average firm's total costs, whereas workers earning less than $14.25 accounted for 17 percent.[34] (For the median firm, workers earning less than $11.75 accounted for 2 percent of total costs, whereas those earning less than $14.25 accounted for 9 percent of total costs.) Overall, we found that labor costs accounted for an average of 63 percent of the total costs of these contractors (or a median of 69 percent).

One phenomenon often associated with low-wage work is high employee turnover and absenteeism. How prevalent are these problems among all our firms? We found that monthly turnover averaged 3.4 percent for nonmanagerial employees—slightly above the national rate of 3.3 percent and slightly below the national rate of 3.5 percent for the service sector.[35] These figures correspond to an annual average of 41 percent. Our firms reported an average of 4.6 sick days per employee per year, translating into 805 days per firm.

To understand the impact of turnover and absenteeism, we asked firms to estimate the total cost—including separation, search, and training—of replacing their lowest-paid workers. The forty-three responding firms reported a median of $2,500 and an average of $9,297 per new hire, with the former representing about 3 percent of the firm's wage bill for workers earning less than $11.75. These figures do not account for productivity lost while new workers become proficient at their job, which can account for as much as 60 percent of total turnover costs, even in low-wage industries.[36] Even if we account for lost productivity, however, it is not clear that these costs are substantial for most firms covered by the Boston law.

As we show in table 10.8, the firms in our survey reported a total of 14,606 employees, with 2,771 working on city service contracts. Although city contract workers represent about 20 percent of all workers in covered firms, for the average firm about 31 percent of its workforce is involved in city contracting.[37]

Service contractors in Boston reported substantial continuity in working with the city: some 72 percent had held the same contract before the adoption of the living wage law. However, 12 percent said they did not immediately comply with the law when it first applied to their contracts. Nonprofits disproportionately accounted for these delays, particularly those working in assisted living and supportive housing, and those with contracts for more than one service.

One very important finding from our survey is that the living wage law forced nearly one-quarter of covered firms to raise wages to comply. Although we did not directly query firms as to how many workers received raises as a result of the law, our estimates indicate that as many as 2,000 current employees did.[38]

Table 10.8. Scope of living wage coverage in Boston, 2001

Total number of employees of firms participating in our survey	14,606
Estimated number of employees in all firms covered by Boston's living wage law	26,440
Number of employees working on city contracts among firms in our survey	2,771
Estimated number of employees working on city contracts among all covered firms	5,177
Average percentage of employees working on covered contracts among firms in our survey	31%
Firms in the survey that delayed implementing the living wage[a]	12%
Firms in the survey with the same contract before the living wage law[b]	72%
Firms in the survey that raised wages to comply with the living wage law[c]	23%

Source: Authors' survey of covered firms.
[a]Number of firms = 60.
[b]Number of firms = 62.
[c]Number of firms = 66.

Comparing Firms That Raised Wages and Those That Did Not

We now have a picture of the firms covered by Boston's living wage law. However, our main goal is to determine how firms forced to raise wages under the law dealt with rising costs. To do this, we want to compare their experience with that of firms not forced to raise wages. Concretely, that means we need to compare changes experienced by these two groups of firms between 1998 and 2001 on a number of counts. In so doing, we attribute any differences in how the two groups reacted to the impact of the law.[39]

The fact that we conducted our survey nearly 3 years after the living wage law took effect raises the risk that any changes in these two groups over time may reflect other influences. However, this time lag also better enables us to uncover firms' long-term adjustments to the Boston living wage law, including approaches such as reorganizing workplaces and adopting new technologies. Because 10 percent of our firms reported delays in raising pay to comply with the law, our time horizon also ensures that we have not missed any adjustments that occurred because of a lag in implementation.

To see if unaffected firms would provide a good control group for our study, we compared them to the affected firms on a couple of fundamental characteristics. We found that firms that raised wages were roughly the same size as firms that did not, with both employing roughly two hundred people at the time of our survey. Both sets of firms were roughly similar in terms of revenues as well, with affected firms reporting median revenues of $8.9 million, versus $6.6 million among unaffected firms.[40]

Not surprisingly, affected and unaffected firms differed in a few key areas related to the living wage. Affected firms were overwhelmingly nonprofit, 80 percent versus just one-third of unaffected firms. And, as we would expect, affected firms reported more workers earning near the living wage threshold; an average of 37 percent of their employees earned less than $11.75, versus 12 percent at unaffected firms. Affected firms also averaged significantly higher labor costs as a share of total costs, 73 percent versus 60 percent for unaffected firms. Affected firms also had a much higher turnover rate among nonmanagerial employees, 7.4 percent per month versus 2.6 percent per month for unaffected firms.

As we show in table 10.9, we found that firms that raised wages to comply with the Boston law varied dramatically by type of service even within the nonprofit human services sector. The largest concentration of affected firms occurred in special education, in which 57 percent of all firms reported raising wages. One-third of child-care firms raised wages, as did over

Table 10.9. Firms that raised wages under the Boston living wage law, by type of service

Type of service	Percentage
Education and training services	27%
Repair and construction	8%
Assisted living/supportive housing	0%
Special education services	57%
Engineering/architecture/ other consulting	9%
Childcare	33%
Computer consulting	0%
Trash/janitorial/security	0%
Multiservice contractor	17%
All firms	23%

Source: Authors' survey of affected firms.

one-quarter of firms in education and training. None of the assisted living/supportive housing firms, in contrast, reported raising wages.

How the Two Groups Reacted to the Living Wage Law

Did firms that raised wages and firms that did not raise them react to the living wage law differently? For example, perhaps the former shrank in size to cope with higher labor costs or grew at a slower pace than they otherwise would have. Perhaps they reduced the number of hours worked by their staff or substituted more part-time employees. Perhaps they coped with higher labor costs by hiring more experienced or more skilled workers at the higher wages. These are all possible methods of adjustment. But did firms in fact rely on those or other adjustment channels in the face of higher wages?

We did find evidence, presented in table 10.10, that employment grew more quickly among unaffected firms than among affected firms between 1998 and 2001. Among the former, it grew by an average of 17 percent (from roughly 156 to 183 employees), whereas among the latter it grew 11 percent (from 183 to 203).[41]

However, these figures do not account for changes in the number of full-time versus part-time employees. Did affected firms react to higher costs under the living wage law by reducing the number of full-time employees? Upon examination, we did not find that to be the case. In fact, we found nearly identical trends for affected and unaffected firms. The number of full-time jobs at affected firms actually *rose* by an average of 13 percent (from 166 to 188), whereas the number of such jobs similarly rose 14 percent among unaffected firms (from 153 to 175). Moreover, the average number of part-time staff actually declined substantially among affected

Table 10.10. Comparing firms that did and did not raise wages, before and after the living wage law

Variable	Raised wages			Did not raise wages		
	1998	2001	Difference	1998	2001	Difference
Number of employees	183	203	21	156	183	27
Number of full-time-equivalent employees	166	188	22	152	175	22
Percentage part-time employees	34%	23%	−11%	11%	10%	−0.9% *
Number of employees working on city contracts covered by the living wage[a]	69	87	18	15	15	−0.2 **
Percentage of employees earning < $9.25	23%	4%	−19%	3.4%	2.6%	−0.8% **
Percentage of employees earning < $11.75	41%	41%	0%	11%	12%	1.0%
Average monthly turnover rate[b] (percentage of non-supervisory employees)	4.8%	5.6%	0.8%	3.6%	1.6%	−2.0%
Average annual absenteeism rate[c] (days per employee per year)	5.3	5.7	0.4	4.4	4.2	−0.2

Source: Authors' survey of affected firms.

Note: Number of firms = 51.

*Indicates a statistically significant difference in the trend from 1998 to 2001 between firms that raised wages and those that did not, at a 95 percent confidence level.

**Indicates a statistically significant difference in the trend from 1998 to 2001 between firms that raised wages and those that did not, at a 99 percent confidence level.

[a]Only 36 firms reported valid information on the number of contract workers in both years, including 10 firms that raised wages and 26 that did not.

[b]Only 43 firms reported valid data on turnover in both years, including 10 that raised wages and 33 that did not.

[c]Only 36 firms reported valid data on absenteeism in both years, including 9 that raised wages and 27 that did not.

firms—from 34 to 23 percent—versus a much more modest decline among unaffected firms, from 11 to 10 percent.[42] These findings are striking because they reveal that affected firms did not respond to higher wages by laying off staff, cutting hours, or shifting to more part-time employees. Quite the opposite—there was growth in overall employment and a shift away from part-time and toward full-time staff.

How else might firms have adjusted to higher wages? Rather than reducing the overall number of jobs or employees' hours in response to higher wage mandates, could firms have responded by cutting the number of employees working on city contracts while expanding the number of employees performing other work? Again, we did not find that to be the case. The number of employees working on covered contracts grew much faster among firms forced to raise wages than among firms not forced to raise wages. The average number of contract workers at affected firms rose from 69 in 1998 to roughly 87 in 2001; at unaffected firms the number remained relatively stable at 15.[43] We found virtually identical results when we analyzed changes in the number of contract jobs on a FTE basis and changes in the percentage of contract workers.

Perhaps the living wage law raised wages for only a marginal number of workers at affected firms. As one of us notes in related work, many localities do not implement or enforce living wage ordinances effectively (see Luce 2004). If we find little direct evidence that firms raised wages in response to the living wage law, that may explain why we failed to detect any negative effects on employment or hours and, instead, found an increase in firms' use of full-time staff.

The evidence, however, does not support this proposition. Affected firms saw a substantial decline—from 23 percent in 1998 to 4 percent in 2001—in the proportion of workers earning below $9.25. Firms unaffected by the law, in contrast, reported a decline of less than 1 percentage point.[44] The proportion of workers earning less than $11.75 did not change for either group of firms. That implies that affected firms saw a substantial degree of wage compression; that is, the number of workers earning mid-range wages grew from 1998 to 2001. This is important evidence that firms raised wages for a substantial number of workers and that the living wage ordinance was effectively enforced.

If firms did not reduce the number of employees or the hours worked in the face of higher wages, what other avenues could they have pursued to adjust to the Boston living wage mandate? One possibility is that firms offset higher direct labor costs by trying to reduce turnover and absenteeism, which are essentially indirect costs to firms. Examining the evidence, however, we found that average turnover and absenteeism actually rose among firms forced to raise wages, whereas firms unaffected by the law saw a sharp drop in turnover and a more modest reduction in absenteeism. This seemingly contradictory finding is most likely the result of the extraordinarily low unemployment rate in Boston between 1998 and 2001, which averaged less than 3 percent for the entire period. This tight labor market (coupled with the substantial increases in the state minimum wage over this period) may have actually made alternative employment more attractive for some covered employees. At a minimum, it significantly reduced the cost of finding (and perhaps taking) a new job.

What other methods could firms have used to adjust to higher wage costs? We present the relevant evidence in table 10.11. Perhaps higher wages boosted productivity by spurring greater worker effort, thereby enabling

Table 10.11. How firms reported adjusting to the Boston living wage law

Variable	Percentage
Greater employee effort	25%
Higher employee morale	25%
Raised bid prices on city contracts	15%
Raised prices for other services	8%
Lowered profits	39%
Changed hiring standards	0%
Changed hiring methods	27%
Changed production techniques	0%

Source: Authors' survey of affected firms.
Note: This information is based on reports from 13 firms.

firms to absorb these higher costs. There is solid empirical evidence that such effects exist, although analysts disagree on whether the greater employee effort results from positive forces, such as higher morale, or negative ones, such as fear of losing a higher-paying job (see Capelli and Chauvin 1991; Levine 1992; and Campbell 1993). A quarter of affected firms reported that employee effort and morale had improved somewhat or significantly under the living wage law. Although we have no way of assessing whether this greater effort and higher morale translated into higher productivity, such impacts are unlikely given the modest number of firms reporting such improvements.

Another alternative to lowering employment or hours among firms with rising labor costs is raising prices. This adjustment method seems to explain a lack of job losses in the fast-food industry after increases in federal and state minimum wage levels. According to one study of the fast-food industry, "Pretax prices rose 4 percent faster as a result of the minimum-wage increase in New Jersey—slightly more than the increase required to fully cover the cost increase caused by the minimum-wage hike" (Card and Krueger 1995, 54). Another study similarly found that restaurant prices in the United States and Canada generally rise with changes in the wage bill and that these changes typically occur in the first quarter after a minimum wage increase (Aaronson 2001).

In Boston, however, only 15 percent of our affected firms reported raising the prices they bid for city contracts after the living wage took effect, and only 8 percent reported raising prices for other customers. This evidence is consistent with our previous finding that overall contract costs did not rise after living wage implementation in Boston. One explanation for the scant evidence of higher bid prices in the wake of higher labor costs is the fact that funding for many of the Boston covered contractors ultimately comes from state and federal sources. Because many state and federal programs set reimbursement rates associated with their programs, firms cannot pass costs through to the city. This situation is particularly true for nonprofit human service providers.

Rather than passing on higher costs, firms may be lowering profits to adjust to the law.[45] And indeed, 39 percent of affected firms reported doing so. This suggests that firms may have been maintaining high profit margins—or, in the case of nonprofits, large operating surpluses—before the living wage law took effect. Such a situation is not uncommon with government contracting, in which markets are often thin or otherwise uncompetitive. However, analysts do not typically attribute such behavior to the types of nonprofit social service agencies covered by the Boston living wage law.[46]

If substantial operating surpluses are indeed prevalent among nonprofit government contractors, these firms may have greater incentive than their for-profit counterparts to lower such surpluses in the face of higher wages. That is because nonprofit status—although conferring many advantages to firms—also comes with legal restrictions on the use of operating surpluses. More research is needed to fully understand whether many nonprofits do, in fact, reap operating surpluses and whether they have more incentive than for-profit firms to lower those surpluses in the face of higher wages.

Another possibility is that firms may have responded to higher wage mandates by replacing existing workers with better-educated or otherwise more-skilled employees. Such an outcome would not necessarily lead to changes in employment or hours, but it could limit or erase any benefits to low-wage workers. However, no firms in our study reported changing hiring standards after the passage of the Boston living wage law.

A related concern is that firms might also change their methods of hiring in the wake of living wage implementation and that these changes might undercut poor workers. And we did indeed find that more than one-quarter of affected firms reported changing their methods of hiring. Upon investigating further, however, we uncovered two types of adjustments. Firms expanded their use of city-sponsored referral centers, as mandated by the living wage law, and they also increased their use of the Internet to advertise jobs. The former may enlarge the pool of job applicants from disadvantaged neighborhoods, whereas the latter is likely to undercut the chances of job seekers without regular Internet access.

A final option for firms in adjusting to higher wages is to change production techniques, either reorganizing the way work is performed or substituting machinery or equipment in an attempt to minimize the use of (now more expensive) labor. One example might be to eliminate security personnel in a multilevel parking garage by installing remote security cameras.

Another would be to shift to responsibility-sharing teams as a way to reduce the number of people involved in cleaning an office building. However, we found that no firms reported changes in their production techniques after the living wage law took effect. Boston contractors do not seem to have displaced low-wage labor with machines and other equipment or to have reduced employment with other types of work reorganization.

On balance, our study confirms other research showing that living wage laws affect a minority of firms. Yet we did find that the law exerted a significant effect on the pay of low-wage workers. Although unaffected firms saw virtually no changes in the proportion of workers earning less than $9.25, affected firms reported a drop from nearly 25 percent to less than 5 percent in the number of such workers.

In summary, firms did not respond to the Boston living wage ordinance—and its higher wage mandates—by reducing employment or hours. Indeed, firms that were forced to raise wages actually significantly expanded the number of staff assigned to their city contracts compared with firms that did not have to raise wages. Nor did affected firms raise prices—to the city or other customers—to accommodate higher labor costs.

In the absence of changes in jobs or hours, firms might have lowered the indirect costs linked to turnover and absenteeism to offset higher labor costs. However, turnover and absenteeism actually rose among affected firms, whereas unaffected firms saw a substantial decline. Employee effort and morale rose somewhat at affected firms, but those forces alone were not enough to offset rising labor costs. We also found little evidence that firms adjusted to living wage mandates by substituting higher-skilled workers or equipment for their low-wage workforce. The one clear move a large number of affected firms made was to accept lower profits.

THE IMPACT OF THE BOSTON LIVING WAGE LAW ON WORKERS

Proponents of living wage laws contend that they can be an effective mechanism for improving the living standards of low-wage workers. Do employees covered by these laws in fact experience such benefits?

As we see in chapters 8 and 9, studies of proposed living wage ordinances show that potential beneficiaries are likely to be overwhelmingly adults supporting at least one family member and living below or slightly above a realistically defined poverty level. Far fewer studies have examined the impact on workers after living wage ordinances have actually been implemented. Notable exceptions are an analysis of workers at San Francisco International Airport (Reich, Hall, and Jacobs 2003) and an analysis of home care workers in San Francisco County (Howes 2002). Both these studies shed light on the job tenure and earnings of living wage beneficiaries, finding marked reductions in turnover and (unsurprisingly) substantial wage gains for workers covered by the living wage vis-à-vis their counterparts not covered by the law. But neither study examines the family situation of covered workers, in particular whether living wage ordinances help lift families out of poverty.

To shed light on these unanswered questions, we conducted an in-depth telephone survey between November 2001 and May 2002 of workers covered by the Boston living wage law. Our findings mirror prior research showing that workers covered by living wage ordinances—particularly those likely to receive mandated raises—are overwhelmingly adults well into their working lives. In Boston, living wage beneficiaries are also primarily women and people of color. The high incidence of poverty among these workers before the implementation of the living wage law attests that it is well targeted to the working poor. We found significant wage gains among covered workers after the law took effect, and the incidence of poverty fell sharply. However, close to one-third of these workers remained poor even after the law took effect, if we define poverty realistically and take into account the high cost of living in Boston. Not surprisingly, therefore, we found that the living wage level was generally not sufficient to lift covered workers and their families up to a still-modest but more substantial living standard that allows them to fulfill basic needs.

Defining Poverty and Basic-Needs Thresholds

The approach we use here is basically the same as that described in chapter 8 for Santa Monica, California. The figures also correspond to those presented briefly in chapter 2, specifically with respect to Boston. We work with three poverty benchmarks: severe poverty, which is the official federal poverty line; poverty, corresponding to 160 percent of the official poverty line; and near-poverty, which we define as 185 percent of the official line. We present our various thresholds in table 10.12.

We have defined the basic-needs threshold based on two separate measures. The first—the self-sufficiency standard—was created in 1998 by the Massachusetts Women's Educational and Industrial Union (WEIU), in conjunction with Wider Opportunities for Women (WOW). The second measure—the basic family budget—comes from research on the cost of living conducted by the Economic Policy Institute (EPI).[47] Both the EPI and WEIU/WOW thresholds are substantially above not only the federal poverty line (which we believe is more accurately described as a measure of severe poverty) but also our adjusted poverty thresholds for Boston. In fact,

Table 10.12. Living standard thresholds for Boston, 2001

	Family type	
	1 adult, 2 children	2 adults, 2 children
Severe poverty		
(Official poverty line)		
Annual income	$14,270	$17,960
Hourly wage rate for full-time job	$6.86	$8.63
Poor		
(160% of official poverty line)		
Annual income	$22,830	$28,740
Hourly wage rate for full-time job	$10.98	$13.82
Near-poor		
(185% of official poverty line)		
Annual income	$26,400	$33,230
Hourly wage rate for full-time job	$12.69	$15.97
Self-sufficiency standard		
(Women's Educational and Industrial		
Union and Wider Opportunities for		
Women)		
Annual income	$44,700	$48,600
Hourly wage rate for full-time job	$21.49	$11.68
Basic family budget		
(Economic Policy Institute)		
Annual income	$48,550	$54,190
Hourly wage rate for full-time job	$23.34	$13.03

Sources: Official poverty line is from the U.S. Census Bureau, http://www.census.gov/hhes/poverty/threshld/thresh01.html; basic family budget is from Boushey et al. (2001, tables A4.2 and A4.5); self-sufficiency standard is from Bacon, Russell, and Pearce (2000, table 1).

Note: Calculations of the hourly wage assume one wage earner per family. All figures are in 2001 dollars.

the EPI family budget for a one-adult, two-child family is more than three times the official poverty line and more than double our adjusted poverty threshold.

Even though substantially above our poverty thresholds, these two measures are not extravagant. Both aim "for a safe and decent standard of living, accounting for major family expenditures related to housing, childcare, food, transportation, health care, other miscellaneous expenses, and taxes" (Boushey et al. 2001, 7). Both also reflect the cost of living "in the regular 'marketplace' without public or private subsidies—such as public housing, food stamps, Medicaid or childcare—or private 'informal' subsidies such as free baby-sitting by a relative or friends" (Bacon, Russell, and Pearce 2000, 4). These measures include no savings, even for retirement or education, or any expense for restaurant meals, movies, or vacations. Both measures also assume that both parents in a two-adult, two-child family work.[48]

EPI calculated its measure for six family types living in twelve regions of Massachusetts, whereas WEIU/WOW calculated its measure for more than seventy family types in forty regions of the state. We combined those two standards to establish the outer bounds of a decent, yet modest living standard that we call basic needs. That standard implies a wage of $12–13 per hour for a family with two wage earners and $21–23 per hour for a family with one wage earner—in contrast to the city's living wage of $9.11 at the time of our study. We used the basic-needs measure—along with 185 percent of the federal poverty line as a measure of near-poverty—to evaluate the impact of the Boston living wage law on the living standards of low-wage workers.[49]

A Profile of Covered Workers in Boston

To develop a profile of workers covered by the law and assess its impact on them, we surveyed 105 individuals employed by covered service contractors, 97 of whom provided usable information.[50] As in many such situations, we could not conduct a random sample of workers covered by the Boston living wage law because a master list of those workers did not exist. We therefore relied instead on a nonrandom sampling technique, soliciting respondents among workers employed in high-impact sectors—those with large concentrations of low-wage workers.[51] Because our firm survey revealed that 93 percent of covered workers who earned less than $11.75 in 2001 worked in child care, assisted living/supportive housing, education and training, and special education, we solicited respondents from those sectors.[52] An overwhelming majority of these respondents worked in nonprofit organizations.

Our respondents sat on the lower rungs of the wage scale among firms covered by the law. As we see in table 10.13, section A, some 70 percent earned between $9.11 (the living wage at the time of our survey) and $12.74, and more than one-third made between $9.11 and $10.74 (one respondent, a teenager, reported an hourly wage of $8.75—the only violation of the law we found).

This workforce was overwhelmingly female—women composed 80 percent of all respondents and at least three-quarters of each wage category. The workforce was also overwhelmingly non-White; 64 percent were people of color, with African Americans composing the largest single ethnic group. Race and earnings appeared to be related because more than 70 percent of workers in two lower wage categories were non-White, whereas less than 50 percent in two upper wage categories were non-White.

Our workers averaged 32 years of age, with the oldest workers concentrated in the lowest-paid jobs. Just 5 percent of our respondents were younger than 20 years old, and they, too, fell mostly in the lowest wage category.

Table 10.13. Individual characteristics of workers covered by the Boston living wage law

A. Basic demographics

	All workers	Hourly wage rate			
		$9.11–10.74	$10.75–12.74	$12.75–14.74	$14.75+
Number of workers	97	34	33	16	13
Percentage	100%	35%	34%	17%	13%
Average age	32	34	32	31	30
Percentage teenagers	5.2%	4.1%	0%	0%	0%
Average tenure on current job *(years)*	2.9	1.9	4.1	2.4	3.0
Percentage female	79%	77%	82%	75%	85%
Percentage black	40%	47%	46%	25%	31%
Percentage Hispanic	22%	24%	24%	13%	15%
Percentage non-white	64%	71%	72%	44%	46%

B. Education levels

	Number of workers	Percentage
Less than high school	7	7%
High school/GED	29	30%
Two- or four-year college degree	50	52%
Master's degree	11	11%

C. Wages and earnings

	All workers	Hourly wage rate			
		$9.11–10.74	$10.75–12.74	$12.75–14.74	$14.75+
Hourly wage					
Average	$11.90	$9.61	$11.83	$13.60	$16.18
Median	$11.60	$9.38	$12.00	$13.46	$15.68
Average hours per week	43	44	42	48	42
Average weeks per year	47	44	49	49	45
Average hours worked last year	2,038	1,918	2,112	2,345	1,863
Average number of jobs	1.3	1.3	1.2	1.4	1.3
Earnings *(2002 dollars)*					
Average	$24,402	$18,590	$25,071	$30,910	$30,008
Median	$23,324	$18,949	$24,960	$28,538	$32,050

Source: Authors' survey of covered workers.

Despite the fact that these workers had participated in the workforce for a number of years, their average tenure in their current position was just 3 years. Job tenure varied significantly by wage group, with workers earning $10.75–12.74 averaging 4.1 years and those earning $9.11–10.74 averaging 1.9 years.

As we see in table 10.13, section B, over one-third of our respondents held no more than a high school degree, more than one-half reported a 2- or 4-year college degree, and 11 percent held advanced degrees. This large divergence in education despite relatively narrow differences in earnings is characteristic of the nonprofit social services sector from which the bulk of our respondents were drawn.

These employees were working a substantial number of hours, with those in all wage groups averaging over 40 hours per week, as we see in table 10.13, section C. The high proportion of full-time work reflects the fact that these employees often worked for more than one firm, averaging 1.3 jobs. Our respondents also worked during a substantial part of the calendar year, averaging 44–49 weeks annually.

These workers averaged $24,402 in earnings, ranging from $18,590 in the lowest wage category to $30,910 in the next-to-highest category. Our respondents reported wages ranging from $9.61 to $16.18, averaging $11.90. Differences in hours worked among people in different wage categories exerted a strong effect on their annual earnings. Workers earning $12.75–14.75 per hour, for example, averaged higher earnings than those making more than $14.75 per hour, largely because the former worked 26 percent more hours.

Turning to the demographic characteristics of our sample in table 10.14, we found that the model of the nuclear family does a poor job of capturing the living situation of these workers. The majority were single heads of household; 43 percent were single with no children, and another 14 percent reported only one adult in a family that included children under 18. Although a majority were supporting only themselves, some 43 percent supported at least one other family member, and some 30 percent lived in families with children. We also found that the number of respondents supporting children was very much in line with the figures for the city as a whole. Our respondents reported a wide range of family incomes—from an average of $18,000 for two-adult families without children to $25,000 among single adults with children, to $39,000–49,000 among families with more than one wage earner.

As we show in table 10.15, section A, these families faced relatively high rates of poverty; 11 percent lived in severe poverty—below the federally defined poverty line—whereas close to one-third fell below an adequate poverty threshold. Nearly 40 percent of these families were near-poor,

Table 10.14. Family incomes and dependency ratios of covered workers in Boston, by family type

Family type	Number of families and percent of total	Dependency ratios[a] (median)	Family income (in 2001 dollars)	
			Average	Median
One adult; no children	41 (43%)	1	$24,085	$25,000
One adult; with children	13 (14%)	2	$24,473	$25,033
Two adults, both wage earners; no children	10 (10%)	1	$43,348	$33,898
Two adults, both wage earners; with children	13 (14%)	2	$39,197	$40,000
Two adults, one wage earner; no children	4 (4%)	2	$18,000	$20,250
Two adults, one wage earner; with children	4 (4%)	3.5	$24,410	$18,995
Multiple adults and wage earners	11 (12%)	1.7	$49,067	$35,000
Total, all family types	97 (100%)	1.5	$30,813	$26,076

Source: Authors' survey of covered workers.

[a]The dependency ratio is the number of family members divided by the number of income earners in the family. This measure indicates the number of people a wage earner is supporting with his or her earnings.

whereas one-half fell below the basic-needs threshold. Our respondents had much lower living standards than similarly situated workers in the Boston-area labor market.[53]

What helps explain the low living standards among covered workers? Perhaps the clearest predictor of poverty is a high dependency ratio—that is, the number of people in these families divided by the number of workers supporting them. More than one-half of workers supporting another person lived in families that were poor. (The exception was two-adult families with two wage earners, of which only 31 percent were poor.) This effect becomes even clearer when we divide our respondents into families with and without children. Some 40 percent of respondents with children were poor, 43 percent were near-poor, and a full 79 percent fell below our basic-needs standard. Although respondents without children were more likely to surpass our poverty thresholds, a substantial fraction of these families also lived on relatively modest means; nearly 25 percent were poor, whereas roughly 38 percent were either near-poor or fell below the basic-needs threshold.

Table 10.15. Poverty and basic-needs status of workers covered by the Boston living wage law, by family type and wage (percentage falling below each threshold)

A. Family type

	Severe poverty	Poor	Near-poor	Basic needs
One adult; no children				
(number of families = 41)	8%	18%	35%	35%
One adult; with children				
(number of families = 13)	8%	46%	46%	100%
Two adults, both wage earners; no children				
(number of families = 11)	0%	11%	11%	22%
Two adults, both wage earners; with children				
(number of families = 13)	8%	31%	31%	44%
Two adults, 1 wage earner; no children				
(number of families = 4)	25%	50%	50%	75%
Two adults, 1 wage earner; with children				
(number of families = 4)	25%	50%	75%	100%
Multiple adults and wage earners				
(number of families = 11)	27%	54%	64%	—
Total, families without children[a]				
(number of families = 64)	9%	25%	38%	37%
Total, families with children[b]				
(number of families = 30)	13%	40%	43%	79%
Total, all family types				
(number of families = 94)[c]	11%	30%	39%	50%

B. Wage categories

	Severe poverty	Poor	Near-poor	Basic needs
All workers	11%	30%	39%	50%
$9.11–10.74	25%	50%	69%	68%
$10.75–12.74	0%	28%	34%	46%
$12.75–14.74	6%	6%	13%	38%
$14.75+	0%	8%	8%	42%

Source: Authors' survey of covered workers.

[a]We cannot define a basic-needs threshold for any household with more than two adults, so the basic-needs calculation is based on only 54 families.

[b]The basic-needs calculation for this category is based on 24 families.

[c]The basic-needs calculation for this category is based on 86 families.

Not surprisingly, we found strong links between lower wages and poverty, as we see in table 10.15, section B. For example, the families of 25 percent of individuals earning $9.11–10.74 were severely poor. Half of these families were poor, 69 percent were near-poor, and 68 percent fell below the basic-needs threshold.[54] None of the families of workers in the

$10.75–12.74 wage bracket lived in severe poverty, but 28 percent were poor. More than one-third were near-poor, and 46 percent fell below the basic-needs threshold. Less than 8 percent of individuals in the two higher wage groups were poor or severely poor, yet roughly 40 percent fell below the basic-needs standard.

Despite the high incidence of poverty among our respondents, as many as half reported incomes above a basic-needs standard—many more than in cities such as Los Angeles and Santa Fe, where as many as 80 percent of potentially affected workers fell *below* such a standard.[55] Who are these Boston workers above the basic-needs threshold?

In several respects, workers living above this threshold were similar to those living below it. The former were, on average, the same age as all covered workers (32 years in both cases), and women appeared in roughly the same proportion (74 percent of workers above the basic-needs threshold were female, compared with 79 percent of the entire sample).[56]

However, workers above the basic-needs level also differed from other respondents in several important respects. For example, one-half of this group was White, versus one-third of all respondents. Workers above the basic-needs threshold also averaged about $1.00 more per hour in earnings compared with all respondents. Employees above the basic-needs threshold, further, averaged some 200 more hours of work per year than all covered workers.

But the most dramatic difference between workers above the basic-needs threshold and those below it is the type of family in which they reside. Close to 70 percent of workers above the basic-needs threshold were single adults, whereas another 16 percent resided in two-adult households with no children and both spouses working. Only 16 percent of workers above the basic-needs threshold had children, and all of those reported a second adult in the household working for wages.

Is the Boston law doing a bad job of targeting workers in poverty, compared with living wage laws in other cities? Our evidence suggests that the Boston law is at least as well targeted as other ordinances across the country. The main difference between our findings and earlier research is that we define basic-needs thresholds for a broader range of family types, including those without children. If we examine only covered workers *with* children, we find that some 80 percent of these families fall below the basic-needs threshold—virtually identical to the situation in Los Angeles. The rates of severe poverty, poverty, and near-poverty among these Boston families with children are also higher than among low-wage workers in Los Angeles.[57]

The Impact of the Living Wage Law on Wages and Earnings

What changes are associated with the implementation of the Boston living wage ordinance? Did the living wage law exert a discernable impact on the poverty status of any of our survey respondents? Did it lift any of these low-wage workers out of poverty or raise them to a higher standard of living that enabled them to meet their basic needs? To answer these questions, we asked our respondents to compare their wages and family incomes in 1998, before the law took effect, with their situation in 2001.[58]

We found that workers who earned below the living wage in 1998 had reaped significant gains by 2001: $2.10 per hour in real terms. We see this in table 10.16, section A. These employees also worked a greater number of hours. Their $10,000 rise in real earnings reflects longer hours along with higher real wages. The boost in hours confirms our finding earlier that covered firms—particularly those forced to raise wages to comply with the living wage law—shifted from part-time to full-time staffing. Living wage beneficiaries also experienced significant gains in family income, which grew on average by $3,650.

Workers who already earned above the living wage in 1998, in contrast, saw little wage growth—a mere $0.09 in real terms—and their real annual earnings remained flat. These workers did see increases in family income, however, reflecting gains by other family members.

We also saw differences in wage and earnings gains between people who changed employers and people who did not, as we report in table 10.17, section A. By far the largest wage gains accrued to individuals earning less than the living wage and working for a different employer in 1998; those employees saw a real increase of $2.88 per hour and $11,880 per year. Affected workers who remained with the same employer saw a much more modest real increase of $0.83 per hour and $6,950 per year. Workers who already earned above the living wage in 1998 and who remained with the same employer saw real earnings decline by $1,590, whereas unaffected workers who changed employers saw real gains of $2,100.

The fact that workers earning less than the living wage in 1998 who changed employers saw the greatest gains runs counter to some claims that higher wage floors prompt employers to substitute lower-paid (and presumably lower-skilled) workers with higher-skilled (and presumably higher-paid) workers. In this case, lower-paid (and possibly lower-skilled) workers appear to be the prime beneficiaries of the living wage law.

These results also suggest the need for a broader understanding of the benefits of living wage policies. Analysts often discuss those benefits solely in

Table 10.16. Wages, family incomes, and poverty status of workers covered by the Boston living wage law, 1998 and 2001

A. Hourly wages, annual earnings, and family income (in 2001 dollars)[a]

	Hourly wage	Annual earnings	Family income
Earned below the living wage in 1998 *(number of workers=21)*			
1998	$9.22	$16,990	$37,310
2001	$11.32	$26,990	$40,960
Difference	$2.10	$10,000	$3,650
Earned above the living wage in 1998 *(number of workers=38)*			
1998	$12.78	$27,350	$33,750
2001	$12.87	$27,800	$36,620
Difference	$0.09	$450	$2,870

B. Poverty and basic-needs status (percentage falling below each threshold)

	Severe poverty	Poor	Near-poor	Basic needs[b]
Earned below the living wage in 1998 *(number of workers=32)*				
1998	34%	41%	50%	54%
2001	13%	28%	41%	54%
Difference (1998–2001)	22%	13%	9%	0%
Earned above the living wage in 1998 *(number of workers=44)*				
1998	9%	32%	46%	63%
2001	0%	23%	30%	48%
Difference (1998–2001)	9%	9%	16%	15%
Difference in trend between the two groups	13%	3%	−7%	−15%

Source: Authors' survey of covered workers.

[a]Annual earnings and incomes refer to the prior year.

[b]We cannot define the basic-needs threshold for any household with more than two adults, so these figures are based on fewer individuals than the other thresholds. That is why, in one case, the proportion of families living under the basic-needs threshold is lower than the proportion of families that is near-poor.

terms of the higher wages that accrue to lower-paid individuals. However, our evidence suggests that the Boston ordinance has benefited more than just the individuals who received raises when the law went into effect. The law has also turned a discrete set of jobs into better-paying jobs—typically with better hours and sometimes better benefits. Our results also show that far from disadvantaging lower-paid workers, the living wage policy has given many a pathway to a better job.

Table 10.17. Effects in Boston of changing employers versus remaining on covered workers' earnings, family income, and poverty status

A. Hourly wages, annual earnings, and family income (in 2001 dollars)[a]

	Hourly wage	Annual earnings	Family income
Same employer			
(number of workers=25)			
Earned below the living wage in 1998			
(number of workers=8)			
1998	$9.81	$21,770	$35,690
2001	$10.64	$28,720	$36,090
Difference	$0.83	$6,950	$400
Earned above the living wage in 1998			
(number of workers=17)			
1998	$12.27	$28,210	$36,310
2001	$13.12	$26,620	$33,900
Difference	$0.85	−$1,590	−$2,410
Different employer			
(number of workers=33)			
Earned below the living wage in 1998			
(number of workers=13)			
1998	$8.86	$14,060	$38,310
2001	$11.74	$25,940	$43,950
Difference	$2.88	$11,880	$5,640
Earned above the living wage in 1998			
(number of workers=21)			
1998	$13.20	$26,660	$31,680
2001	$12.67	$28,760	$38,820
Difference	−$0.53	$2,100	$7,140

Changes in Family Income and Living Standards

Although unaffected workers who changed employers experienced the largest gains in *family* income between 1998 and 2001 (increasing by $7,140), affected workers who changed jobs saw significant increases as well, with family income rising by $5,640. Family income for affected workers who remained with the same employer rose modestly, in contrast, whereas family income among unaffected workers remaining with the same employer fell by $2,410.

How did these shifts in earnings and family incomes affect living standards? We found that for individuals earning *less* than the living wage in 1998, the percentage living in severe poverty dropped from 34 percent to 13 percent, as we see in table 10.16, section B. The proportion of families con-

Table 10.17. Effects in Boston of changing employers versus remaining on covered workers' earnings, family income, and poverty status

B. Poverty and basic-needs status (percentage below each threshold)

	Severe poverty	Poor	Near-poor	Basic needs[b]
Same employer				
(number of workers=26)				
Earned below the living wage in 1998				
(number of workers=8)				
1998	13%	13%	38%	29%
2001	0%	0%	13%	29%
Difference (1998–2001)	13%	13%	25%	0%
Earned above the living wage in 1998				
(number of workers=18)				
1998	0%	28%	44%	56%
2001	0%	22%	28%	44%
Difference (1998–2001)	0%	6%	17%	13%
Difference in trend between the				
two groups	13%	7%	8%	–13%Di
ferent employer				
(number of workers=50)				
Earned below the living wage in 1998				
(number of workers=24)				
1998	42%	50%	54%	64%
2001	17%	38%	50%	64%
Difference (1998– 2001)	25%	13%	4%	0%
Earned above the living wage in 1998				
(number of workers=26)				
1998	16%	35%	46%	67%
2001	0%	23%	31%	50%
Difference (1998–2001)	16%	12%	15%	17%
Difference in trend between the				
two groups	9%	1%	–11%	–17%

Source: Authors' survey of covered workers.

[a]Annual earnings and incomes refer to the prior year.

[b]We cannot define the basic-needs threshold for any household with more than two adults, so these figures are based on fewer individuals than the other thresholds. That is why, in one case, the proportion of families living under the basic-needs threshold is lower than the proportion of families that is near-poor.

sidered poor also fell markedly, from 41 percent to 28 percent. The percentage that were near-poor fell from 50 to 41, but the proportion with family incomes below a basic-needs threshold did not change.

Family living standards among workers earning *above* the living wage in 1998 also improved, with the percentage of severely poor families falling from

9 percent in 1998 to 0 by 2001 and the proportion of poor families dropping from 32 percent to 23 percent. However, the proportion of families living near poverty fell even more markedly—from 46 to 30 percent—whereas the proportion below the basic-needs threshold fell from 63 to 48 percent.

For those in poverty, the living standards of affected workers and their families improved much more substantially than for unaffected workers. How much of this is due to the living wage ordinance? One way to measure this is to compare the trends in living standards between the two groups. Although the design of our survey design does not lend itself to formal statistical testing, we can still reasonably attribute differences in these trends to the living wage law. Making such a comparison, we find—by looking at the difference in the trend between the two groups in table 10.16, section B— that from one-third to one-half of the decline in poverty and severe poverty stems from the living wage ordinance.[59]

However, these benefits seem restricted to those living in poverty or severe poverty. Unaffected workers saw much greater drops in the proportion of families who were near-poor or just below basic needs. Because affected workers were making substantially less money in 1998 compared with 2001, it is not surprising that we see the benefits of Boston's living wage law restricted to the lower reaches of the income distribution. However, although the living wage policy cut the proportion of families living in poverty, it does not appear to have improved living standards for families just above poverty, who remain in some degree of insecurity.

As before, to deepen our understanding of these findings, we considered differences in *family* incomes between workers who changed employers and those who did not. We present these findings in table 10.17, section B. Among workers earning less than the living wage in 1998 who changed employers, the proportion with families in severe poverty fell from 42 percent to 17 percent, whereas the proportion in poverty fell from 50 to 38 percent. The percentage of families in this group living near poverty declined modestly, whereas the proportion below the basic-needs threshold remained the same.

Among workers earning less than the living wage in 1998 who remained with the same employer, the proportion of severely poor and poor families fell from 13 percent in 1998 to 0 percent in 2001, whereas the proportion of near-poor families fell from 38 percent to 13 percent. The proportion of families that remained below a basic-needs threshold did not change. Poor or severely poor workers earning above the living wage in 1998 experienced much more modest gains, whether they stayed with the same employers or changed jobs during that time. By contrast, the gains for families living near poverty or below a basic-needs threshold were much more substantial.

Overall, then, poor workers who received raises as a result of the living wage law experienced much sharper improvements in their living standards than did poor workers already earning more than the living wage. Yet only a modest percentage of affected workers moved above the near-poverty and basic-needs thresholds after the living wage took effect, particularly compared with workers unaffected by the law. By comparing affected workers with similarly situated unaffected workers, we conclude that the Boston living wage ordinance has been relatively effective at lifting workers out of poverty. However, at current wage levels it appears unable to lift all workers out of poverty or to help lower-wage workers achieve a higher standard of living that enables them to meet their basic needs.

Based on our evidence, we also conclude that these benefits have by and large been concentrated among workers who managed to obtain jobs with a covered firm *after* the living wage law took effect. Affected employees who worked for the same employer before implementation experienced much more modest gains. These results suggest that policymakers must expand their concept of who benefits from living wage laws to include not only current but future jobholders as well. Indeed, one of the primary benefits of the Boston living wage law is the fact that it led to qualitative improvements in the jobs themselves. These jobs will remain better jobs as long as they remain covered by the living wage law.

The Impact of the Living Wage Law on Employees' Quality of Life

We also aimed in this study to include more than just a quantitative assessment of the impact of the Boston living wage law on the employees it covers. We also wanted to convey a deeper sense of the concrete impact of wage increases on workers' quality of life. Thus, in the summer of 2003 we conducted follow-up phone interviews with eight employees who had received raises as a result of the living wage ordinance. We selected these respondents randomly from the pool of employees earning less than $9.11 in 1998 (8 percent of the initial sample). The results illuminate the modest but concrete benefits that accompany higher wages, as well as many of the challenges low-wage workers face.

For example, higher wages had enabled virtually all these workers to boost their savings. One worker reported that she had opened her first bank account, and another had created a 401(k) retirement account. Debt was a near-unanimous concern, and six of the eight reported that they had been somewhat successful in reducing their debt burden in the wake of higher wages.

Respondents also signaled small but concrete advances in their personal and professional lives. Five had begun classes, four had been able to take vacations, and four had used the higher disposable incomes to assist their families financially. This ability to help out friends and family was especially meaningful because it signaled a degree of independence and security that these workers had not been able to attain with lower earnings. For example, one woman was able to regularly purchase groceries for her aging mother, and even to save enough money to buy her mother a new set of living room furniture and help her son with college expenses. One man was saving money to help his mother make a down payment on a house. Another woman was able to help two of her family members pay for funeral arrangements. Three individuals used the higher wages to help buy a car, and one young man managed to improve his housing situation by leaving his mother's house to share an apartment with friends. Three respondents reported that they were able to reduce their work hours after receiving the living wage.

All our interviewees confirmed that the living wage law had exerted a positive but modest impact on their lives, but that the higher wages did not provide enough money to avoid trade-offs. For example, the workers who took vacations tended not to offer their families financial support, whereas the ones who bought a car tended not to enroll in classes.

In spite of incremental financial improvements, our respondents also clearly conveyed that the higher wages did not leave them feeling more financially secure. Only two workers indicated a greater sense of financial security; in both cases, these individuals had been able to reduce their debt and increase their savings. The overriding lack of security among these workers mirrors findings by analysts examining living wage effects in San Francisco, which also showed rapid rises in the cost of living. These researchers conclude that higher wages did not permit workers to get ahead, but merely to avoid falling behind (Reich, Hall, and Jacobs 2003).

The Overall Impact of the Law on Workers

Our survey revealed that workers covered by the Boston living wage law have low living standards. In 2001, the families of some 11 percent fell below the official poverty line, which we consider a measure of severe poverty in the Boston area. Using a more accurate measure of poverty for the region, we found that close to one-third of covered workers were poor and nearly 40 percent were near-poor, defined as below 185 percent of the official measure. We found that nearly one-half of covered workers fell below a more comprehensive basic-needs living standard. Further examination revealed that workers with children were much more likely to fall below each of our living standards, with 40 percent of these workers below poverty, 43 percent near poverty, and a full 79 percent below the basic-needs threshold. Although these figures confirm that the Boston living wage law is well targeted toward working poor individuals, they are a sobering reminder that for many people $9.11 is still inadequate to lift their families out of poverty and achieve a higher standard of living.

Nevertheless, we found solid evidence of real wage increases and gains in annual earnings since the implementation of the Boston living wage ordinance. Real wages rose nearly 25 percent for affected workers, and real annual earnings rose by roughly 60 percent. The steep rise in annual earnings reflects a parallel rise in the number of hours worked per week and weeks worked per year. This shift to more full-time employment is consistent with our previous findings, in which we also saw evidence of a shift to more full-time, higher-wage jobs. Upon closer examination, we found that the biggest changes accrued to low-wage employees who took jobs with covered firms *after* the law was implemented, not to those who had worked for these firms beforehand. This means that policymakers should broaden their understanding of the benefits of living wage laws to include the creation of better-paying jobs and more full-time jobs.

We found clear evidence of sharp reductions in the incidence of poverty among workers covered by the Boston living wage ordinance, and we attribute as much as one-half of the reduction in severe poverty and one-third of the reduction in poverty to the law. However, we also found that the Boston living wage law was not enough to lift affected workers to a higher standard of living that better reflects the spirit and intent of the ordinance.

Part 5

TECHNICAL STUDIES
AND DEBATES

The four studies that we present in this part of the book are more technical than those in the previous sections. In particular, we present here in some detail findings of formal econometric models. We realize that at least portions of these chapters may prove daunting to many readers. At the same time, much of the discussion in all four chapters should still be accessible, including the main issues under consideration and our basic approach to analyzing them.

We decided to include these technical papers in the book for two reasons. First, they all deal with absolutely crucial aspects of the debate about the merits of living/minimum wage initiatives. And second, as should become clear, the central substantive findings in all the papers are those that emerge directly from the econometric exercises themselves. If we were to take the econometrics out of the papers, there would be basically nothing left to present other than a brief summary of the findings.

What we have therefore done is include these papers in the book but also explain their main results in an accessible way to nontechnical readers. In this introduction, I provide somewhat detailed discussions that aim both to set the context for the issues being explored and to summarize the main findings. Within each of the papers themselves, we again present the main findings in nontechnical terms.

Chapter 11 by Jeannette Wicks-Lim provides the most thorough consideration to date as to how significant are the ripple effects of living/minimum wage increases—that is, the wage gains that businesses provide to employees that extend beyond what the new minimum wage standard requires. As we have seen in our part 2 studies on New Orleans and Santa Fe, these ripple-effect wage increases can be extensive, bringing both additional benefits to low-wage workers and their families and additional costs to businesses who pay these raises. In cases in which the minimum wage increase itself is modest but its coverage is wide—as when entire states raised their minimum wages from $5.15 to something less than $7.00 per hour in November 2006—the the ripple-effect wage increases can be as large or larger than the mandated raises themselves, even though businesses are under no legal obligation to provide ripple-effect raises. Evidently, we cannot accurately evaluate the impact of living/minimum wage measures without having a clear understanding of what the ripple effects are likely to be.

In our studies of the business costs for the New Orleans and Santa Fe measures in chapters 4 and 5, we present estimates of the ripple effects based on methodologies that we developed at the time of writing. These are solid methodologies that, correspondingly, produced broadly reliable estimates for these two situations. But in her research summarized in chapter 11, Wicks-Lim examines the issue in substantially more depth than we, or other researchers, had previously. As such, it is important that her approach be available to all readers trying to understand the full extent of both the benefits and costs of living and minimum wage raises.

Much of the debate about living wages inevitably reverts back to a discussion of unintended consequences; and in most circumstances, the potential unintended consequence that is most widely discussed is employment losses.[1] We have already addressed this issue at some length, both in the prospective studies on New Orleans and Santa Fe and in the retrospective analysis on Boston. Now, in chapter 12, Mark Brenner, Jeannette Wicks-Lim, and I briefly present still another approach that enables us to consider the negative employment effects. That is, we directly compare the relative employment experiences in recent years of states with and without minimum wage laws above the federal minimum. We focus, in particular, on the restaurant and hotel industries, on which the impact of minimum wage increases is strongest. We present both descriptive statistics and a formal econometric model in this chapter. And here again, at least within the ranges of minimum wage increases that the various states have implemented, we find no evidence supporting the idea that higher minimum wage standards have produced negative employment effects.

Chapters 13 and 14 are critiques of econometric studies by other authors that, despite having been highly technical presentations themselves, were nevertheless widely discussed in the media and policy circles. This, then, explains why we need to also provide an econometric approach in pursuing our critiques.

Chapter 13, by Jeannette Wicks-Lim and myself, addresses a basic question about the increase in 2004 to an $8.50 citywide minimum wage in Santa Fe, New Mexico: Did the $8.50 minimum wage mean reduced job opportunities for low-wage workers in the city? In the introduction to part 2 of this book, I refer to the most basic evidence on this question—the data showing that employment growth had been healthy in the first year after Santa Fe had implemented its $8.50 minimum wage standard. Most notably, this was true for the restaurant and hotel industries that had to absorb the largest proportional cost increases from the $8.50 minimum. We present this evidence more fully in chapter 13.

Nevertheless, such basic data on employment growth cannot in themselves provide the final word as to what the effects have been of the minimum wage increase. This is because these figures do not control for factors other than the living wage law that might also be affecting employment growth. For example, it is possible that businesses in the city may have been willing to hire even more people than they did if they were not forced to operate under the $8.50 minimum wage. If this had been the case, then we might still reasonably claim that the Santa Fe living wage initiative ended up hurting the employment prospects of the people the measure had intended to help. In a 2005 work titled *Santa Fe's Wage Ordinance and the Labor Market*, Aaron Yelowitz of the University of Kentucky makes exactly such a claim. He purports to show that, once one does control appropriately for the other factors that might influence employment in Santa Fe, unemployment in the city did, in fact, rise sharply for the least educated workers seeking employment.

Chapter 13 evaluates this claim by Yelowitz. As we show, one econometric finding in Yelowitz's study is accurate (assuming the data he used for the estimate are reliable). That is, the probability of workers with low educational levels being *unemployed* in Santa Fe did rise between June 2004 and July 2005 after the $8.50 minimum wage was implemented. But what we also show—and what Yelowitz does not consider—is that the probability of being *employed* remained the same in Santa Fe for the same type of workers during this time period. These two findings—that the probability of being unemployed went up while the probability of being employed did not go down for the same group of people over the same time period—may appear to present a contradiction, or worse still, some sort of statistical sleight-of-hand. In fact, the explanation is quite straightforward and, moreover, fully consistent with a standard approach to how labor markets work.

That is, when the minimum wage rose in Santa Fe to $8.50 per hour, more people entered the city's low-wage labor market, applying for jobs that previously were paying in the range of $7.00 per hour but then could offer no less than $8.50. As already mentioned, the number of jobs in Santa

Fe did grow after the minimum wage rose to $8.50, although we are not suggesting that the number of jobs grew *because* of the living wage law. We simply are observing that the number of jobs in fact grew at the same time that the $8.50 minimum wage became law. And our econometric finding tells us that this employment growth was enough to provide people with low educational levels the same level of job opportunities after the living wage was enacted as before (keep in mind that because of population growth, there generally must be employment growth to provide people with the same level of job opportunities over time). Nevertheless, if the number of people seeking work in the city rose at a still faster rate during this period, it then follows that both employment growth and unemployment in Santa Fe would have risen. This is because employment growth measures the increase in the number of people holding jobs, whereas the unemployment rate tracks the number of job holders as a percentage of all the people seeking employment.

Based on these figures, what can we conclude overall about how the Santa Fe measure affected the well-being of low-wage workers and their families in the area? Yelowitz appears to believe that an increase in the likelihood of being unemployed in the city is the only appropriate way to evaluate the effects of the Santa Fe law. By contrast, we argue that because (1) the number of jobs available to low-wage workers in the city appeared to have risen at a healthy rate while (2) the wages being paid to those at the low-end of the job market also rose substantially, it follows that the overall impact of the minimum wage increase was indeed beneficial to the people it was seeking to help. Any possible rise in the unemployment rate for those with low educational levels under these circumstances is thus a by-product of improvements, not declines, in Santa Fe's labor market situation. More people were seeking jobs in the city itself, as opposed to elsewhere in the region, precisely because there were more jobs and better jobs in Santa Fe than elsewhere.

In Chapter 14, Mark Brenner, Jeannette Wicks-Lim, and I evaluate a 2003 paper titled "Do Living Wage Ordinances Reduce Urban Poverty," by David Neumark, of the University of California–Irvine, and Scott Adams, of University of Wisconsin–Milwaukee. Neumark and Adams's study is highly ambitious in its scope. They seek to assess all the living wage ordinances in the United States that had been implemented at the time they wrote their paper in terms of their impact on wages, employment levels, and poverty. These are obviously critical matters that need to be evaluated. In their assessment, the impact of living wage laws has been mixed, but, overall, positive. First, they conclude that wages did go up at the low end of the job market due to the living wage laws. But they also conclude that living wage laws reduced employment opportunities in the covered cities. However, because wages rose more than job opportunities fell, the overall effect of these measures was to reduce poverty in cities that operated under living wage laws. Our critique of Neumark and Adams is with regard to their methodology only, as opposed to their results. However, because we find their methodology unreliable, that also means that we cannot give credence to their findings. This is the case regardless of whether we consider their findings to be being favorable to living wage measures as a policy tool.

In our view, there are two basic methodological errors in the Neumark and Adams paper. The first is with the data they use for constructing their econometric estimates. Unlike other authors who examined the effects of living wage laws, including ourselves, Neumark and Adams made no attempt to gather information on the actual firms or workers covered by living wage laws in the various cities considered in their study. Instead, they base their econometric estimates entirely on the basis of data from the Current Population Survey (CPS) put out by the U.S. Labor Department.

There is certainly nothing intrinsically wrong with using CPS data for evaluating living wage laws or related policy interventions. It is, in fact, an indispensable data source and we rely on it heavily ourselves, as is clear most fully in parts 2 and 3, as well as the chapters 11–13 of this part. However, as with all such data sources, the CPS must be used judiciously and not be employed for tasks for which it cannot adequately serve. The problem with using the CPS for evaluating the effects of living wage laws on workers in different cities is that the number of workers that were covered by these early living wage laws was very low. As we report in chapter 10 for the experience with the Boston living wage ordinance, approximately 2,000 workers received wage increases as a result of the measure as of 2001. This is in a labor force of about 173,000 workers who were earning between the state's $6.75 minimum wage and the $9.11 living wage at that time. The proportions of covered workers relative to the total labor force were similarly modest with comparable living wage laws in other cities. This is not surprising, given that the initial living wage laws were written to cover only a very narrow sector of the labor force in each city (i.e., those employed by private firms holding service contracts with the cities).

Because of the low numbers of workers in each city who received raises due to the living wage law, the CPS is unlikely to sample a sufficient number of these workers to establish reliable estimates of living wage induced changes in wages, employment, or poverty. As such, the Neumark and Adams study is not likely to be observing the effects of living wage ordinances themselves on the workers in the data sample they have.

But there is a second problem with the Neumark and Adams approach, even if we allowed that the CPS were adequate to the task of analyzing the impact of narrowly targeted living wage laws. This is that they assume that virtually all workers in a living wage city are "potentially covered" by the law if its ordinance includes a provision requiring firms to pay living wages if these firms receive some form of financial assistance from the city. As we report in chapter 14, the direct evidence from city records and city officials shows that very few firms, if any at all, are mandated to follow living wage laws because of the subsidies they received from city governments. Once we adjust the econometric model to take account of this fact, we show that the Neumark and Adams results no longer hold up.

Let me emphasize again: in reaching this conclusion, our point is not to counter the Neumark and Adams's finding that living wage laws have been successful in reducing poverty. We obviously believe that living wage laws can indeed make substantial contributions toward improving the living standards of low-wage workers and their families. But we are unwilling to accept as a matter of faith even our own predispositions on the effects of living wage laws. We similarly cannot embrace the conclusions of other researchers—however favorable or unfavorable they may be toward living wage policies—when these conclusions are based on unsound research methods.

—R. P.

11 *Mandated Wage Floors and the Wage Structure*

New Estimates of the Ripple Effects of Minimum Wage Laws

JEANNETTE WICKS-LIM

INTRODUCTION

A recurring issue in the debate around minimum and living wage laws is whether mandated wage floors have a more wide-ranging impact on wages than the legally required raises alone. That is, do employers feel compelled to give workers raises beyond those legally required, also called ripple-effect raises, when a mandated wage floor is increased?

Why would employers feel compelled to give some workers ripple-effect raises? Consider the following scenario. If the current $5.15 federal minimum is increased to $6.15, employers are legally required to raise the wages of all covered workers earning less than $6.15. However, without a ripple effect, workers earning $6.15 prior to the increase will fall in their relative wage position. These workers will no longer be $1.00 above the bottom of the wage structure, they will be at the bottom of the wage structure. Moreover, these workers will be earning the same wages as workers who had previously earned inferior wages. Such a fall in relative wage position could damage worker morale and, therefore, productivity. To avoid this, employers extend raises above the wage floor to maintain a consistent wage hierarchy. Workers earning $6.15 prior to the increase may receive a ripple-effect raise to keep their wage position above the bottom of the wage structure.[1]

Both sides of the political debate around mandated wage floors have a stake in arguing that ripple effects are both large and small. Large ripple effects allow proponents to argue that mandated wage floors are even more effective by expanding the pool of beneficiaries. Opponents, however, can argue that large ripple effects seriously intensify the economic strain on employers from such laws. Small ripple effects enable proponents to minimize the business costs of mandated wage floors. But, likewise, small ripple effects allow opponents to minimize workers' benefits from the laws. Regardless of one's political position, understanding the extent and size of ripple effects is an important part of evaluating mandated wage floors.

Given the political significance of ripple effects, it is surprising that the empirical research on this question is thin. To date, only one serious attempt has been made to rigorously estimate minimum wage ripple effects (Neumark, Schweitzer, and Wascher 2004). Unfortunately, Neumark, Schweitzer, and Wascher's methodology appears to exacerbate the problem of reporting errors evident in their wage growth measure, calling into question their findings.[2] As a result, we still do not have a clear picture of the size and extent of ripple effects.

I fill this gap in research by providing detailed empirical estimates of the ripple effects produced by state and federal minimum wage increases in the United States during 1983–2002. In the next section, I discuss the data and methodology I use to estimate the size and extent of ripple-effect raises. I present the results in the third section. In the fourth section, I discuss the policy implications of these results by answering the following questions: How much do ripple-effect raises contribute to the overall cost of mandated wage floors? How do ripple-effect raises change the pool of workers who benefit from mandated wage floors? Finally, how do the ripple effects of living wage laws compare to the ripple effects of more traditional minimum wage laws? I conclude in the last section.

DATA AND METHODOLOGY

Data

The Current Population Survey (CPS), prepared by the Bureau of the Census for the U.S. Bureau of Labor Statistics, is the primary data source for this analysis. The CPS surveys approximately 50,000 households monthly and asks one-quarter of this sample (referred to as the outgoing rotation groups) detailed earnings questions.[3]

The years covered in this analysis, 1983–2002, roughly cover two business cycles: the 1980s business cycle (1982–1990) and the 1990s business cycle (1991–2000).[4] This timeframe includes two recessions that are preceded by two long expansionary periods. As a result, years from business cycle upswings predominately compose the sample.

During this period, minimum wage laws changed at both the state and federal levels. The federal minimum wage increased four times: 1990 (from $3.35 to $3.80), 1991 (from $3.80 to $4.25), 1996 (from $4.25 to $4.75), and 1997 (from $4.75 to $5.15). The number of states that set their minimum wages higher than the federal rate rose from two in 1983 to eleven in 2002. The effective minimum is the higher of the two rates for covered workers.

Methodology

The strategy I use to observe the effect of minimum wage changes on wages is a basic difference-in-difference approach. I compare the change in wages among workers who are subjected to a wage floor increase (e.g., workers in a state when the effective minimum rises) to the change in wages of similar workers who are not (e.g., workers in a state when the effective minimum does not change). I attribute differences in the wage movements of these two types of workers to the minimum wage.[5] I use regression analysis to take into account other factors (described later) that impact wage growth.

To get detailed estimates of the extent and size of the ripple effect, I need to observe how far up the wage distribution the impact of a minimum wage increase goes and how the size of the impact changes—not just an overall effect. To do this, I use the difference-in-difference approach to compare the change in wage percentiles of workers subjected to a wage floor increase to the wage percentiles of workers who are not. In other words, I estimate the wage impact of changes in states' effective minimum wage levels at thirteen different points of states' wage distributions: the 5th, 10th, 15th, 20th, 25th, 30th, 35th, 40th, 50th, 60th, 70th, 80th, and 90th wage percentiles. The basic model is:

$$(1) \quad \Delta\ln(wage\ percentile_{st}) = \alpha + \beta_1\Delta\ln(min_{st}) + \beta_2\Delta\ln(min_{s,t-1})$$
$$+ \underline{\delta}(\Delta\underline{X}_{st}) + \eta(Half1) + \underline{\gamma}_Y(\underline{Y}_t) + \underline{\tau}_S(\underline{S}_s) + \epsilon_{st}$$

where the subscript s denotes states and the subscript t denotes time period. The dependent variable, $\ln(wage\ percentile_{st})$, is the change in the natural log of the wage percentile of interest in a particular state over a 1-year period starting at time t.[6] The $\ln(min_{st})$ is a measure for the immediate effect of the minimum wage analogous to the dependent variable. To take account of the possibility that the impact of a minimum wage increase may not be immediate, $\ln(min_{s,t-1})$ is included. This measure is equivalent to $\ln(min_{st})$ with the exception that it refers to the change in the minimum 1 year prior to time t. The coefficients on these two measures provide estimates of the immediate and lagged impact of minimum wages on wages across the wage distribution.

The next set of variables $\underline{X}_{st}$ are measures of the demographic, industrial, and occupational shifts in states' workforces. For example, to take into account the effects of shifts in the gender composition of states' workforces on the states' 10th wage percentiles, I include the change in the proportion of female workers earning between states' 5th and 15th wage percentiles.[7] The other demographic characteristics included in the model are race, educational attainment, union membership, full-time work, and work experience.[8]

The year dummy variables $(\underline{Y}_{st})$ take into account national macroeconomic effects that may affect all workers in a particular year (e.g., inflation). State dummy variables $(\underline{S}_s)$ take into account differences in the rates of wage growth between states. Finally, because the data allow for biennial observations, I include a measure to control for seasonal effects $(Half1)$.[9]

Isolating the Impact of Minimum Wage Increases

A common challenge to studying economic phenomena is sorting out the impact of one factor from the many other factors that are changing simultaneously in the economy. If two of these factors simultaneously cause changes in the economic outcome that is being studied, then isolating the separate effect of each factor can be difficult. Worse, this can lead to the spurious conclusion that one factor is responsible for the effect of another. In this section, I discuss two aspects of the minimum wage changes that took place from 1983 to 2002 that may lead to such spurious conclusions about their impact on wages.

First, there is a regional character to state minimum wage laws. New England states changed their state minimum wages much more frequently than other states. As a result, I need to separate the impact of minimum wage increases on wage growth from other aspects of the New England economy. The state dummy variables in the model take account of regional effects that do not change over time. These variables, however, do not take account of regional effects that change over time. The New England states were almost alone in increasing their minimum wages during the economic upswing of the late 1980s. This fact, coupled with the faster growth New England economies experienced relative to other regions during this economic boom, means that accelerated wage growth in New England due to macroeconomic conditions will be hard to separate from wage growth due to minimum wage increases.[10] To avoid conflating any time-varying regional effect on wages with that of minimum wage increases, I estimate the model excluding the New England states.

Second, there is a business-cycle aspect of minimum wage increases because the federal minimum wage increases occurred at pivotal points in the business cycles during this period, first, in 1990 and 1991, at the end of one business cycle and the beginning of another, and then in 1996 and 1997 when the 1990s business cycle began to accelerate. This fact, coupled with the fact that the federal rate is the effective minimum wage for many states, means that business-cycle effects on wages will be hard to separate from the effect of the minimum wage. The year dummy variables provide a partial solution by accounting for year-to-year changes in the national economy. However, they do not account for within-year changes in the national economy. If, for example, both the federal minimum and the rate of national economic growth increase mid-year, wage growth due to national economic trends may appear to be caused by the minimum wage increase.[11] The years 1990 and 1996 stand out as likely to produce this type of spurious result (for a detailed discussion see the appendix to this chapter); I estimate the model excluding these years.

Retail Trade

I single out the retail trade industry[12] for separate analysis because of its high concentration of minimum wage workers.[13] In 2002, for example, the Bureau of Labor Statistics reported that 3 percent of all workers paid hourly earned wages at or below the federal minimum.[14] Among hourly wage workers in the retail trade industry, the proportion was more than twice as high at 8 percent.

How this will affect the size and extent of the ripple-effect raises is unclear. On the one hand, the conspicuous role of the minimum wage in retail may make it an important reference wage. As a result, employers may be strongly motivated to avoid changes in their wage hierarchy and provide more extensive ripple-effect raises. On the other hand, faced with higher costs, these employers may increase their resolve to only provide mandated raises.

THE EXTENT AND SIZE OF RIPPLE EFFECTS

In table 11.1, section A, I present two sets of regression estimates for each of the thirteen wage percentiles. The regression estimates in columns 3 and 4 are based on the full sample. The regression estimates in columns 5 and 6 are based on a sample that excludes the New England states and the years 1990 and 1996 (see discussion above). Each coefficient is a wage elasticity; it is roughly equivalent to the percentage increase in the particular wage percentile given a percentage increase in the effective minimum wage.

Table 11.1. Estimating ripple effects from state and federal minimum wage changes, 1983–2002

A. All industries

(1) Wage percentile	(2) Average wage relative to minimum wage[a]	Total sample		Both exclusions	
		(3) Immediate effect	(4) Lagged effect	(5) Immediate effect	(6) Lagged effect
5th	1.00	0.39 **	0.13 **	0.42 **	0.02
10th	1.12	0.24 **	0.11 **	0.22 **	0.02
15th	1.23	0.16 **	0.08 **	0.16 **	−0.01
20th	1.35	0.05 *	0.05	0.04	0.03
25th	1.47	0.04	0.02	0.01	0.00
30th	1.59	0.01	0.04	−0.01	0.00
35th	1.72	−0.01	0.01	−0.02	−0.01
40th	1.86	0.02	−0.01	0.01	−0.02
50th	2.17	−0.03	0.03	−0.02	0.01
60th	2.53	−0.03	0.02	−0.04	−0.01
70th	2.98	−0.03	0.05 *	−0.02	0.03
80th	3.59	0.01	0.06 **	0.00	0.02
90th	4.50	0.03	0.06 **	0.02	0.04

B. Retail trade industry

(1) Wage percentile	(2) Average wage relative to minimum wage[a]	Total sample		Both exclusions	
		(3) Immediate effect	(4) Lagged effect	(5) Immediate effect	(6) Lagged effect
5th	—	—	—	—	—
10th	0.99	0.49 **	0.21 **	0.58 **	0.15 **
15th	1.03	0.47 **	0.12 **	0.53 **	0.07
20th	1.07	0.36 **	0.13 **	0.35 **	0.07
25th	1.10	0.22 **	0.13 **	0.18 **	0.02
30th	1.15	0.18 **	0.13 **	0.17 **	0.07
35th	1.19	0.20 **	0.12 **	0.20 **	0.01
40th	1.25	0.16 **	0.13 **	0.12 **	0.02
50th	1.38	0.05	0.10 *	0.05	0.00
60th	1.56	0.02	0.10 *	0.06	0.03
70th	1.81	−0.01	0.09	−0.01	0.02
80th	2.21	0.06	0.07	0.04	−0.06
90th	2.95	−0.07	0.23 **	−0.04	0.02

Source: Current Population Outgoing Rotation Group 1983–2002 files, Bureau of Labor Statistics, U.S. Department of Labor.

Notes: ** and * indicate statistical significance at the 0.05 and 0.10 levels, respectively. The standard errors are estimated by Prais-Winsten regression with panel-corrected standard errors. The panel-corrected standard errors are estimated with the following assumptions: 1) first-order panel-specific autocorrelation, 2) heteroskedastic errors across panels, and 3) contemporaneous correlation across panels.

[a]Average wage positions are based on total samples.

Overall, the regression estimates reflect the expected pattern. The impact of minimum wage increases is strongest at the 5th (roughly equal to the minimum wage), 10th, and 15th wage percentiles. The size of these raises diminishes the higher the worker's wage rate.

There is one unexpected result based on the full sample. The positive, statistically significant coefficients in column 4 for the 70th–90th wage percentiles suggest that 1 year after a minimum wage increase, the highest wage-earners receive raises. These unlikely results, however, disappear when the alternative sample excluding New England states and the years 1990 and 1996 is used. In fact, using the alternative sample reduces substantially the impact of minimum wage increases on the wage growth 1 year later for most wage percentiles. This suggests that at least some of the wage growth for most wage percentiles—and all of the wage growth for the highest wage-earners—associated with minimum wage increases indicated by the original set of results is actually due to business cycle or regional economic trends. The remainder of this section focuses on the results based on the alternative sample.

The estimated wage elasticity of 0.44 (0.42 + 0.02) for workers earning wages around the 5th wage percentile indicate that the wages of these workers go up an average of 4.4 percent given a 10 percent minimum wage increase. Take, for example, the federal minimum wage increase of 1997 from $4.75 to $5.15, an 8 percent increase. The wages of workers who earned wages around the old minimum of $4.75 increased, on average, by 3.5 percent ($8.0 \times 0.44 = 3.5$), or $0.17, to $4.92.

Why does the 5th wage percentile not go up exactly as much as the minimum wage (i.e., have a combined wage elasticity of 1)? This is because, although those workers earning *exactly* the minimum wage probably see their wages move in line with the minimum wage, the workers earning wages *around* the minimum wage (i.e., above and below it) do not. From other analyses not presented here, I found that sub–minimum wage workers receive raises that are smaller, rather than equivalent to, the minimum wage when the minimum wage increases.[15] The same is true for workers earning very close to, but above the minimum (see discussion below). As a result, the estimated effect for the 5th wage percentile—which reflects the average experience of workers earning wages below, at, and just above the minimum wage—is below 1.

Workers with wages around the 10th wage percentile receive, on average, a 2.4 percent increase for every 10 percent increase in the minimum wage (i.e., a wage elasticity of 0.24). Applying this to the 1997 federal minimum increase, workers earning around the 10th wage percentile of $5.22 got 2 percent raises ($8.0 \times 0.025 = 2.0$), roughly 10 cents, to $5.32.

The highest point in the wage distribution with a detectable impact from minimum wage changes is the 15th wage percentile. Because there is no detectable impact at the 20th wage percentile, the 15th wage percentile approximates the lower bound of the ripple effect's upper limit. These workers receive, on average, a 1.5 percent raise for every 10 percent increase in the minimum wage (i.e., a wage elasticity of 0.15). The 8 percent federal minimum increase in 1997 produced a 1 percent raise for workers earning around the 15th wage percentile of $5.74 ($8.0 \times 0.15 = 1.2$), or 7 cents, to $5.81.

Taken together, these estimates describe a minimum wage effect that compresses the wage distribution. Consider the example of the 1997 federal rate increase. Prior to the increase, the bottom of the wage floor was almost $1.00 less than the 15th wage percentile. After the increase, the new wage floor was pushed up within 70 cents of the 15th wage percentile.

Retail Trade

Although the minimum wage clearly has a stronger "bite" in the retail trade industry compared to other industries, the impact of minimum wages in the retail trade industry has virtually the same pattern as that found for the entire economy, both in terms of extent and magnitude (see table 11.1, section B). The impact of minimum wage increases extends to the 40th wage percentile of the retail trade industry. Because of the higher concentration of low wages in this industry, the 40th wage percentile among retail trade workers is roughly equivalent to the 15th wage percentile among all workers (see column 2). The wage elasticity for the 40th wage percentile among retail trade workers (0.14) is also roughly equivalent to the wage elasticity for the 15th wage percentile among all workers (0.15).

Instead of producing qualitatively different results, the high concentration of low-wage workers in the retail trade industry simply provides a more detailed view of the minimum wage effect. This is because each wage percentile characterizes a narrower range of wages.[16] As a result, the high wage elasticity of 0.73 for the 10th percentile of the retail trade industry is a more precise estimate for minimum wage workers than the lower wage elasticity of 0.44 for the 5th wage percentile across industries. These estimated wage elasticities also illustrate more clearly the precipitous drop in the size of the raises. Even workers earning wages immediately above the minimum receive raises that are smaller (proportionately) than the full minimum wage increase.

POLICY IMPLICATIONS

The Overall Cost Impact of Ripple Effects

Despite the limited extent of ripple effects, these wage raises considerably expand the overall cost of minimum wage increases. This result is driven by the fact that the workers with wages just above the minimum greatly out-number workers earning the minimum. To illustrate, I present in table 11.2 estimates of the wage raises that occurred in response to the 1997 federal minimum wage. Column 3 presents the number of workers that earned wages around the 5th, 10th, and 15th wage percentiles prior to the federal minimum increase. Because the 5th wage percentile sits right at the $4.75 minimum wage level, the average worker earning wages around the 5th wage percentile received mandated raises only. Based on this example, al-most triple the number workers earning wages around the 5th percentile earned wages around the 10th and 15th wage percentiles. In other words, the high concentration of workers near but above the minimum wage pro-duces a large ripple effect.

I calculate a ripple-effect multiplier to provide a measure of how impor-tant the ripple effect is in the overall cost of minimum wage increases. This multiplier quantifies how much ripple-effect raises multiply the total change in employers' annual wage bills from mandated wage raises alone.

To do this, I estimate the total change in employers' annual wage bills caused by the 1997 federal minimum wage increases due to mandated raises and ripple-effect raises separately. Specifically, I multiplied the number of workers who earned wages around each wage percentile (column 3) by their average raises as estimated by the regression analysis, given an 8.4 percent increase in the federal minimum (column 4), their average hours per week (column 5), and their average weeks worked per year (column 6).

I estimate that employers responded to the federal minimum wage in-crease by providing roughly 4 million workers with $741 million in man-dated raises (column 7). Ripple effects provide another 11.5 million workers with $1.3 billion dollars in raises (column 8), nearly quadrupling the number of minimum wage beneficiaries and almost tripling the overall increase to employers' annual wage bills. In other words, with regard to the overall change in the wage bill, ripple effects multiply the cost increase to employers by 270 percent ([741.0 + 1280.3]/741.0), producing a ripple-effect multiplier of 2.7. Similar calculations based on the other three federal minimum wage increases of the 1990s produce an average ripple-effect multiplier of 2.5.[17]

While the ripple-effect multiplier is large, the actual economic impact of the cost increases associated with minimum wages—from mandated or ripple-effect raises—can only be assessed when put into context with some measure of businesses' capacity to absorb these costs. One way to evaluate this capac-ity is to compare the increased costs to businesses' sales revenue. Robert Pollin, Mark Brenner, and I did such a comparison in a 2004 study of the eco-nomic impact of a proposed $6.15 state minimum wage for Florida, increas-ing the effective minimum wage by $1.00 above the $5.15 federal minimum. We estimated the associated cost increases of the minimum wage proposal for

Table 11.2. Estimate of the ripple-effect multiplier, all industries, based on federal minimum wage increase in September 1997 from $4.75 to $5.15

(1) Wage percentile	(2) Average wage before[a]	(3) Number of workers (millions)[b]	(4) Average raise due to 8.4% federal minimum increase		(5) Average weekly hours[c]	(6) Average annual weeks worked[d]	(7) Mandatory raises (millions of dollars)	(8) Ripple-effect raises (millions of dollars)
			% increase	Dollar amount				
5th	$4.73	4.0	3.6%	$0.17	28.0	39	$741.0	$ -
10th	$5.22	6.1	1.9%	$0.10	30.5	40	$ -	$757.5
15th	$5.74	5.4	1.6%	$0.07	32.5	43	$ -	$522.7
							$741.0	$1,280.3
							Multiplier =	2.7

Source: Current Population Survey Outgoing Rotation Group (CPS-ORG) 1997 files, Bureau of Labor Statistics, U.S. Department of Labor.
[a]Average wages are estimated from workers earning between the wage percentile ± 2. For example, the average wage of workers for the 5th wage percentile is based on workers earning above the 3rd wage percentile and below the 8th percentile. "Before" refers to January–June 1997.
[b]Number of workers is estimated from the same sample of workers as the average wages.
[c]Average hours are estimated from the same sample of workers as the number of workers.
[d]Average weeks worked per year estimates are not available from the CPS-ORG data. Instead, approximations were taken from table 11.3 (see notes to table 11.3).

both mandated and ripple-effect raises as a percentage of businesses' sales revenue. We used a methodology similar to that presented here to estimate the ripple-effect raises.

We found that, on average, the total cost increases associated with the Florida minimum wage proposal amounted to less than 1 percent of businesses' sales revenue. The mandated raises alone accounted for less than one-half of 1 percent of businesses' sales revenue. Viewed in this context, it is clear that the large multiplier effect of ripple-effect raises does not meaningfully change the economic burden of minimum wage laws on businesses. If the typical business in Florida wanted to fully cover the costs of the minimum wage increase through price increases, they would have to raise their prices by less than 1 percent. This is true, even though the number of workers receiving ripple-effect raises in Florida was 550,000, nearly double the 300,000 workers receiving mandated raises under the $6.15 proposal.

The Impact of Ripple Effects on the Pool of Minimum Wage Beneficiaries

These ripple-effect estimates add new information to the debate about whether minimum wage benefits are well targeted. A common critique of minimum wage laws is that some minimum wage beneficiaries are secondary wage-earners (e.g., high school teenagers earning pocket money). If ripple effects quadruple the number of workers affected by minimum wage increases, the demographic profile of minimum wage beneficiaries may be different when ripple-effect raises are considered.

Table 11.3 illustrates how the demographic profile of minimum wage beneficiaries may change when ripple-effect raises are taken into account. Column 1 presents the average demographic characteristics of workers earning wages around the 5th wage percentile ($5.50, averaged across states) in 1999–2000.[18] These workers would most likely receive mandated raises if the federal minimum rose by 13.5 percent to $5.85—an amount similar to the federal increases of 1990 and 1996. Column 2 adds workers earning wages up to and around the 15th wage percentile (6.83, averaged across states). These workers would be expected to receive mandated or ripple-effect raises from the 13.5 percent increase in the federal rate.

The most striking difference between the two demographic profiles is the fall in proportion of workers who are usually identified as secondary wage-earners: teenagers and traditional-age (16–24 years old) students. The proportion of teenagers falls from 33 to 25 percent and the proportion of traditional-age students falls from 31 to 24 percent. As a result, primary wage-earners make up a greater share of the minimum wage beneficiaries when ripple-effect raises are taken into account. The average worker's

Table 11.3. Demographic profiles of workers who would receive raises from a hypothetical federal minimum wage increase in 2000, from $5.15 to $5.85

	(1) Workers who would receive mandated raises ($5.15 to $5.85)	(2) Workers who would receive mandated and/or ripple-effect raises ($5.15 to $7.15)
Number of workers	4.8 million	14.4 million
Percentage of workforce	3.6%	10.7%
Individual characteristics		
Average hourly wage	$5.52	$6.17
	(0.00)	(0.00)
Teenager	33.3%	25.4%
	(0.72)	(0.37)
Student and 16 to 24 years old	31.1%	24.0%
	(0.72)	(0.37)
Teenager or student	38.7%	30.6%
	(0.73)	(0.39)
Non-White	29.7%	30.3%
	(0.62)	(0.35)
Female	57.5%	58.3%
	(0.69)	(0.38)
Usual hours worked per week	30.6	32.7
	(0.18)	(0.10)
Family characteristics		
Family income	$48,088	$46,449
	(720)	(375)
Worker's earnings as percentage of family income	33.9%	38.9%
	(0.48)	(0.30)
Severely poor (federal poverty level)	17.1%	14.3%
	(0.52)	(0.27)
Low-income (200% federal poverty level)	45.5%	44.9%
	(0.69)	(0.38)

Source: Current Population Survey Annual Social and Economic Supplement survey 2000–2002 files, Bureau of Labor Statistics, U.S. Department of Labor.

Notes: Dollar values are in 2000 dollars. Standard errors are in parentheses and in same units as characteristic measure. CPS-ASEC sampling weights were adjusted to account for differences in reporting errors in CPS-ASEC earnings data and CPS Outgoing Rotation Group files wage data.

contribution toward his or her family's income increases from 34 to 39 percent when ripple-effect raises are included.

Is the Ripple Effect Stronger When the Minimum Wage Has a Stronger Bite?

The limited extent of the ripple effect in combination with a relatively high concentration of minimum wage workers in the retail trade industry suggests that ripple-effect raises will contribute less to the overall impact of minimum wage increases in this industry. I repeat calculations analogous to those presented in table 11.2 for the retail trade industry only for the four federal minimum wage increases of the 1990s. As expected, the heavy concentration of workers at the wage floor in this sector reduces the size of the ripple-effect multiplier. These calculations suggest an average ripple-effect multiplier for the retail trade industry of 1.9.

Implications for Living Wage Laws

Living wage laws typically call for much higher wage floors than state and federal minimum wage laws because their levels are explicitly tied to wage rates that provide a "livable income" such as the federal poverty-level income threshold for a family of three. Minimum wage rates are not. This difference has dramatic effects. For example, the 2007 New Mexico state minimum wage is set at $5.15, equivalent to the federal rate. In the city of Santa Fe, New Mexico, however, a citywide living wage rate is set at $9.50, 84 percent higher than the state minimum. Consequently, living wage laws require that, among covered firms, a significantly larger proportion of workers receive mandated raises than in the general case of minimum wage laws. When the Santa Fe living wage was originally set at $8.50 in 2004, Pollin (2003) estimated that 16.4 percent of Santa Fe's workforce would receive mandated raises—more than three times the percentage of workers likely to receive mandated raises from the hypothetical federal minimum wage increase presented in table 11.3.

The findings based on the separate retail trade analysis suggests that a higher concentration of workers receiving mandated raises from a wage floor increase does not lead to more extensive ripple effects. As a result, the cost increases that employers face (and the wage benefits that workers receive) from living wage laws will probably be primarily due to mandated raises rather than ripple-effect raises, the opposite of the general case of minimum wage laws. This pattern is illustrated by the much smaller ripple-effect multiplier (1.9) found for the retail trade industry compared to all industries (2.5).

There are a couple reasons why living wage laws may produce ripple effects that behave differently from the minimum wage ripple effects. First, workers just above the living wage levels (reaching as high as $15.39 in Hartford, Connecticut, in 2006) may have more bargaining power than workers just above minimum wage levels (the highest is only $7.63 in Washington state in 2006) and thus be better able to obtain raises when a living wage law is enacted. In that case, living wage laws may produce more extensive ripple effects because different *types* of workers—perhaps more skilled or more unionized—sit just above the new wage floor.

Second, living wage laws typically cover only employers with financial ties to their municipal government, such as city contractors. As a result, the coverage of living wage laws is typically no more than 2 percent of workers within a city (Neumark and Adams, 2003a). Minimum wage laws tend to have virtually universal coverage. This aspect of living wage laws introduce the possibility of ripple effects *across* firms in addition to ripple effects up the wage scale *within* covered firms. Employers who are not covered by living wage laws may increase the wages of their workers as they compete for workers within the same local labor market as covered employers. This additional source of ripple-effect raises may cause the ripple effect to be larger than suggested here.

However, the empirical evidence so far supports the conclusion that the role of ripple-effect raises tends to be much smaller for living wage laws than for minimum wage laws. Case studies of the San Francisco and Los Angeles living wage laws suggest that ripple-effect raises added only 13–35 percent to the cost increases from mandated raises (Reich, Hall, and Jacobs 2003; Fairris et al. 2005).

CONCLUSION

This chapter presents detailed empirical estimates of the ripple effects produced by state and federal minimum wage increases in the United States during 1983–2002. These estimates help to address some of the policy questions being raised in the wake of a political tide that appears to be turning in favor of higher mandated wage floors.

How much do ripple-effect raises contribute to the overall cost of mandated wage floors? These estimates demonstrate that ripple effects change dramatically the overall impact of mandated wage floors. In the general case, ripple-effect raises typically multiply the overall costs to employers by as much as 2.5. Despite this, ripple-effect raises represent a very small cost burden for employers because the cost of mandated raises—as measured as a percentage of businesses' sales revenue—is so small.

How do ripple-effect raises change the pool of workers who benefit from mandated wage floors? By tripling or quadrupling the number of workers receiving raises from minimum wage increases, ripple-effect raises expand the pool of minimum wage beneficiaries to include an even greater majority of adult workers.

How do the ripple effects of living wage laws compare to the ripple effects of more traditional minimum wage laws? Based on the experience of the retail trade industry, living wage laws should be expected to generate cost increases for employers, as well as benefits for workers, mainly through mandated raises rather than ripple-effect raises, the opposite of the general case of minimum wage laws.

APPENDIX: NOTES ON THE POTENTIAL
SOURCES OF SPURIOUS CORRELATION

In this appendix, I provide more detail on why wage growth caused by national macroeconomic changes may be spuriously linked to minimum wage increases. As noted in the chapter, several times throughout the time period studied the federal minimum wage caused the effective minimum wage to change for virtually all states at the same time. Although the year indicator variables control for changes in national macroeconomic trends between years, they do not control for within-year changes in the national economy.

If macroeconomic factors cause most states to experience similar patterns in wage growth within the same year that there are within-year changes in federal minimum wage increases, some of this wage growth may be attributed to the minimum wage. I present these within-year changes in the last column of table 11A.1. Two years, 1990 and 1996, stand out as likely to be problematic. During these years, large positive differences in federal minimum wage changes, lagged 1 year, overlap with significant upturns in the economy—marked by relatively large increases in the growth rate of the real gross domestic product. If wage growth is a coincident indicator of the macroeconomy, this coincidence may cause the regression estimates of the lagged minimum wage variable to reflect, in part, macroeconomic effects.

For the high wage percentiles in particular, the coincidence between federal minimum wage increases and macroeconomic growth are likely to produce spurious results. This is because real wage growth among high-wage workers is more pronounced than among other workers during the business cycle upturns of the 1980s and 1990s (Mishel, Bernstein, and Boushey 2003).

Table 11A.1. Trends in federal minimum wage changes and macroeconomic growth

A. Federal minimum wage change (lagged 1 year)

Year		(1) Change based on 1st observation in year	(2) Change based on 2nd observation in year	Difference in change within year (column 2 − column 1)
1983		0.0%	0.0%	0.0%
1984		0.0%	0.0%	0.0%
1985		0.0%	0.0%	0.0%
1986		0.0%	0.0%	0.0%
1987		0.0%	0.0%	0.0%
1988		0.0%	0.0%	0.0%
1989		0.0%	0.0%	0.0%
1990	*Fed. min.*	**7.0%**	**13.0%**	**6.0%**
1991	*increase from*	13.0%	12.0%	−1.0%
1992	*$3.35 to $4.25*	6.0%	0.0%	−6.0%
1993		0.0%	0.0%	0.0%
1994		0.0%	0.0%	0.0%
1995		0.0%	0.0%	0.0%
1996	*Fed. min.*	**0.0%**	**6.0%**	**6.0%**
1997	*increase from*	12.0%	11.0%	−1.0%
1998	*$4.25 to $5.15*	8.0%	3.0%	−5.0%
1999		0.0%	0.0%	0.0%
2000		0.0%	0.0%	0.0%
2001		0.0%	0.0%	0.0%

Table 11A.1.—cont.

B. Real GDP annual growth rate

Year		1st quarter (January–March)	3rd quarter (July–September)	Difference in growth within year (column 2– column 1)
1983		8.1%	3.9%	−4.2%
1984		3.8%	6.4%	2.6%
1985		3.9%	3.9%	0.0%
1986		2.7%	3.7%	1.0%
1987		2.0%	2.1%	0.1%
1988		4.1%	2.9%	−1.2%
1989		4.7%	0.0%	−4.7%
1990	*Fed. min.*	**−2.0%**	**1.9%**	**3.9%**
1991	*increase from*	4.2%	4.0%	−0.2%
1992	*$3.35 to $4.25*	0.5%	2.1%	1.6%
1993		4.1%	2.3%	−1.8%
1994		1.1%	3.3%	2.2%
1995		2.9%	3.4%	0.5%
1996	*Fed. min.*	**3.1%**	**5.1%**	**2.0%**
1997	*increase from*	4.5%	4.7%	0.2%
1998	*$3.35 to $4.25*	3.4%	4.8%	1.4%
1999		1.0%	−0.5%	−1.5%
2000		−0.5%	−1.4%	−0.9%
2001		2.7%	2.4%	−0.3%

Source: Bureau of Economic Analysis, U.S. Department of Commerce. Gross Domestic Product: Percent Change from Preceding Period, available at: http://www.bea.gov/bea/dn/gdpchg.xls.

Note: Change in minimum wage (lagged) and GDP growth rate is from the year in column 1 to the next year.

12 *Employment Effects of Higher Minimum Wages*

A State-by-State Comparative Analysis

MARK BRENNER, ROBERT POLLIN,
AND JEANNETTE WICKS-LIM

The evidence we review in chapters 4, 5, and 10 (on living wage and minimum wage measures in New Orleans, Santa Fe, and Boston) provides a strong overall case that business firms covered by these measures are able to absorb the increased costs resulting from the higher minimum wage, primarily through a combination of raising prices and improving productivity by small amounts. This means that in these cases, if not more generally, raising the minimum wage standard is not likely to induce firms to either lay off employees or relocate out of their present place of business to avoid the increased costs of the measure. It means, correspondingly, that in most cases firms will not need to cut into their profits or reduce the wages of higher-paid workers in order to cover their higher wage payments to low-wage workers. We do see, however, in chapter 10 that covered firms in Boston primarily reduced their previously large profit margins as a means of absorbing their increased costs.

Overall, these conclusions are especially pertinent as regards unemployment effects, that is, whether a mandated minimum wage increase within the range that we have reviewed in previous chapters will lead businesses to lay off low-wage workers or be more reluctant to hire them in the future. Certainly, in considering the negative unintended consequences of minimum wage or living wage laws, the potential for creating employment losses among low-wage workers is, rightfully, the single greatest matter of concern. As such, it is appropriate to consider this question in a bit more detail now.

As we discuss in previous chapters, the best-known recent work considering the employment effects of minimum wage laws has been that of David

216

Card and Alan Krueger, especially their 1995 book that we cite above, *Myth and Measurement: The New Economics of the Minimum Wage*. Card and Krueger have consistently found that changes in the minimum wage have not tended to raise unemployment by any discernable amount (and indeed have tended to be associated with slight *increases* in low-wage employment; see also Card and Krueger 2000). However the Card-Krueger research methods and results have been challenged by a number of authors, most notably David Neumark and William Wascher (e.g., 2000). But Neumark and Wascher's most recent findings, although still at variance with those of Card and Krueger, also show either no significant employment effects at all resulting from a minimum wage increase or only small negative effects. The differences between the Card-Krueger and Neumark-Wascher findings have been well summarized by Richard Freeman of Harvard University, who writes that "The debate is over whether modest minimum wage increases have 'no' employment effect, modest positive effects, or small negative effects. It is *not* about whether or not there are large negative effects" (1995, 833; emphasis in original).

Freeman's overall conclusion has also been supported by the findings of a 1998 survey of professional economists at forty leading research universities in the fields of labor economics and public economics by Victor Fuchs of Stanford, Alan Krueger, and James Poterba of MIT. According to this survey, the general professional view is, again, that there were no strong negative employment effects, if any, from raising the minimum wage by relatively modest amounts. More specifically, the Fuchs, Krueger, and Poterba survey asked economists what they thought was the employment elasticity of demand for teenagers of a minimum wage increase—that is, how much employment of teenagers would go down when the minimum wage went up. In the median, the economists' view was that a 10 percent increase in the minimum wage would lead to a 1 percent decline in teenage employment—a relatively modest negative employment effect for a group of workers who are relatively most affected by changes in the minimum wage. The survey did not ask the economists how overall employment would be affected by a minimum wage increase, that is, its impact on adult as well as teenage employment. But given their median position that the effect on teenagers is itself modest, it follows that most economists would regard the employment effect to be significantly more modest still for the adult labor market.

The findings from these general studies to date are also consistent with the series of 2005 studies examining the impact of living and minimum wage increases in San Francisco (Dube, Naidu, and Reich 2005; Reich, Hall, and Jacobs 2005) and Los Angeles (Fairris et al. 2005). None of these studies finds evidence of significant employment reductions associated with the implementation of living wage laws.

This summary of the academic research is also consistent with further evidence that we present here. In particular, we examine here the employment experience of two sets of states (counting the District of Columbia as a state): (1) the eleven states that operated with minimum wage levels higher than the federal minimum for the full period since the last recession, 2001–2005 and (2) the thirty-three states that operated with the federal $5.15 minimum throughout these years. These eleven high minimum wage states were Alaska, California, Connecticut, Delaware, the District of Columbia, Hawaii, Massachusetts, Oregon, Rhode Island, Vermont, and Washington. The minimum wage in these states ranged between $6.15 and $7.50 as of January 2005. We present some basic findings from that comparison in table 12.1.[1]

As we see, in terms of overall employment, the eleven states with a minimum wage higher than the $5.15 federal mandate in these years experienced an average annual rate of employment growth of 0.57 percent, whereas the thirty-three states that did not have statewide minimums that exceeded the federal rate experienced an average annual employment growth rate of 0.52 percent. In other words, there was slightly *faster* growth in the eleven states with higher minimum wages over the full period than in the thirty-three states with statewide minimums at the federal rate.

The table next focuses on employment in the restaurant and hotel industries, the industries that, in all areawide living or minimum wage measures, will be most heavily affected by the rise in the minimum wage. With restau-

Table 12.1. Comparing employment growth for states with above $5.15 minimum wage standards versus states with only federal $5.15 minimum

Average Annual Employment Growth in the Private Sector, 2001–2005

	All 50 states and the District of Columbia	11 states with above $5.15 minimum wage[a]	33 states with only federal $5.15 minimum[b]
Overall employment growth	0.48%	0.57%	0.52%
Hotel industry employment growth	0.07%	0.19%	0.12%
Restaurant industry employment growth	2.29%	2.21%	2.32%

Source: Quarterly Census of Employment and Wages 2001 and 2005, Bureau of Labor Statistics, U.S. Department of Labor.

Notes: See Pollin and Wicks-Lim (2006, app. 2) for details on calculations.

[a]The states that have minimum wage standards that exceed $5.15 during 2001–5 are Alaska, California, Connecticut, Delaware, the District of Columbia, Hawaii, Massachusetts, Oregon, Rhode Island, Vermont, and Washington.

[b]The states that have minimum wage standards equal to $5.15 during 2001–5 include the remaining states excluding the seven states (Florida, Illinois, Maine, Minnesota, New Jersey, New York, and Wisconsin) that have minimum wage standards that exceed $5.15 for part of this time period.

rants, we do see that employment growth is somewhat slower in the eleven states with higher minimum wages—2.2 percent growth versus 2.3 percent for the thirty-three states with statewide minimums at the federal rate. For the hotel industry, the growth in employment was 0.19 percent for the eleven states with higher minimum wage mandates, whereas it was slightly slower, at 0.12 percent, in the thirty-three states with statewide minimum wages at the federal rate.

Overall, there is certainly no evidence in table 12.1 to suggest that a higher minimum wage in a state significantly reduced that state's rate of employment growth. To the contrary, if anything, employment in states with higher minimum wages tended to grow slightly faster than those operating at the federal $5.15 minimum. Of course, many things other than the minimum wage mandate affect employment growth at any given time. For example, the September 11, 2001, terrorist attacks no doubt contributed to the almost nonexistent employment growth in the hotel industry during this period. The national recession in 2001 (which began in March of that year, well before the terrorist attacks) obviously led to a decline in employment growth in all the states. When we recognize these considerations, the data in table 12.1 still shows that instituting a minimum wage law higher than the federal mandate does not, *on its own*, produce a major negative effect on employment—or indeed any significant discernable effect on employment of any kind—relative to all the other influences that may also be affecting employment. If the higher minimum wage laws in the eleven states were, on their own, producing a major influence on employment relative to other factors, then we would observe significantly lower employment growth figures for these states. This obviously did not happen in the years that we are observing, 2001–2005.

Through more formal statistical procedures, we are also able to test how statewide minimum wage laws affect employment in the states, *after* controlling for other factors that could affect employment in the states. In this analysis, we consider the period 1991–2000 and again group the states according to whether they operated with a statewide minimum wage law above the federal minimum. Within this framework, we consider the employment trends in the retail trade, restaurant, and hotel industries. We present this formal statistical analysis in table 12.2. Here we use panel data regression analysis. As table 12.2 reports, we regressed the change in log (Employment) on a series of independent variables.

The model is designed as follows.[2] The dependent variable in the model is the change in log (Employment) in each state during the period 1990–2000. We are testing here for changes in employment in each state resulting from differences in the various states' minimum wage standards. To focus more sharply on minimum wage effects, we do not consider this employment

Table 12.2. Regression analysis of the employment effects of federal and state minimum wage changes

Dependent variable – Change in log (Employment) in:	Retail trade	Restaurants	Hotels
Fraction of workers directly affected by minimum wage increase	0.191*** (5.75)	0.369*** (9.35)	−0.103 (0.97)
Change in the state employment/ population ratio	0.014 (0.23)	−0.049 (0.68)	0.290 (1.48)
Change in the state unemployment rate	−0.453*** (4.13)	−0.483*** (4.05)	−0.556* (1.78)
Change in log (Wage of adult males)	0.010 (0.46)	0.036 (1.40)	0.007 (0.10)
Region effect	−0.004*** (3.91)	−0.006*** (4.40)	−0.003 (1.01)

Sources: Employment totals from 1991–2000 ES-202 data, Bureau of Labor Statistics, U.S. Department of Labor; employment/population ratio and unemployment rate from 1991–2000 Geographic Profiles of Unemployment and Employment, Bureau of Labor Statistics, U.S. Department of Labor; fraction of directly affected workers and average wage of adult males are estimated for each state from the Current Population Survey Outgoing Rotation Group 1991–2000 files, Bureau of Labor Statistics, U.S. Department of Labor.

Note: This model is estimated on 450 state-year observations for the fifty states (excluding the District of Columbia) between 1991 and 2000 using a random-effects generalized least squares regression. t statistics appear in parentheses below the estimated coefficients. * indicates significant at the 10 percent level; ** indicates significant at the 5 percent level; *** indicates significant at the 1 percent level.

variable for the economy as a whole in each state but rather focus on industries in which we know the employment effects of minimum wage increases will be relatively large. These are retail trade, restaurants, and hotels.

The explanatory variables in the model include (1) the fraction of workers directly affected by the minimum wage increase, (2) the change in the state's employment/population ratio, (3) the change in the state's unemployment rate, (4) the change in the log of the average adult male's wages, and (5) a regional effect. The explanatory variable of interest here is the first one. The remaining explanatory variables are included as controls.

What are we attempting to capture with the first explanatory variable, the fraction of workers directly affected by the minimum wage increase? This variable measures the proportion of workers in a state who are expected to get mandated raises when that state's minimum wage increases.

As such, when there is no minimum wage increase in a particular state in a particular year, this fraction is equal to zero—no workers get mandated raises that year. In other words, the minimum wage should have no impact in that state in that year. Correspondingly, when a minimum wage increase does occur in a given state and year, this variable measures the fraction of workers earning between the old minimum wage and the new minimum wage at the time of the increase. These are the people who are therefore scheduled for mandated raises once the higher minimum wage takes effect. Thus, the larger this fraction is, the more of an impact the minimum wage increase should have on employment in the state (the dependent variable in the model).

We now consider this in terms of the specific industries on which we focus. In the restaurant industry in California, for example, the change in employment in California restaurants should be negatively affected in the years when a minimum wage increase is implemented in California, if it is indeed true that implementing a minimum wage has a negative effect on employment. As such, when the fraction of workers directly affected by the minimum wage increase rises, we would expect that it would generate a negative effect on employment—especially in the restaurant, hotel, and retail trade industries, which have relatively high proportions of low-wage workers.

Considering the control variables in the model, the changes in a state's employment/population ratio and unemployment rate are both standard measures of overall labor market conditions. By including them in the model, we are isolating the effects of the minimum wage change from these overall labor market conditions. The change in the average adult male worker's wages is another overall measure of conditions in a state's labor market. Including this allows us to again isolate the minimum wage effect from general wage-setting conditions. We, finally, add a control for overall conditions in each region in the country.

Turning to the results for our explanatory variable of interest, we see that for both the retail trade and restaurants, the relationship between the fraction of workers directly affected by the minimum wage increase and employment in these industries is positive and statistically significant. That is, as a general finding, when there are more people in a state's retail or restaurant industry about to receive a mandated minimum wage increase, employment in those industries tends to *increase*, not *decrease*, all else remaining equal. This finding contradicts the idea that increasing the minimum wage in a state engenders negative effects on employment, all else remaining equal. For the hotel industry, we do see that the employment effect of having more workers getting minimum wage increases is negative. However, in this case, unlike with retail trade and restaurants, the negative employment effect is not statistically significant.

Thus, to summarize the main finding of this analysis: considering the period 1991–2000 and controlling for other factors that influence employment growth, we find no evidence showing that states that increased their minimum wage standards above the federal mandate experienced slower employment growth in either the retail trade, the restaurant, or the hotel industries.

In other words, this formal statistical analysis again supports our main conclusion from previous discussions: that raising the minimum wage within the ranges that we have discussed in previous chapters will not produce any significant change in the employment practices of businesses. Businesses will make small adjustments in their operations due to the higher minimum wage. The primary adjustment they are likely to make will be to slightly raise prices, especially in the hotel and restaurant industries, and most especially among fast-food and other limited-services restaurants. Small improvements in productivity encouraged by the wage increase may also make a modest contribution to absorbing their increased costs, as might small reductions in profits, in cases in which profit margins are high.

13 Comments on Aaron Yelowitz, "Santa Fe's Living Wage Ordinance and the Labor Market"

ROBERT POLLIN AND JEANNETTE WICKS-LIM

Aaron Yelowitz first became involved in the debate over the Santa Fe living wage ordinance through his participation in the April 2004 trial that challenged the validity of the law. Specifically, Yelowitz was hired by the plaintiffs in the trial to rebut the report by one of us (Pollin), who was serving as the city's expert witness in the trial. Yelowitz both provided a written rebuttal and was questioned verbally at length during the trial.

Yelowitz's rebuttal of Pollin's study had serious errors and misrepresentations, including even in the manner that he reported citations of the professional literature and the handling of basic data. As such, Yelowitz's testimony in the trial was dismissed by Judge Daniel Sanchez. The judge wrote that Yelowitz "fails to undermine the credibility of Dr. Pollin," while commending Pollin's own work for the "reliability of his methodology" and "the dependability of [his] data sources."[1]

In a new study, *Santa Fe's Living Wage Ordinance and the Labor Market* (Yelowitz 2005b), Yelowitz claims to demonstrate that the Santa Fe living wage ordinance is responsible for significant negative consequences for the least educated Santa Fe residents, including a 9.0 percentage point increase in the city's unemployment rate among such workers. However, he derives these findings through a presentation of evidence that is misleading and incomplete, misusing the available data.[2]

BASIC EVIDENCE ON SANTA FE EMPLOYMENT GROWTH

The single most useful starting point for assessing the impact of the Santa Fe $8.50 per hour living wage law on employment is the basic data on employment growth in Santa Fe since the living wage law was implemented in June 2004. We present the evidence on this in table 13.1. As we see, overall employment growth in Santa Fe during July 2004–July 2005 was 2.0 percent and employment growth in the leisure and hospitality industry was 3.2 percent. The 3.2 percent employment growth figure in leisure and hospitality is especially significant, given that the highest concentration of workers who would have received wage increases due to the living wage laws are in this industry, which includes Santa Fe's hotels and restaurants as the main components of this industrial category. Given the disproportionately large impact of the living wage measure in this industry, we would expect that employment growth would, if anything, have been slowed in this industry if the measure did indeed lead to reduced employment growth. However, instead, we see that employment growth in leisure and hospitality exceeded overall employment growth in Santa Fe by a substantial amount (for Santa Fe as a whole, the difference between job growth at 3.2 percent and the actual 2.0 percent during July 2004–July 2005 is 738 jobs).

The Santa Fe employment growth statistics, especially again in the leisure and hospitality industry, are also impressive relative to employment trends in the state overall and in other regions of the state. Santa Fe was the only city in the state that operated with a living wage mandate during this period. The rest of New Mexico operated under the federal minimum wage standard of $5.15 per hour. As we see in table 13.1, employment in New Mexico overall grew at 2.0 percent, exactly equal to the employment growth rate in Santa Fe. And although employment growth in leisure and hospitality throughout the state, at 2.3 percent, was faster than the overall state employment growth, this 2.3 percent figure is still well below the 3.2 percent figure for Santa Fe. Here, again, there appears to be no evidence that employment growth in Santa Fe has suffered through implementing an $8.50 living wage mandate in June 2004.

Table 13.1 also provides employment growth data for the three other metropolitan statistical areas (MSAs) in New Mexico. Again, the Santa Fe performance looks quite healthy, both in overall employment and in the leisure and hospitality industry. Employment growth is clearly stronger than in Albuquerque. It is slower overall than in Las Cruces, but well above the Las Cruces 1.6 percent employment growth figure for leisure and hospitality. Employment did grow more quickly in Farmington, both in total and

Table 13.1. Employment growth in New Mexico, July 2004–July 2005

	Total nonfarm employment	Leisure and hospitality industry
Santa Fe MSA	2.0%	3.2%
Statewide	2.0%	2.3%
Albuquerque MSA	1.7%	0.8%
Las Cruces MSA	3.0%	1.6%
Farmington MSA	2.6%	3.9%

Source: New Mexico Department of Labor (2005), *Labor Market Report* 7(3): 8, 13–15.

in the leisure and hospitality industry. But the figures for Santa Fe are still roughly comparable to Farmington, which, in any case, has the smallest base of employment in the state. The overall point that again emerges from these comparisons is that there is no evidence suggesting that Santa Fe has suffered in terms of employment growth since it implemented its $8.50 living wage mandate relative to the other New Mexico MSAs, which continue to operate at a $5.15 minimum wage.[3]

Such figures provide an important basic reference for analyzing the impact on employment over the first year of the Santa Fe living wage law. However, these figures do not in themselves provide a complete picture. This is because they do not control for factors other than the living wage law that could also be affecting employment growth. For example, it is possible that, even given the healthy employment growth in Santa Fe over this period, businesses in the city may have hired even more people if they were not forced to operate under the $8.50 minimum wage. This is the basis for the claim made by Aaron Yelowitz that the Santa Fe measure has increased unemployment in Santa Fe. We therefore now turn to evaluating Yelowitz's specific claims.

DISTORTIONS IN CITATIONS OF THE PROFESSIONAL LITERATURE

1. On the first page of the main text of his study, Yelowitz asserts that "virtually no serious economist would argue that a 65 percent increase in the wage floor would lead to employment growth" (2005b, 3). This is an inaccurate and highly misleading assertion. We deal with only the main distortions.

A) The professional debate is not over whether an increase in the minimum wage itself *increases* employment growth. The only real issue under debate is whether increases in the minimum wage within the ranges discussed by policymakers (including those in Santa Fe) produces only a weak negative effect on employment (i.e., causing little or no employment losses) or whether they cause large employment losses. After many years of research and debate, the professional consensus view is that increases in the minimum wage in the ranges being discussed by policymakers do not produce significant employment losses. We briefly review the range of professional opinion on this question in chapter 12.

B) Yelowitz reports correctly that the wage floor in Santa Fe rose by 65 percent due to the living wage ordinance—that is, from $5.15 to $8.50 per hour. But he fails to note that, even with this increase in the wage floor, the average increase in costs to businesses relative to their sales due to the living wage ordinance was about 1 percent and that, even for the hotel and restaurant industries, the cost increase/sales ratio was about 3 percent. Robert Pollin estimated these ratios based on publicly available data. But his estimates were confirmed virtually to the decimal point by the payroll data provided for the trial by the plaintiffs.

It may be difficult to accept that there could be no employment losses after a 65 percent increase in the wage floor in Santa Fe. But it is far easier to accept that businesses are capable of absorbing their cost increases due to the living wage mandate when it is understood that, on average, these cost increases amount to no more than 1 percent of their total sales; and to no more than about 3 percent even for restaurants such as the plaintiffs in the Santa Fe trial. The main means through which businesses can absorb cost increases of this modest magnitude is to raise prices by similar magnitudes (assuming no decline in customer demand). For example, a meal at one of the plaintiff's restaurants will need to rise from, say, $20.00 to $20.60 to fully absorb the cost impact of the Santa Fe ordinance, assuming business demand does not decline through this price increase.

2. Also on the first page of his September 2005 report, Yelowitz cites an "employment elasticity" estimate of Neumark and Wascher (2000) of –0.22 due to increases in the minimum wage.

This employment elasticity figure means that if the minimum wage were to rise by 10 percent, then employment would fall by slightly more than 2 percent. Yelowitz cites this same –0.22 percent elasticity estimate in his 2004 rebuttal to Pollin's study. However, just as in his 2004 paper, Yelowitz again fails in his current study to point out a fundamental fact about this Neumark and Wascher estimate: that it applies to the *fast-food industry only*. Neumark and Wascher never state that the estimate applies to all workers in all industries, but Yelowitz misleadingly cites the figure as if it were meant to apply generally. Under cross-examination at the April 2004 trial, Yelowitz was forced to concede this major misrepresentation. Yet he continues to recycle this misrepresentation in his current report.

NO DECLINE IN EMPLOYMENT BASED ON DATA
AND MODEL USED BY YELOWITZ

Yelowitz's conclusions are based on an incomplete analysis. Yelowitz's main findings are based on his examination of the unemployment rate only. However, the unemployment rate is only one aspect of the employment situation of a given labor market. Indeed, the unemployment rate can sometimes provide a misleading picture of what is happening to job growth because the unemployment rate may increase at the same time that the number of jobs is constant or increasing.

Because of this, economists often look at other features of a labor market to get a more complete picture of what is happening to jobs or job growth. Two such features are the employment/population ratio (the number of employed individuals relative to the population) and the labor force participation ratio (the number of individuals who are interested in having a job relative to the population). By simply extending Yelowitz's analysis to encompass these other important characteristics of the Santa Fe labor market, we find that Yelowitz's result of an increase in unemployment among those with high school degrees or less is due *entirely* to a large increase in the percentage of such people entering the labor force in the post–living wage period—that is, to an increase in the labor force participation rate. It is not due *at all* to a given number of people finding greater difficulties finding jobs.

To illustrate this point, let us consider some simple descriptive statistics based on the Current Population Survey (CPS) data presented in the columns 1 and 2 of table 13.2. Again focusing, as Yelowitz does, on those with high school degrees or less, we see that the percentage of such adults who are employed (i.e., the employment/population rate) *increased* from 66.7 to 70.0 percent. In other words, the chances of an adult with a high school degree or less getting (or holding onto) a job did *not* decrease after the enactment of the Santa Fe living wage ordinance. The only way for the unemployment rate to increase, given that employment opportunities did not fall, is for the percentage of adults looking for jobs to rise—*not* for the percentage of adults who have jobs to fall. This trend shows up in the sizable increase in the labor force participation rate from 70.3 to 76.6 percent.

The following hypothetical exercise drives home this point. Let us assume that the percentage of people participating in the labor force remained constant at 70.3 percent between the pre–living wage and post–living wage

Table 13.2. Employment data on Santa Fe MSA, pre– and post–living wage ordinance for those with high school degree or less

	(1) Pre–living wage period Jan. 2003– May 2004 *Actual data from CPS*	(2) Post–living wage period June 2004– June 2005 *Actual data from CPS*	(3) Post–living wage period *Assuming constant labor force participation rate*
Adult population	32,199	33,512	33,512
Employed	21,476	23,472	23,472
Employment to population rate (Number of adults employed/ Adult population)	66.7%	70.0%	70.0%
Labor force participation rate (Number of adults in the labor force/Adult population)	70.3%	76.6%	70.3%
Number of people in labor force (= Adult population × Labor force participation rate)	22,631	25,674	23,559
Unemployed	1,155	2,202	87
Unemployment rate (= Unemployed/Number of people in labor force)	5.1%	8.6%	0.4%

Source: Current Population Survey Basic Monthly January 2003–June 2005 files, Bureau of Labor Statistics, U.S. Department of Labor.

periods rather than rising from 70.3 to 76.6 percent. Let us then also assume that the same number of people with high school degrees or less were holding jobs in the post–living wage period. If both of these assumptions are true, then, as we see in the last column of table 13.2, there would be 23,559 people in the labor force and 23,472 employed. That is, the number employed would be just eighty-seven people shy of the total labor force. This is a rough estimate, of course, but the basic point is clear: there would be effectively *full employment* among those with high school degrees or less in the Santa Fe MSA if the labor force participation rate did not increase from the pre– to the post–living wage period, given the employment level in the post–living wage period.

The result from this simple exercise is purely illustrative. Among other things, it does not take into account all the other factors that could be influencing employment in Santa Fe. However, we reach basically the same conclusion when we conduct a formal replication of Yelowitz's own model that includes controls for other factors potentially influencing employment in the Santa Fe MSA. In that formal replication of Yelowitz's model, which we present in table 13.3, we find the following main results:

Table 13.3. Replication and extension of Yelowitz probit models of probability of unemployment, employment, and labor force participation

	Probit model of probability of:		
	(1) Unemployment during month (among labor force participants)	(2) Employment during month (among adults)	(3) Labor force participation during month (among adults)
Indicator for living wage ordinance	0.480 (0.205) *0.090*	−0.004 (0.098) *−0.002*	0.144 (0.088) *0.051*
Santa Fe indicator	−0.420 (0.153) *−0.044*	0.208 (0.078) *0.079*	0.119 (0.068) *0.043*
Las Cruces indicator	0.088 (0.068) *0.013*	−0.082 (0.042) *−0.032*	−0.064 (0.043) *−0.024*
Rest-of-state indicator	0.103 (0.051) *0.014*	−0.138 (0.028) *−0.053*	−0.127 (0.026) *−0.047*
Married	−0.288 (0.044) *−0.040*	0.077 (0.024) *0.030*	0.004 (0.023) *0.001*
Head of household	−0.018 (0.038) *−0.002*	0.089 (0.023) *0.034*	0.099 (0.022) *0.036*
Male	0.020 (0.035) *0.003*	0.392 (0.024) *0.151*	0.461 (0.024) *0.168*
High school dropout	0.214 (0.045) *0.031*	−0.386 (0.025) *−0.150*	−0.395 (0.028) *−0.146*
White	−0.406 (0.044) *−0.067*	0.234 (0.031) *0.092*	0.155 (0.034) *0.058*
Hispanic	0.252 (0.043) *0.034*	−0.116 (0.026) *−0.045*	−0.052 (0.026) *−0.019*
Veteran	0.051 (0.100) *0.007*	−0.233 (0.048) *−0.092*	−0.266 (0.046) *−0.101*

(*continued*)

Table 13.3.—cont.

	Probit model of probability of:		
	(1) Unemployment during month (among labor force participants)	(2) Employment during month (among adults)	(3) Labor force participation during month (among adults)
Household size	−0.017 (0.012) *−0.002*	−0.009 (0.010) *−0.003*	−0.020 (0.010) *−0.007*
Time trend included?	Yes	Yes	Yes
CPS sample size	9,294	14,529	14,529

Source: Current Population Survey Basic Monthly January 2003–June 2005 files, Bureau of Labor Statistics, U.S. Department of Labor.

Notes: Standard errors are in parentheses, and are corrected for clustering at the MSA × Month × Year level of aggregation. Probability derivatives are in italics. To be included in the sample for column 1, the individual must (1) live in New Mexico, (2) be ages 16–64, (3) have a high school degree or less, and (4) be in the labor force. To be included in the samples for columns 2 and 3, the individual must (1) live in New Mexico, (2) be ages 16–64, and (3) have a high school degree or less. In addition to the variables shown, all models include a constant term and dummy variables for ages 16–64. We also produced estimates using Yelowitz's alternative model, which includes dummy variables for each month and each year; the results are basically unchanged.

1. As with Yelowitz, we find that the probability of *unemployment* within the Santa Fe MSA for labor force participants with high school degrees or less rose by 9 percent in June 2004–June 2005 relative to a pre–living wage base period of January 2003–May 2004 (column 1).

2. However, for all adults with high school degrees or less, using Yelowitz's own model, we also find that the probability of *employment* did not change at all—that is, that the living wage ordinance is not associated with any decline at all in the availability of jobs among those with high school degrees or less (column 2).

3. Finally, still using Yelowitz's own model, we find that the probability of being in the labor force (i.e., employed or looking for a job) rose by 5.1 percent in the post–living wage period (column 3).

Thus, again, according to the CPS data set used by Yelowitz and his own model, we find that it is the rise in the number of people looking for jobs—not the decline in employment opportunities—that has caused the rise in the unemployment rate.

The interpretation of this result is very straightforward in terms of mainstream economic theory—the rise in wages associated with the living wage ordinance attracted more people into the labor market seeking better-paying jobs. There has been no decline in the number of jobs available in the post–living wage period in the Santa Fe MSA, even relative to the population level in the post–living wage period. But there has been an increase in the number of people seeking jobs in the MSA. This is how it is possible for there to be an increase both in the *growth of employment* (total number of jobs) and in the *unemployment rate* (total number of people not getting jobs/total number of people seeking jobs).

DECREASED HOURS AND INCREASED EARNED INCOME

Yelowitz also presents evidence that the weekly hours of those workers who had jobs after the ordinance was passed decreased. Specifically, he finds that workers with a high school diploma or less worked 3.5 fewer hours per week after the living wage ordinance was enacted. Let us assume for now that this figure is accurate. Yelowitz presents this result as an unambiguous hardship for workers. In fact, assuming the figure is accurate, what is most likely is that most workers are earning significantly more money even while working somewhat fewer hours.

Based on findings presented in Pollin's 2004 expert testimony, we provide a rough estimate of the likely impact on workers' earnings in table 13.4. In his expert testimony, Pollin estimates that workers earning less than $8.50 in Santa Fe prior to passage of the living wage ordinance had an average hourly wage of $6.91. This means that establishing the $8.50 minimum wage in Santa Fe would bring an average wage increase to these workers of $1.59—from $6.91 to $8.50.

These workers, on average, also worked 33 hours per week and 50 weeks per year in Pollin's initial estimate. Assuming that their hours did not change after the living wage law was implemented, they would have earned an additional $2,647 per year due to the $8.50 living wage minimum, from $11,505 to $14,152 during the year. But, assuming that their hours did change by the 3.5 hours that Yelowitz estimates, that still means that their annual earnings would have risen by $1,160 due to the $8.50 living wage, to $12,665. This would happen even though the average low-wage employee worked 3.5 fewer hours per week. That is, their wage earnings over the year would have risen by 10 percent due to the living wage ordinance, even while working fewer hours.

Living wage ordinances are not designed to accelerate the growth in the number of jobs. Rather, they are designed to improve the quality of jobs by raising wages while, at the same time, avoiding losses in the availability of jobs. As we have shown, using the same data and model as Yelowitz himself, the Santa Fe ordinance did not produce any decline at all in the avail-

Table 13.4. Change in annual earnings for the average affected worker, assuming Yelowitz's estimate of reduction in hours

	Estimates assuming no change in work hours/week	Estimates based on Yelowitz's estimate of reduced hours/week
Average wage before living wage ordinance	$6.91	$6.91
Mandated raise due to living wage ordinance	$1.59	$1.59
Average hours per week	33.3	29.8 (with 3.5 hours reduction)
Average weeks per year	50	50
Average yearly earnings prior to living wage ordinance	$11,505 (with 33.3 hours/week of work)	$11,505 (with 33.3 hours/week of work)
Average yearly earnings increase due to living wage	$14,152 (=$2,647 earnings increase)	$12,665 (=$1,160 earnings increase)
Average percentage earnings increase due to living wage	23.0%	10.0%

Source: March 9, 2004, Expert Report of Robert Pollin, submitted to the First Judicial District Court of Santa Fe, New Mexico, in the case of *New Mexicans for Free Enterprise, the Santa Fe Chamber of Commerce, Pranzo, Zuma Corporation, Robbie Day, and Pinon Grill at the Hilton of Santa Fe, Plaintiff, vs. The City of Santa Fe, Defendants,* no. D-101-2003-00468, hearing April 15, 2004.

Note: Revised estimate based on the expected reduction in hours estimated by Yelowitz (2005b).

ability of jobs. Moreover, our estimates suggest that the living wage ordinance did increase earned income for the average worker affected by the ordinance, even if we accept Yelowitz's estimates on reduced hours of work. In short, even while relying on Yelowitz's own model and estimates, we find that, to date, the Santa Fe ordinance has succeeded in achieving its main aims: to improve the quality of jobs for low-wage workers in Santa Fe without reducing their employment opportunities.

14 Detecting the Effects of Living Wage Laws

A Comment on Neumark and Adams

Mark Brenner, Jeannette Wicks-Lim, and Robert Pollin

Since 1994 over a hundred municipal governments in the United States have adopted living wage ordinances. Although the specifics of these various measures differ, their common theme is that they require firms doing business with local governments to pay minimum wage rates that are well above both federal and state minimum wage levels. The aim of these laws is to set a wage floor high enough so that a full-time worker can support a family of three or four at a living standard above the official poverty line. Most of the laws apply to large-scale city service contractors, although a limited number also apply to firms receiving financial assistance, tax abatements, or other subsidies.

Most of the existing research has recognized the benefits of these laws for those workers who receive living wage increases and their families (e.g., Pollin and Luce 1998; Reich, Hall and Hsu 1999; Fairris et al. 2005; as well as chaps. 8 and 10 in this book). But this research has also been clear in acknowledging the limitations of these measures in terms of affecting large numbers of the working poor. Indeed, most studies of both proposed and enacted living wage ordinances find that these measures affect a very small number of private-sector firms in a given locale and that the benefits of higher wages are concentrated among a small fraction of the overall workforce within any given municipality (e.g., Pollin and Luce 1998; Niedt et al. 1999; Nissen 1998). The findings of these studies are derived from considering, through a range of standard techniques, the number of low-wage workers who are employed by the actual firms that are covered by such ordinances and the existing wage levels of these covered workers.

A paper by David Neumark and Scott Adams, "Do Living Wage Ordinances Reduce Urban Poverty?" (2003b) takes a dramatically different methodological approach. Unlike previous authors, Neumark and Adams do not attempt to gather information on the actual firms or workers covered by living wage laws in the various cities contained in their study. Instead, they construct econometric models aimed at estimating the wage, employment, and poverty effects of living wage laws, basing their analysis entirely on data from the Current Population Survey (CPS), a survey administered by the Census Bureau for the U.S. Bureau of Labor Statistics.

Given the dramatically different approach taken by Neumark and Adams to researching the impact of living wage laws, it is not surprising that the results they obtain are, correspondingly, dramatically at odds with previous studies. They find, in particular, that living wage laws affect a far larger number of workers than what previous studies had concluded. Their research shows, first, that wages may rise for as much as 11 percent of the lowest-wage workers in cities that have adopted these measures compared to an average estimate of 1.3 percent by other researchers. They also conclude that living wage laws reduce employment by 1.4 percent for every 10 percent increase in the wage floor for these low-wage workers. In short, they find a clear trade-off between higher wages and fewer jobs that does not just occur at the level of individual firms but, rather, within an entire low-wage labor force in the relevant cities. They also conclude that the positive wage effects are stronger than the negative employment effects, finding that living wage laws have indeed reduced urban poverty by a significant extent.

Their findings have important implications for how we understand living wage laws. First, Neumark and Adams's results suggest that the impact of living wage laws extend far beyond what has widely been assumed in the past. Second, they attribute this broad effect to living wage laws that apply to business-subsidy recipients. They find, in other words, that living wage laws with business-assistance clauses extend the coverage of these laws far beyond the coverage of those that apply only to city contractors. If their analysis is correct, then policymakers, researchers, and living wage advocates and opponents need to incorporate in their assessments of future living wage laws this new information.

In this chapter, we critically review Neumark and Adams's findings. Our analysis focuses principally on the effect these laws have on wages because, as the Neumark and Adams acknowledge, if living wage laws do not succeed in boosting wages of low-wage workers, "then it is unlikely that any positive (or negative) effects will flow from them" (2003b, 503). However, we also extend our analysis to their findings on employment.

Our overall conclusion is that Neumark and Adams's findings are neither methodologically sound nor statistically or substantively robust. First and foremost, we argue that Neumark and Adams have erred in relying on the CPS data for this analysis. This follows from the fact that it unlikely that there is a sufficient number of workers actually covered by living wage ordinances in the CPS sample for living wage–induced wage increases to be observable, let alone statistically significant. Second, as we demonstrate for both the wage and employment effects, even assuming the CPS data were adequate to the task of analyzing living wage ordinances, the Neumark-Adams results do not stand up to more accurate classifications of which workers are likely to be covered by living wage laws. The central issue here is that Neumark and Adams assume that virtually all workers are potentially covered in a city if its ordinance includes a provision requiring firms to pay living wages if they receive some form of financial assistance from the city. But the direct evidence from city records, city officials, and retrospective studies by other researchers shows that very few firms, if any at all, have been mandated to follow living wage laws because of the subsidies they are receiving from their city government.

Based on these methodological critiques and empirical results that contradict their findings on the impact of living wage laws on wages and employment, we conclude that the positive effects on urban poverty that they observe are unlikely to flow from living wage laws. Note that our critique neither affirms nor refutes the potential for living wage laws to reduce poverty. In other research, including our presentations in chapters 8 and 10, we suggest that living wage laws do indeed reduce poverty among families with low-wage workers. Our point here is that Neumark and Adams use a flawed methodology. As a result, their study cannot reliably determine negative *or* positive living wage law effects.

PROBLEMS WITH THE NEUMARK-ADAMS METHODOLOGY

The Basic Model

Neumark and Adams begin their article with an extended examination of the effects of living wage laws on wages and employment. To estimate the size of these effects, they construct a pooled cross-section of individual observations from the Outgoing Rotation Group (ORG) of the CPS during the 1996–2000 period.[1] Using a difference-in-difference method, Neumark and Adams attempt to identify the effects of living wage laws by comparing the economic outcomes of low-wage workers in cities with such laws to the outcomes of low-wage workers in cities without such laws over these years.

Focusing on the analysis of wage effects, equation (1) presents Neumark and Adams's Model 1.

$$(1)\quad \ln(w_{icmy}) = \alpha + X_{icmy}\omega + \beta\ln(w^{min}_{cmy}) + \gamma\max[\ln(w^{liv}_{cmy}), \ln(w^{min}_{cmy})] +$$

$$\delta_Y Y_y + \delta_M M_m + \delta_C C_c + \varepsilon_{icmy}$$

The authors specify here a wage equation, where w is the hourly wage; X is a vector of dummy variables controlling for gender, race, education, and marital status; w^{min} is the higher of the federal and state minimum wage, and w^{liv} is the higher of the prevailing minimum wage or applicable municipal living wage (our notation throughout this chapter follows that in Neumark and Adams's article). Y, M, and C are year, month, and city controls. The unit of analysis (denoted by the subscript icmy) is the individual worker (i), within a given city (c), month (m), and year (y). In this specification, β captures the effect of the minimum wage (state or federal) on an individual's wages, and γ captures the wage effect of the living wage law.

Neumark and Adams also modify the specification of Model 1, substituting a pair of interaction terms for the living wage variable to differentiate the effect of living wage laws on workers who are potentially covered by the laws from the effect of living wage laws on workers who are unlikely to be covered. These interaction terms are comprised of dummy variables, representing whether a worker is potentially covered by the living wage law [Cov] or likely to be uncovered [Uncov], multiplied by the natural logarithm of the living wage level.[2] Equation (2) presents their Model 2.

$$(2)\quad \ln(w_{icmy}) = \alpha + X_{icmy}\omega + \beta\ln(w^{min}_{cmy}) + \gamma\max[\ln(w^{liv}_{cmy}) \times Cov_{icmy}, \ln(w^{min}_{cmy})] +$$

$$\gamma'\max[\ln(w^{liv}_{cmy}) \times Uncov_{icmy}, \ln(w^{min}_{cmy})] + \delta_Y Y_y +$$

$$\delta_M M_m + \delta_C C_c + \varepsilon_{icmy}$$

In this specification, γ captures the impact of the living wage law on the wages of workers potentially covered by the living wage law and γ' captures the effect of the living wage law on the wages of workers who are assumed not to be covered by the living wage law.

Neumark and Adams estimate these two models for different segments of the wage distribution, concentrating their analysis on the low-wage workforce. The bulk of their attention is given to estimates for workers in the lowest decile of the wage distribution of their respective city in the month they are surveyed, but Neumark and Adams also comment on estimates for workers between the 10th and 25th centiles.

In addition, they estimate each model with three alternative specifications of the living wage variable. The first allows for an impact immediately after a law has been enacted. The second allows for an impact to occur 6 months after a law has been enacted (i.e., lagged 6 months). And the third specification allows for an impact to appear only 12 months after a law has been enacted (i.e., lagged 12 months).

Neumark and Adams use a linear probability model analogous to their Model 1 to assess the effects of living wage laws on employment. One significant difference is that the employment model incorporates individuals not currently in the labor force. This feature of their employment analysis substantially increases the number of cities included in the pooled cross-section. It also forces the authors to impute wages for people not in the labor force in order to place them within the overall wage distribution. For consistency, Neumark and Adams use imputed wages for all workers in their employment analysis.

Insufficient Sample Sizes

The first concern we raise about Neumark and Adams's approach is their inattention to sample size. Sample sizes in the CPS are, of course, more than adequate for labor market analysis at the national level. However, studying local-area labor markets is frequently impossible within the CPS due to relatively small sample sizes. This is particularly true if the analysis focuses attention on a particular subset of the local-area labor market.[3] Although Neumark and Adams include data from a number of different cities, their analysis is fundamentally one of local-area labor markets because their difference-in-difference methodology relies on comparisons of trends between cities with and without living wage laws or between covered and uncovered workers within living wage cities.

As such, it is essential to assess the likelihood that Neumark and Adams's models can detect the effects of living wage laws in their "treatment" cities. This, in turn, requires some sense of the scope of living wage coverage in these cities, which we attempt to gauge in table 14.1, section A. In column 2, we report the various independent estimates of the total number of workers expected to covered by the living wage in each metropolitan statistical area (MSA). Although these estimates employ various techniques for measuring the scope of the living wage ordinance in each city, their methodological commonality is that, unlike the Neumark-Adams approach, they all rely on actual city contract data as the basis for their calculations. To put these numbers into context, we present the average annual employment level for each MSA during 1996–2000 in column 1. Considering these estimates as a whole, we can only conclude that living wage laws cover a tiny fraction of total MSA employment, usually less than 0.2 percent. Moreover, if we assume that all covered workers in living wage cities are concentrated

Table 14.1. Estimated scope of living wage coverage and sample sizes for living wage cities

A. Total employment and living wage coverage in living wage cities

City	(1) Average employment in the MSA 1996–2000	(2) Number of covered workers (est.)	(3) Covered workers as a percentage of the lowest decile	(4) Source for coverage estimate
Baltimore	1,244,455	1,500	1.2%	Niedt et al. (1999)
Boston	1,756,785			
Chicago	4,005,477	1,760	0.4%	Tolley, Bernstein, and Lesage (1999)
Dayton	454,021			
Detroit	2,180,670	2,300	1.1%	Reynolds, Pearson, and Vortkampf (1999)
Durham	608,951			
Hartford	566,106			
Jersey City	263,707			
Los Angeles	4,266,435	7,500	1.8%	Pollin and Luce (2000)
Milwaukee	779,175			
Minneapolis	1,636,074			
Oakland	1,143,258	3,111	2.7%	Zabin, Reich, and Hall (1999)
Portland	995,456			
San Antonio	726,727			
San Jose	923,641	1,500	1.6%	Benner and Rosner (1998)
Total/weighted average	21,550,937	17,671	1.3%	

among the lowest wage-earners—those earning wages in the lowest decile of the wage distribution—they make up no more than 1.3 percent of bottom-decile wage-earners, on average, as illustrated in column 3 of table 14.1, section A. This very modest concentration of workers covered by living wage laws makes it highly unlikely that any observed changes in wages, employment, or poverty within living wage cities are driven by actually covered workers.

We illustrate this problem with a simple numerical example. In Neumark and Adams (2003b, table 3), they report that the average wage for the lowest decile is $5.35. The average living wage increase in Neumark and Adams's "treatment" cities is approximately 45 percent over the prevailing minimum wage. If the coverage estimates presented in table 14.1, section A, are accurate, this implies that living wage laws would substantially increase

Table 14.1. Estimated scope of living wage coverage and sample sizes for living wage cities

B. "Treatment" sample sizes for wage analysis at the 12-month lag

| City | Model 1[a] All workers in living wage cities | | Model 2[b] Covered workers | |
	(1) Unweighted N	(2) Weighted percentage	(3) Unweighted N	(4) Weighted percentage
Baltimore	325	12.6%	23	1.7%
Boston	157	3.5%	20	0.8%
Chicago	476	10.4%	44	1.9%
Dayton	95	2.1%	1	0.0%
Detroit	230	5.0%	215	8.7%
Durham	96	2.3%	31	1.4%
Hartford	9	0.3%	7	0.4%
Jersey City	15	0.3%	1	0.0%
Los Angeles	1,196	27.5%	1,136	49.1%
Milwaukee	250	8.0%	25	1.6%
Minneapolis	369	10.4%	344	18.2%
Oakland	106	4.2%	94	7.0%
Portland	360	8.4%	13	0.6%
San Antonio	79	2.6%	73	4.5%
San Jose	69	2.6%	58	4.2%
Total	3,832	100%	2,085	100%

[a] In Model 1, the treatment sample is made up of those workers who live in a city with a living wage ordinance in effect (lagged 12 months).

[b] In Model 2, the treatment sample is made up of those workers who live in a city with a living wage ordinance in effect (lagged 12 months) and are classified as potentially covered according to their industry affiliation.

wages for a very small fraction of the lowest decile, approximately 1.3 percent. With such a low extent of coverage, even a wage increase on the order of 45 percent would have only modest effects on average wages in treatment cities. Indeed, from these figures we can see that living wage laws would increase average wages in "treatment" cities on the order of 3 cents, or 0.6 percent of the average for the lowest decile as a whole ($5.35 \times [(0.987 \times 1.00) + (0.013 \times 1.45)] = \$5.38$). These estimates are far below the 7–11 percent average wage increase implied by Neumark and Adams's results.

In related work, the authors acknowledge that their estimates are much larger than expected, given the scope of existing living wage ordinances (Neumark and Adams 2003a). They conclude that such sharp variance with prior research necessitates further empirical analysis to determine whether their results do in fact capture the effect of living wage laws rather than detecting some other influences.

To establish a causal link between living wage laws and the large wage increases they observe, Neumark and Adams estimate their Model 2, which distinguishes between the effect of living wage laws on workers who are potentially covered by living wage laws and those who are not. As they note, finding living wage effects concentrated among covered workers would bolster ". . . the case that the effects of living wage laws that we estimate are real" (Neumark and Adams 2003b, 509). The authors also acknowledge that "certainly the reverse finding, with stronger wage effects for workers less likely to be covered, would cast doubt on a causal interpretation of the positive overall wage effects reported in Table 3" (2003b, 509). Although we agree that this extension would be a useful way to determine more firmly whether living wage laws are behind the wage increases they observe, our second major concern is precisely how they identify which workers are likely to be covered by living wage ordinances. We turn to this issue next.

Identification of Covered Workers

In classifying workers as potentially covered or as uncovered, Neumark and Adams make an important distinction between living wage ordinances that apply exclusively to city service contracts and those that also apply to firms receiving some form of financial assistance from the city. "Contractor-only" ordinances usually include such services as landscape maintenance or security guard and janitorial services. Neumark and Adams define workers potentially covered under this type of contract as those individuals working in selected service industries (usually about 10–20 percent of the workforce). For measures that fall within the second category of "business-assistance" ordinances, Neumark and Adams define potentially covered workers as all private-sector workers (usually about 90–95 percent of the workforce) because any business in the private sector could potentially receive financial assistance from its local government.[4] As we show in the next section, this issue of how Neumark and Adams define coverage is crucial to generating their statistically significant findings.

As we mention at the outset, they assign workers to the categories potentially covered and uncovered without reference to data from the relevant cities about the actual extent of coverage of these ordinances. Moreover, the CPS data set on which they rely offers no way of identifying who might actually be included among the covered workers. To use the CPS data in this way, a researcher would require information about individuals' primary employers, as well as information from the city as to which private-sector firms are affected by the living wage law.

To consider how the Neumark-Adams method of assigning coverage works in practice, let us consider the case of Los Angeles. Based on the

Neumark-Adams classification technique, 90 percent of Los Angeles low-wage workforce—workers who earn wage less than the 25th wage percentile—is potentially covered by that city's living wage law. By this method of approximation, Neumark and Adams conclude that approximately 960,000 low-wage workers are potentially covered by the ordinance. By contrast, Pollin and Luce (2000) draw on the records of the city of Los Angeles to estimate that a total of only six firms fell under the specific stipulations of the Los Angeles ordinance that applied to financial-assistance recipients. The ordinance was specific in limiting coverage only to businesses receiving financial assistance for "economic development," and then only if this assistance was in an amount in excess of $1 million total or $100,000 annually on an ongoing basis. Pollin and Luce offer a high-end estimate that these six firms employed about 3,700 workers total. Adding to these 3,700 workers the 3,900 workers expected to be covered because of their employment with city contractors, Pollin and Luce's high-end estimate of all workers covered by the Los Angeles ordinance is 7,600. In other words, the Neumark and Adams estimate of covered workers is on the order of 125 times the Pollin and Luce estimate.

Fortunately, given the passage of time, we now have information on how living wage laws have actually been implemented in the cities included in the Neumark-Adams sample. The Pollin-Luce figure, like most of those reported in table 14.1, section A, is a projection of the extent of coverage in Los Angeles for firms receiving city subsidies.

We discuss next the experiences of three cities with business-assistance living wage clauses—Los Angeles, Minneapolis, and Oakland. We then evaluate business-assistance living wage laws more generally.

Our discussion begins with these three cities for two reasons. First, for each of these cities we have multiple sources of retrospective information on which we can draw. These include both our own interviews of city officials, interviews conducted by Adams and Neumark (2005), and independent research and/or city reports on the actual implementation of these living wage laws.[5] Second, as pointed out by Adams and Neumark, among cities with business-assistance clauses in their living wage laws, these three cities have had living wage laws on the books the longest. As a result, the vast majority of workers that Neumark and Adams's models assume would be affected by living wage laws reside in these three cities. Any conclusions based on these cities should, therefore, apply broadly to Neumark and Adams's results.

To see this, we present in table 14.1, panel B, a breakdown of the number of workers in their sample that their models assume are affected by living wage laws in each of the fifteen living wage cities included in their study. More specifically, these are the lowest-wage workers (i.e., workers earning at or below the 10th decile of the wage distribution in each city) who were living in each of these cities 12 months after the passage of these laws and are assumed to be affected or covered by living wage laws. We consider only the 12-month lagged specification because Neumark and Adams do not find any observable impact of living wage laws immediately after enactment or 6 months after enactment. In column 1, we present the actual number (i.e., unadjusted by sampling weights) of workers, by city, in their sample who are assumed to be affected in Model 1's 12-month lagged specification. In column 2, we show how these workers are distributed across the cities when weighted with the sampling weights used in Neumark and Adams's regression analysis. We see that 42 percent of the affected workers reside in Los Angeles, Minneapolis, and Oakland.

We consider these same statistics for the 12-month lagged specification of Model 2 (columns 3 and 4). This time the numbers are for workers who reside in each of the living wage cities *and* are categorized as covered according to Neumark and Adam's classification technique. We see that covered workers are even more concentrated in these three cities—now almost three-quarters of the workers assumed to be covered by living wage laws 12 months after the laws' enactment reside in one of these three cities. Based on this, we believe the experiences of these three cities should provide compelling evidence about whether Neumark and Adams's technique for identifying covered workers is appropriate. We discuss each city in turn next.

Los Angeles

The experience of Los Angeles highlights the important difference between the implementation of the business-assistance clauses of living wage laws and their actual impact. Adams and Neumark report in their response to our criticisms of their methodology (2005, 91) that they interviewed a city official in the Office of Contract Compliance (presumably they are referring to the Bureau of Contract Administration, BCA) and were told that the law had been implemented soon after its enactment. But Adams and Neumark do not provide any information about the number of firms (or the number of workers employed in these firms) to which the living wage requirements were applied. This piece of information is particularly important in the case of Los Angeles. Although the living wage law was officially implemented in April 1997, the Los Angeles City Council took away the authority of the BCA to implement the law in 1999 due to its ineffectiveness (Luce 2004; Sander and Lokey 1998; Fairris et al. 2005). This city council action suggests that few, if any, employers were required to meet the living wage requirement prior to 1999. This conclusion is consistent with our interview with a city official in the City Administrator's Office—the office given the authority to implement the living wage law after it was revoked from the BCA—who reported that the business-assistance clause had not been applied to any firm as of 1999.[6]

Fairris et al. (2005) provide additional evidence on the limited impact of the business-assistance clause. To date, this is the most comprehensive analysis of the Los Angeles living wage law. Fairris et al. find that, by 2001, only 7 percent (about 672 jobs) of the approximately 9,600 jobs affected by the Los Angeles living wage law (i.e., jobs covered and below the living wage rate prior to the enactment of the living wage law) were affected by the business-assistance clause. If we include the jobs that have living wage requirements attached to them under a separate policy of the Community Redevelopment Agency, this number is expanded by four hundred, for a total of about 1,100.[7] In other words, based on this comprehensive retrospective study, the business-assistance clause covers only a tiny fraction of the workers covered by the ordinance, let alone of all low-wage workers in Los Angeles.

Based on this evidence, we conclude that coverage of the Los Angeles living wage law is only modestly expanded by the business-assistance clause. Specifically, these 1,100 jobs make up just over one-tenth of all affected jobs $(1,100/10,900 = 0.1)$.[8] In other words, the city contractor clause of the Los Angeles living wage law provides significantly greater coverage than the business-assistance clause—the reverse of Neumark and Adams's assumptions.

Regardless of whether coverage is based on city contractor or business-assistance status, the overall coverage rate of the Los Angeles living wage law, as indicated by the Fairris et al. study, is limited. The number of all affected jobs combined makes up less roughly 1 percent of the low-wage workforce of Los Angeles (as estimated by the lowest quartile of the workforce based on CPS data, or 10,900/1,066,609). In other words, 99 percent of the Los Angeles low-wage workforce is more appropriately classified as uncovered. Neumark and Adams's coverage definition, which classifies 90 percent of the Los Angeles low-wage workforce as potentially covered, incorrectly classifies almost all of these low-wage workers. Based on the best estimates available to date of the number of workers actually affected by the Los Angeles living wage policies, Neumark and Adams's classification of workers is almost entirely incorrect.

Minneapolis

The Minneapolis living wage law differs from most other living wage laws in that its original form did not include a city contractor clause. Rather, businesses were subject to the living wage law only if it had a special relationship with the city through some form of business subsidy.

Adams and Neumark report that a city official in the Minneapolis Community Development Agency (MCDA) office, self-described as the "living wage point person," stated that, "uniform implementation and enforcement guidelines" were put into place about 12–18 months after the living wage law was enacted (2005, 91). However, they again do not provide any information about the number of firms that were actually held to the living wage standards stipulated in the guidelines. According to our interview of Kent Robbins, the workforce coordinator of the MCDA, no firms had been held to the living wage standard as of 1999.[9]

In 2002, Robbins submitted the first full report documenting the number of workers and firms affected by living wage–related programs to the Minneapolis City Council. In this report, he identifies only thirty-six jobs as being covered by the business-subsidy clause of the Minneapolis living wage law as of 2001. If we accept that the number of affected jobs in 2001 is a good approximation of the number of affected jobs in 2000, then this report indicates that the Minneapolis living wage law covered a negligible proportion of workers in the lowest quartile of the Minneapolis wage distribution from the year of its enactment (1997) to 2000: one-hundredth of 1 percent (36/409,019 = 0.0001).

Although the living wage ordinance requires that only businesses that receive subsidies exceeding $25,000 meet living wage requirements, there are two other MCDA programs that link business assistance to improving wages. The first is the Job Linkages program through which businesses that receive business assistance, but do not qualify as receiving a business subsidy, enter into voluntary agreements with MCDA to establish 5-year wage and employment goals. Although this program is not directly tied to the Minneapolis living wage law, it began to use the living wage rate as a benchmark to evaluate the jobs of employers participating in the program after the 1997 living wage law passed. In 2001, 888 jobs with wages at or above the 2001 living wage rate ($9.33 per hour) were provided by employers in this program. The second program is the Enterprise Zone Incentive Grant Program. This program is even less directly connected to the Minneapolis living wage law. However, it does provide a financial incentive for employers receiving such grants to increase their wages over time. So, although the living wage rate is not itself used as a benchmark, the city does use its financial assistance as leverage to encourage employers to provide jobs with wages that improve over time through this program. In 2001, 124 of the 218 jobs covered by this program had wages in excess of the living wage rate of $9.33.

Summing together all the jobs that pay wages at or above the living wage rate in 2001 and that are covered by either the Minneapolis living wage law or the two other business-assistance programs that the city uses to promote higher wages produces a total of 1,048 affected jobs. Assuming that this number is indicative of the coverage rate in each of the years in 1997–2000, the approximate coverage rate for Minneapolis low-wage workers (again using the CPS estimate of the number of workers in the lowest quartile) is about one-quarter of 1 percent, or 0.26 percent (1,048/409,019 = 0.0026).

Based on this report, we reach the same conclusion about the accuracy of Neumark and Adams's coverage classification. In the case of Minneapolis, as with Los Angeles, the overwhelming majority of workers whom Neumark and Adams classify as covered in their analysis are classified incorrectly; in other words, the vast majority of workers classified as potentially covered by Neumark and Adams are actually not covered.

In fact, according to Robbins, the living wage law was amended in 2005 to include city contractors, and it is the city contractor clause that is anticipated to greatly expand the law's coverage.[10] This observation again is consistent with our view that business-assistance clauses do not have dramatically higher coverage rates than city contractor clauses. If anything, the reverse appears to be true.

Oakland

Two separate studies indicate that the actual number of businesses that are subject to the business-assistance clause in Oakland is extremely limited. Based on interviews with an Oakland city contract compliance officer, Zabin, Reich, and Hall document that "56 workers on service contracts and 31 workers employed by City financial assistance recipients had received wage increases as of October 1999" (1999, 6). This total number of workers affected by the Oakland living wage law is a miniscule fraction of Oakland's low-wage workers—two-hundredths of 1 percent of the workers in the lowest quartile of the wage distribution ($67/285,185 = 0.0002$). Even if we assume that the number of covered workers is ten times this estimate—which is beyond the anticipated four hundred affected workers that city officials projected for a fully implemented law—the coverage rate would still amount to less than 1 percent of low-wage workers (Zabin, Reich, and Hall 1999, 6). Moreover, the majority of affected workers received their raises because they are covered by the contractor clause rather than the business-assistance clause, contrary to Neumark and Adams's assumptions.

Elmore (2003) interviewed city officials and administrators from twenty cities and counties, ten of which had business-assistance clauses. He finds that in 2001 only one project in Oakland that had received business assistance from the city had living wage conditions applied to it. Although he does not provide details with regard to the number of workers employed on this project, his findings are consistent with Zabin, Reich, and Hall's finding that the effective coverage of the business-assistance clause does not extend beyond a small fraction of the Oakland workforce.

Adams and Neumark report that "beginning with the effective date, living wage requirements were imposed in Oakland" (2005, 91). They base this conclusion on their reported conversation with the responsible contract compliance officer in the Oakland city manager's office. However, again, the more important piece of information required to support their research strategy is how many workers were employed by firms required to adhere to the living wage law. And, in fact, our own interview with a city official found that, as of 1999, no firm had been held to the living wage requirement due to business subsidies.[11] This distinction is important because it is the much larger scope of coverage—beyond city contractor clauses—that underlies Neumark and Adams's coverage definitions and drives their empirical results. If only a handful of firms were covered by the business-assistance clause, then the timing of the law's application is not as relevant as the scope of the coverage.

Based on these retrospective studies of living wage law implementation, we conclude that Neumark and Adams's classification of 92 percent of the Oakland low-wage workers as covered is incorrect.[12] These reports on how the living wage law was actually applied in Oakland indicate that, contrary to Neumark and Adams, only a small minority of workers were covered by the living wage law.

The Challenges of Businesses-Assistance Clauses

These retrospective studies point out an important policy issue with regard to living wage laws. Passage of such laws does not guarantee that the laws are actually applied to any employers. In fact, the findings that city administrations have applied the living wage business-assistance clauses to few, if any, firms, is consistent with Luce's (2004) extensive study on the successes and pitfalls of implementing living wage ordinances.

Luce's research finds that provisions that require business-subsidy recipients to pay living wage rates are especially difficult to implement. Several factors work against their effective application. First, business subsidies come in many forms and are not given out in any systematic way. Rather, such deals are often worked out on a case-by-case basis, so simply centralizing information about business subsidies—let alone evaluating them for living wage coverage—is challenging. Second, the lack of centralized information is coupled with problems of understaffing and insufficient training for the departments in charge of implementing living wage ordinances. In other words, even if the information were centralized, processing the information requires a certain level of staffing capacity and expertise that has rarely been afforded to the task of implementing a living wage ordinance. Finally, government officials trying to attract businesses to their cities with subsidies have incentives to find ways around living wage ordinances. As such, the officials can circumvent living wage requirements by exercising their option to grant waivers in cases in which this is possible or by obscuring agreements that provide firms the types of subsidies that would qualify them as covered by the living wage law.[13] Luce concludes, "While over 40 percent of living wage ordinances (as of 2002) include provisions that mandate that employers receiving grants, loans, tax breaks, or other public subsidies pay a living wage, very few cities can point to actual instances where the living wage has been applied to an economic development project" (2004, 153).

Luce's findings are corroborated by our interviews with officials in San Antonio, San Jose, and Detroit, the remaining three cities that are included in Neumark and Adams's 12-month lagged specification. Only in San Antonio did city officials report that they had actually applied the business-assistance provision of their living wage ordinance to any private-sector businesses in 1995–1999. Even so, as of 2001, only ten firms in San Antonio were determined to be covered by their business-assistance provision.[14]

The evidence we have presented here compels us to conclude that Neumark and Adams's potentially covered worker category should be limited to only those workers in service industries likely to be affected by living wage laws with city contractor clauses, even in cities that have living wage requirements for business-assistance recipients. We find that business-assistance living wage laws were in practice no broader in their coverage than the more common contractor-only measures. This dramatically reduces the size of the covered category from 90–95 percent of the low-wage workforce in each MSA with a business-assistance clause down to 10–20 percent. One exception is Minneapolis, which did not have a city contractor clause in its ordinance, so no worker in Minneapolis is appropriately classified as covered prior to 1999.

CORRECTING THE COVERAGE CLASSIFICATION IN BUSINESS-ASSISTANCE CITIES

Wage Effects

In light of these concerns, we now reexamine Neumark and Adams's econometric results on the wage effects of living wage ordinances. To assess how Neumark and Adams's findings would be altered by classifying workers in a way that corresponds to the actual application of living wage ordinances, we reestimated Neumark and Adams's Model 2. In doing so, we classified workers in business-assistance cities as potentially covered only if they worked in service industries that are most likely to include city contractors and, thus, more likely to be affected by living wage laws. The results from this exercise are presented in table 14.2. Here we focus our attention on the results for the workers in the lowest decile (where Neumark and Adams obtain statistically significant results), and we present both the 6- and 12-month lagged specifications. In table 14.2, section A, we simply replicate

Table 14.2. Effects of living wage laws on wages, alternative coverage classifications

A. Model 2: Potentially covered and uncovered workers using Neumark and Adams business assistance coverage

	Uncovered workers	Covered workers
Centile range:	<=10	
Specification 2	−4.62	5.66**
Living wage, 6-month lag	(3.07)	(2.56)
Specification 3	0.61	10.61**
Living wage, 12-month lag	(3.49)	(2.72)
Unweighted *N*	34,196	

B. Model 2: Potentially covered and uncovered workers using corrected business assistance coverage

	Uncovered workers	Covered workers
Centile range:	<=10	
Specification 2	0.21	−4.21
Living wage, 6-month lag	(2.49)	(4.16)
Specification 3	5.69**	0.36
Living wage, 12-month lag	(2.68)	(4.91)
Unweighted *N*	34,196	

Source: Current Population Survey Outgoing Rotation Group 1996–2000 files, Bureau of Labor Statistics, U.S. Department of Labor.

Notes: The dependent variable is log (Wages). Estimated coefficients have been multiplied by 100. Standard errors reported in parentheses are robust to heteroskedasticity and non-independence within city-month cells. A city's observations are included in the sample in a particular month and year if it has at least twenty-five observations for that particular month and year. See text for other controls included in the regression. * indicates statistical significance at the 0.10 level. ** indicates statistical significance at the 0.05 level. Corrected coverage definition is based on the actual implementation of living wage ordinances (see text for full description).

Neumark and Adams's results; in section B of the table, we provide estimates based on our corrected coverage classification.

As can be seen for both the 6- and 12-month lagged specifications, our elasticity estimates are orders of magnitude smaller than those obtained by Neumark and Adams and are now statistically indistinguishable from zero. What we now find under our revised approach to classifying workers as either covered or uncovered is that the living wage laws have a positive and significant effect on the wages of *uncovered workers* only. On the one hand, this result suggests that MSAs with living wage laws had relatively large wage growth over this time period. On the other hand, this wage growth cannot be convincingly linked to living wage laws because it is the uncovered workers, rather than the potentially covered workers, who experienced the wage growth.

Employment Effects

As noted earlier, Neumark and Adams analyze the employment effects of living wage laws by estimating a linear probability model with the same basic structure as Model 1 on the lowest decile of the imputed wage distribution for all working-age adults. But because they include nonworking individuals in their sample, they are unable to reproduce the covered/uncovered distinction around which they organize their analysis of wage effects; this is because there are no industry and occupation data for people who are not working. However, by making a slight modification to the Neumark-Adams approach, we are able to preserve the distinction between covered and uncovered workers.

Our modification of the Neumark-Adams model derives from the fact that the CPS incorporates information on industry and occupation for all individuals who are or have been in the labor force over the previous year, even if the surveyed individuals are not in the labor force at the time of the survey itself. Thus, if we restrict our sample to only those individuals who were employed at some point in the past 12 months, we can then use, for the purposes of this employment analysis, the Neumark-Adams approach to classifying workers as either covered or uncovered. Working with this restriction is also appropriate in substantive terms because it is within the set of individuals with at least some marginal attachment to the labor force that we should expect to find any employment effects from living wage laws.

In table 14.3, we report the results from our estimates of Neumark and Adams's Models 1 and 2, working with our restricted data sample. We examine only the lowest decile of the imputed wage distribution and present the results for all three lag specifications. In table 14.3, section A, we estimate Model 1 using the restricted sample. As is clear, we still generate results that mirror Neumark and Adams's findings. Indeed, the living wage variable, lagged 12 months, is statistically significant at the 5 percent level, with a magnitude of −5.38, very close to Neumark and Adams's original point estimate of −5.62 (Neumark and Adams 2003b, 513, table 6). This indicates that restricting the sample to individuals with some marginal attachment to the labor force does not, in itself, significantly alter Neumark and Adams's original findings. Moreover, as we show in table 14.3, section B, even with our restricted sample, when we apply the potentially covered classification scheme following the Neumark-Adams definition, we still obtain results in line with their original estimates—that is, a negative and statistically significant coefficient on the living wage variable for covered workers.

However, as we show in table 14.3, section C, if we classify workers as covered or uncovered in a manner consistent with the *actual* application

Table 14.3. Effects of living wage laws on employment, alternative samples and classifications

A. Model 1: New sample (only those in the labor force or NILF and worked last year)

Centile range:	<=10
Specification 1	−0.65
Living wage	(2.50)
Specification 2	−1.58
Living wage, 6-month lag	(2.55)
Specification 3	−5.38**
Living wage, 12-month lag	(2.74)
Unweighted N	47,759

B. Model 2: Potentially covered and uncovered workers, Neumark's classification—new sample (only those in the labor force or NILF and worked last year)

	Uncovered workers	Covered workers
Centile range:	<=10	
Specification 1	−1.06	−1.35
Living wage	(3.28)	(2.96)
Specification 2	−2.26	−3.16
Living wage, 6-month lag	(3.40)	(3.21)
Specification 3	−5.70	−6.65*
Living wage, 12-month lag	(3.83)	(3.55)
Unweighted N	46,133	

C. Model 2: Corrected classification , new sample (only those in the labor force or NILF and worked in last year)

	Uncovered workers	Covered workers
Centile range:	<=10	
Specification 1	−0.47	−1.45
Living wage	(2.62)	(4.71)
Specification 2	−2.00	−2.04
Living wage, 6-month lag	(2.77)	(5.27)
Specification 3	−4.69	−6.55
Living wage, 12-month lag	(3.04)	(6.12)
Unweighted N	46,133	

Source: Current Population Survey Basic Monthly 1996–2000 files, Bureau of Labor Statistics, U.S. Department of Labor.

Notes: The dependent variable is Employment status. Estimated coefficients have been multiplied by 100. Standard errors reported in parentheses are robust to heteroskedasticity and non-independence within city-month cells. A city's observations are included in the sample if it appeared in the wage analysis sample. See text for other controls included in the regression. * indicates statistical significance at the 0.10 level. ** indicates statistical significance at the 0.05 level.

of living wage laws, as we do with our previous wage analysis, we no longer observe a statistically significant coefficient for covered workers. Indeed, none of the living wage variables for covered or uncovered workers is statistically distinguishable from zero, although all are negative in sign. Thus, as with our analysis of wage effects, we conclude that Neumark and

Adams's results are not robust to coverage specifications that more accurately reflect the actual application of living wage laws across the country.

CONCLUSION

This critical replication of Neumark and Adams's (2003b) paper challenges their conclusion that living wage ordinances, particularly those in cities with business-assistance provisions, increase wages for a far larger proportion of low-wage workers than has been previously estimated. We also challenge their findings that living wage laws cause disemployment to a significant extent in cities that have adopted these measures. As noted in the introduction, Neumark and Adams base their analysis of poverty effects on the evidence they derive regarding wages and employment—that is, the wage increases they observe should serve to reduce poverty, whereas the job losses would tend to worsen poverty. However, the findings we report on wages and employment—that no statistically significant living wage effects emerge once we properly categorize workers as being either potentially covered or uncovered—undermine the Neumark-Adams conclusions concerning poverty effects as well.

On methodological grounds we have shown that the CPS is not an appropriate data set for analyzing the effects of living wage laws. This is because living wage coverage is limited to a very small number of workers in cities that adopt such measures. As such, the raises afforded to this small subset of workers, even if they are concentrated in the lowest decile of the wage distribution, are unlikely to increase average wages sufficiently for them to be detected within the CPS.

We also show that even accepting the authors' use of the CPS on its own terms, their statistically significant results regarding wage and employment effects hinge on the way that they define covered workers in business-assistance living wage cities. We have shown that their broad-brush approach to defining potentially covered workers is largely inaccurate. We base our conclusions on both prospective and retrospective evidence on how cities actually apply living wage ordinances that include business-assistance provisions, as well as a more detailed look at the three cities that have had the business-assistance provisions the longest.

When we reclassify workers within the CPS as either covered or uncovered based on this new evidence, we find a positive effect on wages for uncovered workers but not for those potentially covered by the living wage laws. This strongly suggests that the positive and statistically significant wage effects that Neumark and Adams obtain for all cities with living wage ordinances are driven by factors other than the living wage laws. In particular, because of the heavy representation of Los Angeles, Oakland, and Minneapolis among the observations of covered workers (when assuming a 12-month lag in the implementation of living wage laws) and the fact that the overwhelming majority of workers classified as covered are actually not covered, Neumark and Adams's results most likely reflect MSA-wide trends in these three cities. Put another way, Neumark and Adams's definitions, which categorize almost all workers in these cities as covered, effectively cause the living wage measure to gauge MSA-wide low-wage labor market trends among these cities in the late 1990s.

Adams and Neumark raise the possibility that passing living wage laws with business-assistance clauses may be the cause of such trends in the local low-wage labor market of cities with such clauses saying, "we have to remember that our estimates can reflect broader effects of living wage campaigns, which conceivably had greater effects on low-wage labor markets where business-assistance provisions were ultimately included in the living wage ordinances that were passed" (2005, 91). However, the logic of this proposition is weak. As discussed, the actual application of these types of living wage laws are, in practice, basically indistinguishable from city contractor living wage laws because the number of firms actually affected by the business-assistance clauses is very small. Consequently, there is no empirical basis for concluding that business-assistance clauses of living wage laws produce greater, let alone MSA-wide, effects.

Our results on employment follow a similar pattern. The negative and statistically significant employment effects observed by Neumark and Adams disappear once we reclassify workers as either covered or uncovered using the same method we followed in our wage analysis—that is, according to the evidence provided by the cities as to how the business-assistance provision of these laws operate in practice. The fact that we observe no citywide effects on wage rates or employment due to living wage laws also means that it is unlikely that these laws have produced any citywide effects on poverty rates.

The overall conclusion that we reach is clear: Neumark and Adams's analysis of the effects of living wage laws in the United States does not stand up to the scrutiny of this critical replication exercise. Of course, our results do not speak to the broader substantive question of how living wage laws have affected low-wage workers in terms of wages, employment, or the poverty status of their families. These questions, which we take up elsewhere in this book, remain the central matters of concern for understanding how living wage laws affect the lives of low-wage workers in the United States.

Notes

1. Introduction

1. The terms of the original Los Angeles ordinance were $7.25 per hour in wages plus $1.25 in health benefits.

2. The standard reference for updated information on the status of living wage campaigns throughout the country is the indispensable ACORN Living Wage Resource Center, at http://www.livingwagecampaign.org/index.php?id=2071.

2. Economic Logic and Moral Imperative of Living Wages

This is an updated and revised version of a lecture presented at the University of Tel Aviv, Israel, December 16, 2001.

1. This quotation from Roosevelt is cited in Stabile (1993, 13).

2. United Nations (1948), Universal Declaration of Human Rights of the United Nations, available at http://www.un.org/Overview/rights.html.

3. Despite such large-scale wage cost savings, the results of government outsourcing have been decidedly mixed even in the narrow sense of achieving savings for governments. Thus, in his 1998 survey in the academic journal *Public Administration Review*, George Boyne notes that only about half of all quantitative studies have found that contracting out lowers government spending and improves efficiency. Many local governments are validating these mixed reviews. For example, the International City/County Management Association conducted a survey in 2002 that reported that more than one in five local governments had brought privatized services back in-house. Nearly three-quarters of these localities cited unsatisfactory service quality and more than half cited insufficient cost savings as their primary motivation (International City/County Management Association 2003). Experts have identified several problems associated with contracting out, including the challenge of assuring service quality, the costs associated with monitoring contractors, the service disruptions that can result when contractors attempt to renegotiate contract prices or renege on contracts entirely, and the possibility of corruption or mismanagement.

See Dilger, Moffett, and Struyk (1997); Hirsch (1995); Pack (1989); Sclar (1997); Steel and Long (1998).

4. Alan Greenspan, biannual report to the Congress, July 1997. Available at http://www.bog.frb.fed.us.boarddocs/hh/1997/July/testimony.htm.

5. Mollie Orshansky, a researcher at the Social Security Administration, who did the initial work developing the poverty line, in fact developed two sets of poverty measures, one based on the "economy food plan" and the other on its "low-cost food plan." Welfare agencies had long used the low-cost plan "as a basis for food allotments for needy families," but federal officials decided to opt for the economy plan—the lower of the two thresholds—thereby lowering the number of people officially living in poverty (Fisher 1992).

6. Alan Greenspan's comment during his testimony before the House Financial Services Committee, July 18, 2001, as quoted by Gosselin (2001).

3. Debating Living Wage Laws

Krugman's book review was originally published in the *Washington Monthly* 30 (9): 42–45. Pollin's response appeared in the "Letters" section of the *Washington Monthly* 30 (11): 3.

Part 2. Impacts on Business

1. These examples are derived from the excellent unpublished opinion article by Arindrajit Dube of the University of California–Berkeley, "Katrina Made Us Aware of the Working Poor: Now What Do We Do About It?"

4. A $6.15 Minimum Wage for New Orleans

A longer version of this chapter appeared as Robert Pollin, Mark D. Brenner, and Stephanie Luce (2002), "Intended versus Unintended Consequences: Evaluating the New Orleans Living Wage Ordinance," *Journal of Economic Issues*, 36(4):843–75. The 2002 paper, in turn was, excerpted from Robert Pollin, Stephanie Luce, and Mark Brenner (1999), *Economic Analysis of the New Orleans Minimum Wage Proposal*, PERI Research Report no. 1, Amherst, Mass.: Political Economy Research Institute, available at http://www.peri.umass.edu/fileadmin/pdf/research_brief/RR1.pdf.

1. Beyond simple accounting, we can also draw on either the standard Hicks-Marshall law of derived demand or a dynamic monopsony framework, such as that advanced by Card and Krueger (1995), for identifying these as the five possible paths through which covered firms in New Orleans could adjust to a higher citywide minimum wage.

2. Some legal interpretations of the ordinance, as it was passed in February 2002, contend that sub–minimum wage workers are actually covered by the law. The final determination remains unmade as of this writing. However, we have generated a separate set of estimates that include the costs that would be associated with giving raises to sub–minimum wage workers as well. These results are available from the authors.

3. We do not have accurate data for the number of weeks worked by low-wage workers in New Orleans in 1998. In 1990, low-wage workers who lived in poverty averaged only 38 weeks of work during the year. However, at least in part, this number may be low because 1990 was a recession year. In any case, our assumption of a 50-week working year for low-wage workers is almost definitely high. This means that estimates of the impact of the minimum wage increase—both its costs and benefits—are also probably overstated.

4. In our questionnaire, we did not specify a definition of *operating costs* for the responding firms. We rather allowed each firm to report a figure based on its own accounting procedures. Our general understanding of the term is that it includes all current account expenditures but does not include capital expenditures or depreciation of capital goods.

5. Consistent with the definition used by the Small Business Administration, the Levy Institute survey defined a small business as one having no more than five hundred employees.

6. This approach builds from the well-known analysis by Elzinga and Hogarty (1973) concerning the geographic boundaries of markets, that is, that "a market encompasses the primary demand and supply forces that determine a product's price and the geographic market area is the area that encompasses these buyers and sellers" (47). Other authors (e.g., Benson 1980) have expanded usefully on the Elzinga and Hogarty framework but not in ways that affect our assignments here of alternative competitive environments. These and other useful papers on the economics of location are collected in Greenhut and Norman (1995).

7. HRG & Torto Wheaton Research, The Single Market Hotel Outlook, New Orleans, 2002, available at http://www.tortowheatonresearch.com.

8. The HRG study also reports on a third submarket, called the French Quarter. However, their data from this market also include hotels located outside New Orleans. As such, with this submarket, we cannot observe clearly the distinction between hotels inside and outside New Orleans proper.

9. The relevant data on hotel prices by market segment are presented in full in Pollin, Brenner, and Luce (2002) and Pollin, Luce, and Brenner (1999).

10. Beyond this one case of the New Orleans market, researchers have consistently recognized that the elasticity of demand in the hospitality industry is relatively weak within a fairly wide band of price variation—certainly within the 1–2 percent price increases due to a minimum wage cost pass-through in New Orleans. See, for example, Lewis and Shoemaker (1997).

11. According to a 1994 Food Marketing Institute survey (Miller 1994), food price was only the fourth most important factor—ranking slightly behind quality, store cleanliness, and courteousness of employees—in determining where shoppers purchased food.

12. Two studies documenting differences in food prices between different neighborhoods, racial groups, and income levels are Chung and Myers (1999); Finke, Chern, and Fox (1997).

13. See U.S. Department of Agriculture (2000) for 1997 estimates of food stamp participation rates. According to these estimates, 70–80 percent of those eligible in Louisiana used the program in 1997. But participation rates have fallen significantly as a result of welfare reform, as described, for example, in Revkin (1999) and Mehren (2000). This is why we report only the lower-bound participation estimate of 70 percent in our discussion here.

14. The calculation is as follows: (1.5 percent, food price increase)×(0.33, food as a percentage of total family budget)×(0.50, food budget not covered by food stamps). Our method for deriving the average 50 percent ratio for food-budget coverage through food stamps is presented in Pollin, Luce, and Brenner (1999). Note, however, that a wide range of poverty researchers argue that the government's assumption that food costs absorb one-third of a poor family's total living expenditures is too high. See Citro and Michael (1995).

15. Pollin, Luce, and Brenner (1999, app. 4) explains our methodology for generating $2 million as the amount of lost sales tax revenues.

16. They will not experience, however, an absolute decline in spending because, considered in the context of a growing economy over time, overall incomes and productivity will be rising.

17. We define *lower-income neighborhoods* as those in which average household income is below $26,000 (in 1998 dollars). This figure is equal to $20,000 in 1990 dollars, 1990 being the census year from which our neighborhood-income figures are derived.

18. About 73 percent of those getting raises live in New Orleans, and of these, about 53 percent live in the lower-income neighborhoods. The $20 million net income increase takes account of changes in government subsidies after workers get their minimum wage increases.

5. Santa Fe Citywide Living Wage Measure

An earlier version of the material in this chapter was presented as a section of the March 9, 2004, Expert Report of Robert Pollin, submitted to the First Judicial District Court of Santa Fe, New Mexico, in the case of *New Mexicans for Free Enterprise, the Santa Fe Chamber of Commerce, Pranzo, Zuma Corporation, Robbie Day, and Pinon Grill at the Hilton of Santa Fe, Plaintiff, vs. The City of Santa Fe, Defendants,* no. D-101-2003-00468, hearing April 15, 2004. Because of legal formalities, Robert Pollin was listed as the sole author of the initial Expert Report. However, the study has at all stages been a collaboration between Pollin and Mark Brenner. The full 2004 Expert Report is available at http://www .peri.umass.edu/fileadmin/pdf/other_publication_types/santa_fe_expert_report.pdf.
Throughout this chapter, *the 2004 Report* refers to this expert report.

1. Santa Fe, New Mexico, Ordinance No. 2003-8, section 4, part B. Available at http://www.santafenm.gov/cityclerks/living-wage-2003-8.pdf.

2. The calculations of business costs are drawn from three sources: the 2001 County Business Patterns (CBP) zip code database, published by the U.S. Census Bureau; the 1997 Economic Census (EC) for the county of Santa Fe, also published by U.S. Census Bureau; and the Current Population Survey's Outgoing Rotation Group (CPS-ORG) published jointly by the U.S. Bureau of Labor Statistics and the Census Bureau. The estimates of local supplier cost pass-throughs are taken from IMPLAN, a regional input-output model developed by researchers at the University of Minnesota. This model, in turn, is also developed on the foundation of U.S. government business survey data. The data on low-wage workers in Santa Fe are also taken from the CPS-ORG.

3. The major exemptions to the federal and state minimum wage laws are maintained with the Santa Fe ordinance. As such, our estimates here operate on the assumption that workers who are earning below the current minimum wage, and are therefore exempt from coverage, will remain exempt from coverage under the Santa Fe living wage.

4. *New Mexicans for Free Enterprise et al. versus the City of Santa Fe,* "Plaintiff Pranzo's Responses to Defendant's Third Set of Interrogatories and Fourth Set of Document Requests," 2004, p. 2.

5. In the 2004 Report, app. 1. we discuss how we derive our estimate for total sales for this representative firm. We present figures for the median rather than the mean firm here because the median figures are not distorted by a small number of outlier firms with very high or low ratios of costs/sales. But we also emphasize that the figures for the means are not substantially different than those for the median. The mean cost increase/sales ratio is, for example, 1.2 percent rather than 1.0 percent.

6. Note also that these local suppliers will be passing through their increased costs to noncovered businesses as well.

7. This section of the paper has been revised since the version that was presented as Robert Pollin's expert testimony in March 2004 (the 2004 Report). The reason for the revision is that calculations presented there were based on payroll data submitted by the plaintiffs prior to the trial. Under cross-examination at the trial itself, it emerged that the plaintiffs had not accurately presented their payroll data in their initial submission of materials to the court. Once their payroll data were corrected during the trial, it became clear that our estimating procedure on costs for Santa Fe restaurants, based on publicly available data only, was even more accurate in estimating these plaintiffs' own cost increases than we had initially believed.

8. This general view has been supported in two papers, one published in 2004 by Linda Canina and Cathy Enz, of the Cornell University School of Hotel Administration's Center for Hospitality Research, and Mark Lomanno, president of Smith Travel Research; and the other in 2006 by Canina and Enz. Canina and Enz (2006) studied pricing behavior in over 6,000 brand-name hotels in the United States in 2001–2003; they conclude from their re-

search that "the results were clear that hotels in direct competition make more money when they maintained comparatively higher prices and did not discount to fill rooms" (2006, 6).

9. The UNM study does provide evidence on prices and occupancy rates for Santa Fe hotels for 1993–September 2003. These figures show that occupancy rates for downtown hotels were generally falling over this period from a peak of 78.5 percent in 1993 to 67.1 percent through 2002, the last full year for which data are available. Meanwhile, after adjusting for inflation, room rates for the downtown hotels were basically flat—at $160 in 1993 and $156 in 2002 (both measured in 2003 dollars). However, we are unable to evaluate the performance of these hotels in a manner comparable to the Santa Monica, California, experience because, unlike with Santa Monica, the UNM study does not provide systematic data on room supply or on the performance of the hotels by their distinct market segments. The study does note, however, that "The Albuquerque market has seen large additions to the stock of hotel rooms in recent years and this has probably contributed to keeping down both occupancy and room rates" (2004, 60). The point here seems to be that, in the face of rapidly rising supply, maintaining flat or even slightly lower prices did not, by itself, raise demand.

10. The Pennsylvania firms may have increased their prices anyway, to take advantage of the rising prices in New Jersey, but they would not have raised prices to cover mandated cost increases.

11. *New Mexicans for Free Enterprise et al. versus the City of Santa Fe*, "Revised Affidavit of Elizabeth Draiscol in Support of Motion for Preliminary Injunction," 2004, p. 3.

12. For the past 20 years, academic economic research on efficiency wages and internal labor markets has explored at length how higher wages and a more cooperative work environment can enhance firm productivity. For a brief set of references on these topics, see Akerlof and Yellen (1986); Campbell (1993); Pendergast (1999); Lazear (1999); Fairris (2004). For historical perspectives on these questions, see Raff and Summers (1987); and Owen (1995).

13. There are only two significant differences between the Pranzo and the Zuma data. First, Pranzo supplied data for twenty-one payroll periods out of a full twenty-six for the year. Second, Pranzo did not provide a figure for peak employment over this payroll period. However, we still need to estimate the turnover rate without including seasonal separations in employment as a component of turnover. We, therefore, estimate a peak employment rate for Pranzo as being equivalent to the actual peak employment rate we observe for Zuma. Based on the Zuma ratio of actual October/peak employment, we estimate a peak employment figure for Pranzo of 109. From this, we then follow the same steps as with Zuma to generate an estimate of an annual turnover of 92 percent and a number of separations of 100. Again, working from the industry figure of $5,000 per separation, this means that the costs of turnover for Pranzo are $500,000 per year, which is 4.7 times greater than the $107,170 we have estimated as their mandated costs from the living wage ordinance.

14. For example, according to the software's creators, the state of New Mexico's Departments of Tourism, Agriculture, and Labor all use IMPLAN, as does the New Mexico Office of Management and Budget and the New Mexico Legislative Finance Committee. For more on IMPLAN and similar input-output modeling software, see Rickman and Schwer (1995).

15. For Pranzo, see *New Mexicans for Free Enterprise et al. versus the City of Santa Fe*, "Plaintiff Pranzo's Responses to Defendant's Third Set of Interrogatories and Fourth Set of Document Requests," 2004, pp. 2–3. For Robbie Day, see *New Mexicans for Free Enterprise et al. versus the City of Santa Fe*, "Plaintiff Robbie Day's Responses to Defendant's Third Set of Interrogatories and Fourth Set of Document Requests," 2004, p. 5. For Zuma, see *New Mexicans for Free Enterprise et al. versus the City of Santa Fe*, "Plaintiff Zuma Corporation's Responses to Defendant's Third Set of Interrogatories and Fourth Set of Document Requests," 2004, p. 7.

16. *New Mexicans for Free Enterprise et al. versus the City of Santa Fe*, "Plaintiff Robbie Day's Responses to Defendant's Third Set of Interrogatories and Fourth Set of Document Requests," 2004, 5 (emphasis added).

6. Spending Injections from Arizona's Minimum Wage Increase

This chapter is excerpted from Robert Pollin and Jeannette Wicks-Lim (2006), *Economic Analysis of the Arizona Minimum Wage Proposal,* Washington D.C.: Center for American Progress and the Political Economy Research Institute, available at http://www .americanprogress.org/issues/2006/10/pdf/az_min_wage.pdf.

1. A technical description (with references) of how we derived this figure is in Pollin and Wicks-Lim (2006, app. 1).

Part 3. Benefits to Workers and Families

1. We were certainly active participants in that debate. See, for example, Pollin (2000).

2. This information on Santa Monica was provided to us by Vivian Rothstein of the Los Angeles Alliance for a New Economy (LAANE).

3. These states include Alaska, Arizona, Arkansas, California, Colorado, Connecticut, Delaware, Florida, Hawaii, Illinois, Maine, Maryland, Massachusetts, Michigan, Minnesota, Missouri, Montana, Nevada, New Jersey, New York, North Carolina, Ohio, Oregon, Pennsylvania, Rhode Island, Vermont, Washington, West Virginia, and Wisconsin. Note, however, that the West Virginia state minimum wage is exceptionally narrow in its scope because it excludes businesses that are involved in interstate commerce as well as small businesses.

7. What Is a Living Wage?

This is an edited excerpt from Robert Pollin (2002), "What Is a Living Wage? Considerations from Santa Monica, California," *Review of Radical Political Economics* 34 (fall 2002): 267–73. This paper was, in turn, built from research on Santa Monica developed in Pollin and Brenner (2000).

1. The discussion here closely parallels that in chapter 2. We nevertheless include this chapter in the book for three reasons. First, it provides more depth than the brief discussion in chapter 2 on this obviously central question. Second, it also considers the issue in a different place and time—Santa Monica in 2000 as opposed to Boston in 2005—thereby offering some guidance as to how to apply the general approach under different specific circumstances. Finally, by developing living wage standards that are expressed in 1999 dollars, it provides a reference for the discussion in chapter 8 on how workers in Santa Monica would have been affected by the living wage proposal there.

2. The NRC study includes a consideration of relative as well as absolute measures of poverty. *Relative poverty*, as the term suggests, takes into account problems resulting from pronounced inequality in a society, even if that society's average living standard is relatively high. However, we focus here only on absolute poverty measures. For an insightful overview of these themes, as well as current poverty trends throughout the world, see Griffin (2000).

3. At the same time, the ACCRA index has limitations for our purposes. The problem is that the ACCRA index is explicitly designed to measure relative living costs in different regions at what ACCRA describes as a "midmanagement standard of living." Our aim is to understand living costs for low-wage workers, which, obviously, will be in a different category than that for midmanagers. Thus, to make use of the ACCRA data, we first have to consider the extent to which differences in living costs at this midmanagement level reflect similar relative cost differences at a living standard appropriate to low-wage workers. In Pollin and Brenner (2000), we provide evidence that the ACCRA index is a reasonable standard for measuring relative costs of living for low-wage workers as well as for midmanagers in various U.S. cities.

4. These figures were taken from the CBP's figures in 1998 dollars and adjusted upward based on the Consumer Price Index for All Urban Consumers (CPI-U) inflation rate to report the amounts in 1999 dollars.

5. The CBP derives transportation expenditures based on the 1998 Internal Revenue Service mileage allowance of 32.5 cents per mile. This figure reflects the cost of gasoline, oil, tires, repairs, insurance, depreciation, and related expenses.

8. How Santa Monica Workers Would Have Benefited from a $10.75 Living Wage

This chapter is excerpted from Robert Pollin and Mark D. Brenner (2000), *Economic Analysis of Santa Monica Living Wage Proposal*, PERI Research Report no. 2, Amherst, Mass.: Political Economy Research Institute, available at http://www.peri.umass.edu/fileadmin/pdf/research_brief/RR2.pdf. That earlier full study included several other contributors as coauthors for different sections of the study. Stephanie Luce and Jeannette Wicks-Lim both contributed to the section of the 2000 study that we excerpt here.

1. The CPS figures are from the 1999 survey. But the questions asked in that survey related to conditions for families in 1998. By contrast, our survey of Santa Monica workers took place in March–May 2000, but the questions we asked related to conditions over 1999. Thus, to make the figures comparable, we converted the CPS figures into 1999 dollars. Details of our methods in deriving the figures from both samples are presented in Pollin and Brenner (2000, apps. 9–10).

2. In Pollin and Brenner (2000, app. 10), we explain the basis on which we conclude that the survey is reliable. But, in addition, we can use the results from the CPS survey as a check on the accuracy of our survey findings.

3. In Pollin and Brenner (2000, app. 9), we explain in some detail why making this restriction in our data set increased the overall reliability of our results. However, one by-product of this methodological choice is that we understate the total share of teenagers in this sample. A better measure of their proportion, including those employed fewer than 250 hours per year, is 6.8 percent. Still, even with this higher figure for teenagers, it is clear that the overwhelming majority of workers in the survey are middle-age people on their long-term occupational trajectory.

4. The figures are not exactly equal to those obtained by simply multiplying average wages by the average working year. The small differences result because we have calculated the average figures in the table on an observation-by-observation basis, that is, as the averages of each individual's total wages multiplied by his or her total hours.

5. In Pollin and Brenner (2000), we provide the mean, as well as the median, earnings and income figures. Here we report only the generally more representative median figures.

6. The full list of additional income sources listed in the CPS includes unemployment, workman's compensation, Social Security or railroad retirement, Supplemental Security Income, public assistance or welfare payments, veterans' payments, survivors income, disability, retirement income, interest, dividends, income from estates or trusts, net rental income, child support, alimony, and private financial assistance.

7. To add some additional perspective on the teenagers in our sample, if we consider the workers who were 17–20 years old at the time of their CPS interview, their total median family incomes was about 38 percent above those for the overall sample. Thus, the families that include these teenage workers are better off than the average family in the sample, although not dramatically so.

8. We provide a copy of our survey instrument in Pollin and Brenner (2000, app. 10). We also provide there details on our survey methodology.

9. Note that the higher concentration of teenagers in this sample does not contribute to the somewhat smaller average family size because the teenagers live in families that average

3.9 people. The median family income for the families with teenagers is also higher but, at $30,000, not dramatically above the overall median of $23,500. Indeed, the median $8,905 contributions of the teenagers to their families' incomes is itself a major factor in raising these families' overall incomes above the sample median.

10. The benefits accruing to workers and their families due to various living wage increases were calculated based on information from federal and state government agencies, including federal and state taxes; food stamps; and Medi-Cal, including the Healthy Families program. Details of how these calculations were done can be found in Pollin and Luce (1998). Sources include Internal Revenue Service, U.S. Government, *1999 Individual Tax Return Form 1040A,* available at http://www.irs.gov/pub/irs-prior/f1040a-1999.pdf; California Franchise Tax Board, State of California, *1999 Resident Personal Income Tax Booklet Form 540A,* available at http://www.ftb.ca.gov/forms/99_forms/99_540A.pdf.; Food and Nutrition Services, U.S. Department of Agriculture, *Food Stamp Regulations,* www.usda. gov; California Department of Health Services (1999a, 1999b).

11. Neumark and Adams (2000), among others, have correctly criticized our previous work on this issue for having constructed living wage–impact scenarios based on family types that were not drawn from average characteristics of low-income families. We are fortunate in this project to have had the opportunity to look more thoroughly into this question. At the same time, we should be clear that the scenario we seek to portray here would apply only to those families in which one working member did receive a living wage increase. These prototypical families are not meant to portray the situation for the average low-wage family in the Los Angeles area, the overwhelming majority of which would not be affected by the ordinances considered. The scenario would also not apply to the families of low-wage workers within the Coastal Zone itself that are employed by firms either with less than $3 million in gross receipts or that are exempt from coverage through a tipped worker provision.

12. Note that Family 1, like Family 2, would not qualify for no-cost Medi-Cal coverage under any of the wage rate scenarios because families qualify only if their income is below the official poverty threshold. But Family 1 would qualify for the joint state-federal Healthy Families Program under all the wage rate scenarios. Eligibility for this program, which partially subsidizes the costs of health care for children, requires that a family's income fall below 250 percent of the official poverty threshold. In all cases, therefore, Family 1's status with respect to government-supported health insurance programs will not change under any of the three living wage scenarios that were being considered in 2000.

9. How Workers and Their Families Will Benefit from the Arizona Minimum Wage Increase

This chapter is excerpted from Robert Pollin and Jeannette Wicks-Lim (2006), *Economic Analysis of the Arizona Minimum Wage Proposal,* Washington D.C.: Center for American Progress and Political Economy Research Institute, available at http://www. americanprogress.org/issues/2006/10/pdf/az_min_wage.pdf.

1. When we refer to Phoenix, Tucson, and Yuma, we are referring to the metropolitan statistical areas used by the Census Bureau.

2. By *representative* we mean the median statistic for the various data categories. We also present in Pollin and Wicks-Lim (2006, app. 3) the means and standard errors for the same data sets, and we discuss why median data are more representative in this situation than the means.

3. This characteristic is reflected in the fact that Yuma's mean number of wage earners is 2.4, versus 2.0 for Phoenix, Tucson, and the state of Arizona overall (see Pollin and Wicks-Lim 2006, app. 3).

4. Economic Policy Institute (2005), Basic Family Budget Calculator, available at http://www.epi.org/content.cfm/datazone_fambud_budget.

5. The data sample for measuring the percentage of families below the basic-needs threshold does not include all families but only those family types for which Boushey et al. (2001) provide estimated budget figures. Those family types are (1) one parent with one, two, or three children under 12 and (2) two parents with one, two, or three children under 12. The budget figures for these various family types are available at <http://www.epinet .org/content.cfm/datazone_fambud_budget>.

6. Details and references on how we generated these figures are in Pollin and Wicks-Lim (2006, app. 4).

7. This is for the workers in the types of families for which we have basic–needs thresholds. (See note 5.)

8. Low-income households in Arizona are eligible for other subsidies as well, including child-care subsidies, housing subsidies, and home-energy assistance. However, for most low-income families in the state, the participation rate in these other programs is low and the effects of the minimum wage increase on their eligibility for these additional programs are not large enough to significantly affect our calculations of the average changes in disposable income due to the minimum wage increase. We discuss the details of our calculations, including the participation rates of additional subsidy programs, in Pollin and Wicks-Lim (2006, app. 4).

9. See chapter 10 for an examination of the effect of the Boston living wage law on the lives of workers who received raises due to the law. Reich, Hall, and Jacobs (2005) document the effect of living wage laws on workers at the San Francisco airport. Their survey evidence includes the qualitative finding that low-wage workers who did not receive a living wage increase experienced a decline in their living conditions, whereas the majority who did receive the raise felt that their living conditions were at least not falling.

10. Note that with some family types, EITC benefits can rise along with the wage increase.

Part 4. Retrospective Analyses

1. See, for example, the retrospective studies of Los Angeles' living wage laws (Fairris et al., 2005); San Francisco Airport's living wage policies (Reich, Hall, and Jacobs 2005); San Francisco's citywide minimum wage laws (Dube, Naidu, and Reich 2005); and Miami's living wage ordinance (Nissen and Wolfe Borum 2006).

10. Living Wage Laws in Practice

This chapter is excerpted from Mark Brenner and Stephanie Luce (2005), *Living Wage Laws in Practice: The Boston, New Haven, and Hartford Experiences*, Amherst, Mass.: Political Economy Research Institute, available at http://www.peri.umass.edu/fileadmin/pdf/research_brief/RR8.pdf.

1. The average difference over the year may be more or less than the difference at any given point within the year because governments adjust the living wage and the minimum wage at different times.

2. Boston first passed an ordinance in 1997 that required service contractors to publicly disclose wage and hour records as part of their compliance. However, the city revised the law in 1998 after firms threatened legal action over this provision.

3. Are negotiated contract costs an accurate benchmark of the real costs of procuring services? Bidders may submit artificially low bids to win contracts, only to renegotiate more

favorable terms after a contract is awarded. One analyst has labeled this the hold-up phenomenon (Hirsch 1991). If such a practice is common, our analysis will understate the true costs of living wage laws. Interviews with officials in all three cities revealed no evidence that renegotiation is occurring. For example, Diane Collins, who oversees the living wage for the Boston Public Library, held that library staff members invest time up front to ensure that bids describe the work accurately and that vendors cannot renegotiate the terms of their contract. According to Collins, one director told a vendor "that if they wanted to go that route, the library would exercise their right to void the contract and re-award it 30 days later to another firm." Mark Pietrosimone, New Haven controller, recounted a similar incident in which the city rebid a cleaning contract after the firm tried to renegotiate it.

4. For details of the first Baltimore study, see Weisbrot and Sforza-Roderick (1996); for details on the second, see Niedt et al. (1999).

5. For the review of twenty living wage ordinances, see Elmore (2003). For details on Corvallis, Oregon, see Brewer (2001).

6. Steve Mermell, Pasadena purchasing administrator, interview with Mark Brenner and Stephanie Luce, January 14, 2002.

7. Multnomah County data come from Facilities and Property Management Division (n.d.). For more on relational contracting, see Sclar (2000).

8. The contracts that were effectively exempt from Boston's law fell into a category known as requirement contracts. These are contracts for services that may be performed if the city has a need for them (e.g., auto glass repair, locksmith services, and plumbing and electrical repair). Living wage requirements are applied only should the city make use of more than $100,000 of these services, a phenomenon that we found rarely, if ever, occurs.

9. Recall that Boston dramatically expanded its living wage ordinance in September 2001, raising the wage floor to $10.25 per hour, lowering contract thresholds to $25,000, and lowering the FTE threshold to twenty-five employees for nonprofits. Because of the long process of phasing in these new provisions, we restricted our analysis to contracts covered under the original provisions of the law.

10. See Brenner, Wicks-Lim, and Pollin (2002) for a discussion of how often cities apply living wage laws to recipients of economic development assistance.

11. We excluded special-education contracts here because Boston does not award them through competitive bidding. Instead, special-education facilities must first receive state certification and then win selection by the Boston Public Schools as placement sites.

12. Mark Pietrosimone, New Haven City Controller, interview with Mark Brenner and Stephanie Luce, June 13, 2003.

13. Pat Paboway, Argus Security Group, interview with Mark Brenner and Stephanie Luce, June 12, 2003.

14. Rod Murdoch, Tri-City Security Services, interview with Mark Brenner and Stephanie Luce, June 12, 2003.

15. Donald Coursey, Al Washington and Associates, interview by Mark Brenner and Stephanie Luce, June 11, 2003.

16. Mark Cratin, Lance Investigations, interview by Mark Brenner and Stephanie Luce, June 11, 2003.

17. Some contracts are annual, whereas others span multiple years, so we calculated the annual costs for each. Like most cities, Boston, Hartford, and New Haven implemented the living wage law gradually as contracts expired and were rebid or renewed. To account for this phasing in, we compared a contract from the cycle before the living wage took effect to the one negotiated during the ensuing cycle. When the scope of services had clearly changed over time, we adjusted contract values accordingly.

18. Without additional information on the actual overhead costs of the winning contractor, we could not evaluate whether its profit margins actually rose or fell after living wage implementation.

19. One exception was the New Haven nutrition programs for children, for which costs declined even though the city bids the contracts on a unit-cost basis. That result probably reflected the high proportion of nonlabor costs involved in preparing meals compared with other services bid on a unit-cost basis.

20. Of course, consolidating contracts will not be practical for many services. See Pollin, Luce, and Brenner (1999) for a more detailed discussion.

21. See Brenner and Luce (2005, app. 1) for details on cutting cost pass-throughs.

22. Dianne Collins, Boston Public Library, interview by Mark Brenner and Stephanie Luce, June 12, 2003.

23. Joann Keville-Mulkern, Boston Public Schools, interview with Mark Brenner and Stephanie Luce, June 12, 2003.

24. Mimi Turchinetz, Boston Living Wage Division, testimony before the Providence City Council, March 5, 2002.

25. For a review of the living wage literature, see Brenner (2004).

26. These ideas reflect those of economists writing earlier in the twentieth century, such as Clark Kerr, Richard Lester, Lloyd Reynolds, and Sumner Slichter.

27. In most cases we collected information at the establishment level. However, several multi-establishment contractors reported data for operations covered by the law on a consolidated basis. Thus, our unit of analysis is more accurately the firm, not the establishment. Of course, our information does not represent the national operations of large companies.

28. Brenner and Luce (2005, app. 2) presents the full questionnaire.

29. Details on the respondents to the survey are presented in Brenner and Luce (2005, chap. 3).

30. We include educational and training services as well as special education, assisted living, supportive housing, and child care in the human services category because all fall under the purview of caring labor. See Folbre (1995, 2001) for a more detailed treatment of caring labor.

31. Indeed, the relatively low pay of human service providers in Massachusetts prompted advocates to introduce a statewide living wage bill for human service workers in 2000, which would have required providers to pay a wage of $12.89 to employees working on state contracts.

32. For a review of the theoretical and analytical issues separating the behavior of non-profit and for-profit firms, see Glaeser (2003); Malani, Philipson, and David (2003); and Hansmann, Kessler, and McClellan (2003). A study that examines the impact of the Detroit living wage ordinance on nonprofits is Reynolds and Vortkamp (2000).

33. Annual figures are based on 2,080 hours of work per year.

34. In Santa Monica, by contrast, Pollin and Brenner (2000) estimate that labor costs for workers earning less than $10.75 accounted for close to 17 percent of revenues of firms potentially affected by a proposed living wage ordinance. Had the city implemented its law, those low-wage labor costs would have risen to more than 23 percent of total revenue. Note that we estimated low-wage labor costs based on the approach presented in chapter 4, on New Orleans business costs.

35. We relied on data from the Bureau of Labor Statistics to calculate the turnover rate because they correspond most closely to our survey question: "In the last month, how many nonmanagerial employees have quit, been discharged, or laid-off?" To calculate the turnover rate, we divided a firm's response by the number of nonmanagerial employees.

36. For more on the costs associated with employee turnover, see Hinkin and Tracey (2000).

37. In this approach, we averaged the ratio of such workers at each firm rather than calculating the percentage of all city contract workers among all firms.

38. Brenner and Luce (2005, app. 3) presents more detail on this point.

39. Because we are using firms unaffected by the living wage mandate as a control group, our study closely parallels Katz and Krueger's (1992) analysis of the impact of a minimum wage increase in Texas.

40. Brenner and Luce (2005, chap. 3) presents more detail on similarities between firms that raised wages and those that did not.

41. The first increase was only weakly statistically significant, probably because of the relatively small number of firms, whereas the second increase was statistically significant. Although the difference between the two groups is not statistically significant, we cannot dismiss this finding entirely. For example, it is possible that the relatively small size of our sample has limited the power of our statistical test.

42. The difference between the percentages of part-time staff is highly statistically significant. To test the robustness of this finding, we limited our analysis to human service firms reporting valid information for both years. Although the reduced sample sizes drastically limit the power of the statistical tests, the resulting patterns for employment, FTE employment, and hours are broadly similar to those for the complete sample.

43. This difference in the numbers of contract workers is also highly statistically significant.

44. The difference between the proportions of workers earning below $9.25 per hour is statistically significant.

45. In the context of our survey, nonprofit respondents used *profits* as a shorthand for operating surpluses. It is, therefore, important to note that nonprofits differ from for-profit entities, not in their ability to accrue such surpluses but merely in the ways they are allowed to distribute them.

46. For more on the dynamics of government contracting, in particular the character of nonprofit contracting, see Boyne (1998); Steel and Long (1998); Sclar (2000); Milward and Provan (2000); Van Slyke (2003).

47. The two standards are detailed in Bacon, Russell, and Pearce (2000) and Boushey et al. (2001). The WEIU/WOW standard is historically significant because WEIU released a study of working women in Massachusetts in 1911 as part of its campaign to establish a statewide minimum wage, a goal achieved in 1912. See Luce (2002).

48. If we adjusted transportation and child-care costs to allow for only one working parent in the two-adult, two-child family, the resulting threshold would be about 75 percent of the two-adult, two-child standard—that is, $40,502 for the EPI measure and $35,531 for the WEIU/WOW standard. Health-care costs are based on a self-purchased family plan, adjusted to reflect the fact that some 60 percent of families have some form of employer-provided coverage. See Brenner and Luce (2005, app. 4) for more information on the standards.

49. See Brenner and Luce (2005, app. 4) for the thresholds for each family type.

50. See Brenner and Luce (2005. app. 5) for more information on our survey.

51. For a review of the merits and limitations of nonrandom sampling, see Pollin and Brenner (2000).

52. Our survey respondents resided throughout the Boston metropolitan area, with the single largest concentration in the Dorchester neighborhood (twenty people), followed by the city of Boston (eleven people) and the Jamaica Plain neighborhood (ten people). The rest of the respondents resided in twenty-six different cities and towns throughout the Boston metropolitan area. The employees in the assisted living/supportive housing sector worked for establishments classified as multiservice contractors in table 10.9.

53. See Brenner and Luce (2005, app. 6) for a profile of all low-wage workers in the region.

54. Table 10.15 reports a slight decline in the proportion of workers earning $9.11–10.74 who are near-poor versus below a basic-needs threshold. This is due to the fact that the basic-needs threshold is not defined for all family types; therefore, several individuals included in the calculations for the near-poor are not included in calculations for those below basic needs.

55. The 80 percent figure is for workers earning $5.75–10.75 in Los Angeles in 1999, as reported in chapter 8 on Santa Monica.

56. A more complete profile of workers living in families above the basic-needs threshold is presented in Brenner and Luce (2005, chap. 3).

57. Another example showing that the law is well targeted comes from the results of Brenner and Luce (2005, app. 6). There we show that covered workers in Boston are substantially worse off than similarly situated workers in the Boston-area labor market. Indeed, workers in the Boston-area labor market earning less than the living wage were, nonetheless, better off than covered workers already receiving a living wage, reporting lower rates of severe poverty and poverty, for example.

58. Because firms that reported raising wages to comply with the law reported an annual turnover of 89 percent and because our respondents averaged a job tenure of just 3 years, we had little chance of surveying many current employees who had worked for the same employer before the law took effect. We therefore considered all our respondents who reported earning less than $9.11 in 1998 as direct beneficiaries of the law.

59. For example, we find that severe poverty dropped by 22 percentage points among affected workers but dropped by 9 percentage points for unaffected workers. The difference between these two—which we attribute to the living wage ordinance—is 13 percentage points. This is more than half the total decline.

Part 5. Technical Studies and Debates

1. The unemployment rate is one way of specifying the broader term under consideration, employment losses. We consider this in more depth in chapter 13.

11. Mandated Wage Floors and the Wage Structure

This chapter is an updated version of results presented in Jeannette Wicks-Lim (2005) Mandated Wage Floors and the Wage Structure: Analyzing the Ripple Effects of Minimum and Prevailing Wage Laws, PhD diss., University of Massachusetts, Amherst, available at http://www.peri.umass.edu/fileadmin/pdf/Wicks_Lim_Dissertation.pdf.

1. Ripple effects may also be caused by employers' substituting low-skilled workers with high-skilled workers. In response to an increase in the wage floor, employers may increase their demand for high-skilled workers, who typically earn wages above the minimum. This increased demand for high-skilled workers can push their wages upward. However, past research (see chapter 4, for example) indicates that the costs to businesses typically associated with minimum wage increases are modest in size, making this type of labor substitution, which has its own costs, unlikely. Further research on this issue, however, is needed. Regardless of the cause, however, minimum wage increases have the potential to raise the wages of more jobs than those bound by the minimum wage through ripple effects.

2. Their estimates suggest that minimum wage increases produce two unexpected outcomes: (1) raises for not only low-wage workers but also for those earning very high wages and (2) slower wage growth for workers at almost every wage level 1 year after a minimum wage increase. Their unusual findings have important political implications. If high-wage workers receive some of the benefits from a minimum wage increase, then this suggests that the minimum wage poorly targets low-income workers. Moreover, if these wage increases are then followed by slower wage growth the next year, the benefits are fleeting. The benefits are felt for only 1 year and then disappear. (See Wicks-Lim [2005] for a full critique of their methodology.)

In fact, the findings of this study challenge the conclusions drawn by Neumark, Schweitzer, and Wascher (2004). In particular, I do not find that high-wage workers obtain raises from increases in the minimum wage nor do I find that wage growth slows in response to a minimum wage change for any workers.

3. Hourly earnings data are either (1) taken as reported by hourly wage workers or (2) imputed by dividing weekly earnings by usual weekly hours. Only workers who are part of the civilian labor force, at least 15 years old, and not self-employed and who have positive wage earnings within the range of $0.50–100.00 (in 1989 dollars) are included in this analysis. The last qualifier is used to minimize reporting errors in the wage measure.

4. My sample begins in 1983 because an important demographic variable—union membership—was not asked of all the outgoing rotation groups before 1983. As a result, only data from 1983 on provide sufficient samples sizes to carry out the analyses with the union status variable. The sample ends in 2002 because of the comprehensive change in industry classification systems from the Standard Industrial Classification (SIC) system to the North American Industry Classification System (NAICS). This change precludes creating a consistent data series on the industry variables used in the analysis.

5. Note that because state and federal minimum wage rates change over time and state and federal minimum wage rates are frequently different from one another, comparisons can be made between workers from different states at a point-in-time and between workers within the same state at different points in time.

6. I use the natural log of wages and minimum wages so that relative changes are uniform in size instead of the absolute changes.

7. Measures for other wage percentiles are similarly based on workers earning wages around the wage percentile of interest.

8. These are measured as proportion non-White, proportion with a high school degree only, proportion with some college, and proportion with at least a bachelor's degree, union density, average work experience, and proportion working full-time. The CPS does not have a direct measure of work experience. To approximate work experience I use the measure "potential labor force experience," which originated with Mincer (1974). This measure is equivalent to the number of years a worker has probably been in the labor force given his or her age and years of schooling.

9. Given the sample sizes of the CPS and its monthly survey design, I can construct two observations from each year. For example, the first observation from 1990 measures the change in wages of workers sampled during the first 6 months (January–June) of 1990 to workers sampled in the first 6 months (January–June) of 1991. The second observation from 1990 measures the change in wages of workers sampled during the second 6 months (July–December) of 1990 to workers sampled in the second 6 months (July–December) of 1991. The indicator variable Half1 equals 1 for observations taken from January to June and 0 otherwise.

The biennial character of the data allows this specification to include year dummy variables in the regression analysis without eliminating the minimum wage variation that arises from federal minimum wage changes. Past research using annual data has been criticized by Burkhauser, Couch, and Wittenberg (2000) for including such year dummy variables to control for macroeconomic conditions. As they note, if much of the variation in the minimum wage is not allowed to identify the effect of the minimum wage, the regression may not be able to produce precise results (i.e., large standard errors). Also, if much of the movement in the minimum wage is due to the federal minimum wage and this variation is captured by year dummy variables, then the estimated minimum wage effect may not provide a result that can be generalized. In other words, the estimated effect may be specific to the subset of states that raise their state minimums above the federal level.

10. Although it is possible that increases in the minimum wage contribute to faster economic growth and therefore higher wages, this is different from what this analysis is trying to observe: the wage changes due to mandated and ripple-effect raises from higher wage floors.

11. The federal rate increased in April 1990 and 1991, October 1996, and September 1997.

12. Note that the industry classification system (SIC) used here includes eating and drinking places in the retail trade industry.

13. A few modifications had to be made to the basic methodology described above aside from restricting the data sample to workers who report their industry affiliation as the retail trade industry. First, small sample sizes prohibited estimating the demographic variables from segments of each state's retail trade industry workforce. Instead, these variables were estimated from each state's entire retail trade industry workforce. Second, the smaller samples sizes of the retail trade sector produce unreliable estimates for the 5th wage percentile, and therefore the regression estimates start at the 10th wage percentile. Finally, the industry variables are excluded.

14. Bureau of Labor Statistics (2003), Characteristics of Minimum Wage Workers: 2002, available at http://www.bls.gov/cps/minwage2002.htm.

15. One reason for this is that some sub–minimum wage workers are subject to tip credit allowances that do not automatically change when minimum wage levels are changed.

16. To see this, consider that the 10th wage percentile is equal to, on average, 99 percent of the minimum wage. The 15th wage percentile, the next percentile for which I produce estimates, is only 4 percentage points higher than the 10th wage percentile in terms of its position relative to the minimum, at 103 percent of the minimum wage. Across industries, the 5th wage percentile—the percentile closest to the minimum—is, on average, 100 percent of the minimum wage. The 10th percentile, the next percentile for which I produce estimates, is much further from the minimum than the 5th wage percentile, at 112 percent of the minimum wage.

17. Interestingly, my ripple-effect multiplier exceeds only somewhat Gramlich's (1976) 2.00 estimate, which was derived using a different methodology and for a different time period (1954–1975). A likely cause of the smaller ripple effect estimated by Gramlich is the higher real value of the minimum wage during those years (and, thus, a greater number of workers likely to received mandated raises).

18. These years are chosen in order to pick a time that is neither very close to nor very far from a federal minimum wage increase because the type of workers near the bottom of the wage distribution may be affected by the relatively high or low real value, respectively, of the federal minimum.

12. Employment Effects of Higher Minimum Wages

This chapter is based on work presented both in Pollin, Brenner, and Wicks-Lim (2004) on the Florida minimum wage proposal and in Pollin and Wicks-Lim (2006) on the Arizona proposal.

1. The findings we present here are broadly similar to two other recent studies, Burton and Hanauer (2006) and Parrott and Kramer (2006), which compare employment, business, and payroll growth among small businesses and small retail businesses in states with minimum wages that exceed the federal rate to those in states with minimum wages equivalent to the federal rate of $5.15 during roughly the last decade. Although they study the trends for a different set of years (1997–2003) from our analysis and focus specifically on small businesses, their findings are generally consistent with ours: businesses in the states with higher minimums fared at least as well as, if not better than, businesses in states with $5.15 minimums.

2. This model is a close adaptation of that developed by Card and Krueger (1995, 144–45).

13. Comments on Aaron Yelowitz, "Santa Fe's Living Wage Ordinance and the Labor Market"

This study first appeared as Robert Pollin and Jeannette Wicks-Lim (2005), *Comments on Aaron Yelowitz, "Santa Fe's Living Wage Ordinance and the Labor Market."* PERI Working Paper no. 108. Amherst, Mass.: Political Economy Research Institute, available at http://www.peri.umass.edu/fileadmin/pdf/working_papers/working_papers_101–150/WP108.pdf.

1. Judge Daniel Sanchez, "Findings of Fact and Conclusions of Law," First Judicial District Court, State of New Mexico, County of Santa Fe, Cause No. D-0101-CV-2003-468, June 24, 2000, p. 30. The Pollin study referred to here is the expert testimony (the 2004 Report) that we excerpt in chapter 5 of this book. We note again, as we do in the notes to chapter 5, that in fact this work was a full collaboration between Pollin and Mark Brenner. In this chapter, we have retained the reference to the "Pollin study" because that is how the work was referred to in all the trial documents.

2. Yelowitz offers a response to our critique in his December 2005 paper, *How Did the $8.50 Citywide Minimum Wage Affect the Santa Fe Labor Market?*

3. The University of New Mexico's Bureau of Business and Economic Research also concluded in its city-commissioned report that the Santa Fe living wage ordinance did not affect either overall employment in Santa Fe, or employment in the accommodations and food services sector in particular (Potter 2006).

14. Detecting the Effects of Living Wage Laws

1. Individual observations are included in the Neumark and Adams sample if they are employed, earning an hourly wage greater than $1 and less than or equal to $100, between the ages of 16 and 70, and residing in a city with at least twenty-five observations in a given month of the calendar year.

2. Because Neumark and Adams's coverage estimates vary for each city, they also include a set of dummy variables in Model 2 to control for level differences among the various covered-worker subgroups.

3. For our discussion here, we follow Neumark and Adams, taking the local-area labor market to be roughly equivalent to the metropolitan statistical area (MSA).

4. They specifically present estimates of the proportion of potentially covered workers in the bottom quartile of the wage distribution (i.e., the 25 percent of the workforce earning the lowest wages) in their paper (Neumark and Adams 2003b, table 4).

5. Neumark and Adams conducted their interviews of city officials in these cities in response to an earlier draft of this paper (see Adams and Neumark 2005).

6. June Gibson, office of the CAO, City of Los Angeles, telephone interview with Mark Brenner, October 18, 2001. We focused our interviews on the years through 1999 because we interpreted literally Neumark and Adams's results that living wage effects did not appear until the laws were effectively applied for 12 months. Because their sample covered only 1996 to 2000, this interpretation meant that laws had to be effectively implemented by 1999 to be observed in their sample, which extends to 2000. An alternative—and more likely—interpretation of their results is that the effective implementation did not start until 12 months after enactment, in which case, it would have been useful for us to gather information from city officials about the year 2000. Even so, our interviews cover 4 of the 5 years in Neumark and Adams's sample.

7. Although this policy was not formally adopted until 2003, the policy had been attached to three development funds during the late 1990s (Fairris et al. 2005).

8. This total number of affected jobs includes the 9,600 affected by the original living wage ordinance, 900 city jobs that were given wage increases due to a city ordinance enacted

in 1998, and 400 jobs that had living wage requirements because of their association with economic development projects (Fairris et al. 2005, 25).

9. Kent Robbins, Minneapolis Community Development Agency, interview with Mark Brenner, October 23, 2001.

10. Kent Robbins, Minneapolis Community Development Agency, interview with Jeannette Wicks-Lim, December 3, 2005.

11. Vivian Inman, City of Oakland, telephone interview with Mark Brenner, October 30, 2001.

12. See an earlier draft of their paper (Neumark and Adams 2000, table 1) for an estimate of the coverage rate of workers in the lowest quartile of the wage distribution for Oakland. They do not present an estimate in their later (2003b) paper; this appears to simply be an oversight.

13. For specific examples, see Luce (2004, chap. 4).

14. Carol Apney, Contract Department, City of Detroit, telephone interview with Mark Brenner, October 30, 2001; Nina Greyson, City of San Jose, telephone interview with Mark Brenner, October 15, 2001; Trey Jacobson, Redevelopment Office, City of San Antonio, telephone interview with Mark Brenner, October 29, 2001.

References

Aaronson, Daniel. 2001. "Price Pass-Through and the Minimum Wage." *Review of Economics and Statistics* 83 (1): 158–69.

Adams, Scott, and David Neumark. 2005. "New and Improved Evidence." *Economic Development Quarterly* 19:80–102.

Akerlof, George, and Janet Yellen. 1986. *Efficiency Wage Models of the Labor Market.* New York: Cambridge University Press.

Bacon, Jean, Laura Henze Russell, and Diana Pearce. 2000. *The Self-Sufficiency Standard: Where Massachusetts Families Stand.* Boston: Women's Educational and Industrial Union and Wider Opportunities for Women.

Benner, Chris, and Rachel Rosner. 1998. *Living Wage: An Opportunity for San Jose.* San Jose, Calif.: Working Partnerships.

Benson, Bruce L. 1980. "Spatial Competition: Implications for Market Area Delineation in Antimerger Cases." *Antitrust Bulletin* (winter): 729–43.

Bewley, Truman F. 1999. *Why Wages Don't Fall during a Recession.* Cambridge, Mass.: Harvard University Press.

Bhaskar, V., Alan Manning, and Ted To. 2002. "Oligopsony and Monopsonistic Competition in Labor Markets." *Journal of Economic Perspectives* 16 (2): 155–74.

Blatchford, Robert. 1895. *The Living Wage and the Law of Supply and Demand: A Letter to the Colliers.* London: Clarion.

Boushey, Heather, Chauna Brocht, Bethney Gundersen, and Jared Bernstein. 2001. *Hardships in America: The Real Story of Working Families.* Washington, D.C.: Economic Policy Institute.

Boyne, George A. 1998. "Bureaucratic Theory Meets Reality: Public Choice and Service Contracting in U.S. Local Government." *Public Administration Review* 58 (6): 474–84.

Brenner, Mark D. 2004. "The Economic Impact of Living Wage Ordinances." In *Living Wage Movements: Global Perspectives*, edited by Deborah Figart, 188–209. New York: Routledge.

Brenner, Mark D., and Stephanie Luce. 2005. *Living Wage Laws in Practice: The Boston, New Haven, and Hartford Experiences.* Amherst, Mass.: Political Economy Research Institute, University of Massachusetts. Available at http://www.peri.umass.edu/fileadmin/pdf/research_brief/RR8.pdf.

Brenner, Mark D., Jeannette Wicks-Lim, and Robert Pollin. 2002. *Measuring the Impact of Living Wage Laws: A Critical Appraisal of David Neumark's How Living Wage Laws Affect Low-Wage Workers and Low-Income Families.* PERI Working Paper no. 43. Amherst, Mass.: Political Economy Research Institute, University of Massachusetts.

Brewer, Nancy. 2001. *CMC 1.25 Living Wage Ordinance Review.* Corvallis, Ore.: Finance Director's Office.

Burkhauser, Richard V., Kenneth A. Couch, and David C. Wittenburg. 2000. "Who Minimum Wage Increases Bite: An Analysis Using Monthly Data from the SIPP and the CPS." *Southern Economic Journal* 67 (1): 16–40.

Burton, John, and Amy Hanauer. 2006. *Good for Business: Small Business Growth and State Minimum Wages.* Cleveland: Policy Matters Ohio.

California Budget Project. 1999. *Making Ends Meet: How Much Does It Cost to Raise a Family in California?* Sacramento: California Budget Project.

California Department of Health Services. 1999a. *Healthy Families Handbook.* Sacramento: California Department of Health Services.

——. 1999b. *Medicaid Coverage.* Sacramento: California Department of Health Services.

Campbell, Carl M. 1993. "Do Firms Pay Efficiency Wages? Evidence with Data at the Firm Level." *Journal of Labor Economics* 11:442–70.

Canina, Linda, and Cathy Enz. 2006. "Why Discounting Still Doesn't Work: A Hotel Pricing Update." *Center for Hospitality Research Report* 6 (2).

Canina, Linda, Cathy Enz, and Mark Lomanno. 2004. "Why Discounting Doesn't Work: The Dynamics of Rising Occupancy and Falling Revenue among Competitors." *Center for Hospitality Research Report* 4 (7).

Cappelli, Peter, and Keith Chauvin. 1991. "An Interplant Test of the Efficiency Wage Hypothesis." *Quarterly Journal of Economics* 106 (3): 769–87.

Card, David, and Alan B. Krueger. 1994. "Minimum Wages and Employment: A Case Study of the Fast-Food Industry in New Jersey and Pennsylvania." *American Economic Review* 84 (4): 772–93.

——. 1995. *Myth and Measurement: The New Economics of the Minimum Wage.* Princeton: Princeton University Press.

——. 2000. "Minimum Wages and Employment: A Case Study of the Fast-Food Industry in New Jersey and Pennsylvania: Reply." *American Economic Review* 90 (5): 1397–420.

Chung, Chanjin, and Samuel L. Myers. 1999. "Do the Poor Pay More for Food? An Analysis of Grocery Store Availability and Food Price Disparities." *Journal of Consumer Affairs* 33 (2): 276–96.

Citro, Constance F., and Robert T. Michael, eds. 1995. *Measuring Poverty: A New Approach.* Washington, D.C.: National Academy Press.

Cleeland, Nancy. 1999. Lives Get a Little Better on a Living Wage. *Los Angeles Times,* February 7, 1.

Debare, Ilana. 1999. Living-Wage Wildfire: Cities Ponder Laws to Raise Workers' Pay. San Francisco Chronicle, April 9, B1. Available at http://sfgate.com/cgi-bin/article.cgi?=/chronicle/archive/1999/04/09/BU93193.DTL.

Dilger, Robert J., Randolph R. Moffett, and Linda Struyk. 1997. "Privatization of Municipal Services in America's Largest Population Cities." *Public Administration Review* 57:21–26.

Dube, Arindrajit. 2005. Katrina Made Us Aware of the Working Poor, Now What Do We Do about It? Unpublished manuscript, University of California–Berkeley.

Dube, Arindrajit, Suresh Naidu, and Michael Reich. 2005. Can a Citywide Minimum Wage Be an Effective Policy Tool?: Evidence from San Francisco. Institute of Industrial Relations Working Paper Series no. 111-05, Institute of Industrial Relations, University of California–Berkeley.

Edin, Kathryn and Laura Lein. 1997. *Making Ends Meet: How Single Mothers Survive Welfare and Low-Wage Work*. New York: Russell Sage Foundation.

Elliott, Kimberly Ann, and Richard B. Freeman. 2003. *Can Labor Standards Improve under Globalization?* San Francisco: Institute for International Economics.

Elmore, Andrew. 2003. *Contract Costs and Economic Development in Living Wage Localities: A Report from Cities and Counties on the Impact of Living Wage Laws on Local Programs*. New York: Brennan Center for Justice.

Elzinga, Kenneth G., and Thomas F. Hogarty. 1973. "The Problem of Geographic Market Delineation in Antimerger Suits." *Antitrust Bulletin* (spring): 45–81.

Facilities and Property Management Division, Multnomah County, Oregon. n.d. *Living Wage and Benefit Project*. Portland, Ore: Facilities and Property Management Division, Multnomah County.

Fairris, David. 2004. "Internal Labor Markets and Worker Quits." *Industrial Relations* 43 (3): 573–94.

Fairris, David, David Runsten, Carolina Briones, and Jessica Goodheart. 2005. *Examining the Evidence: The Impact of the Los Angeles Living Wage Ordinance on Workers Businesses*. Los Angeles: Los Angeles Alliance for a New Economy.

Fernsten, Jeffrey A., and Steven A. Croffoot. 1986. "Relationship of turnover and productivity to bottom line profitability." In *The Practice of Hospitality Management II*, edited by Robert C. Lewis, Thomas J. Beggs, Margaret Shaw and Steven A. Croffoot, 281–88. Westport, Conn.: AVI Publishers.

Finance Director's Office. 2000. *Living Wage Ordinance*. Hayward, Calif.: Finance Director's Office.

Finke, Michael, Wen S. Chern, and Jonathan J. Fox. 1997. "Do the Urban Poor Pay More for Food?: Issues in Measurement." *Advancing the Consumer Interest* 9 (1): 13–17.

Fisher, Gordon M. 1992. *The Development of the Orshansky Poverty Thresholds and Their Subsequent History as the Official U.S. Poverty Measure*. Washington, D.C.: U.S. Bureau of the Census.

Folbre, Nancy. 1995. " 'Holding Hands at Midnight': The Paradox of Caring Labor." *Feminist Economics* 1 (1): 73–92.

———. 2001. *The Invisible Heart: Economics and Family Values*. New York: The New Press.

Freeman, Richard. 1995. "What Will a 10% . . . 50% . . . 100% Increase in the Minimum Wage Do?" *Industrial and Labor Relations Review* 48 (4): 830–34.

Fuchs, Victor R., Alan B. Krueger, and James M. Poterba. 1998. "Economists' Views about Parameters, Values, and Policies: Survey Results in Labor and Public Economics." *Journal of Economic Literature* 36 (3): 1387–425.

Glaeser, Edward. 2003. *The Governance of Not-for-Profit Firms*. Chicago: University of Chicago Press.

Glickman, Lawrence. 1997. *A Living Wage: American Workers and the Making of Consumer Society*. Ithaca: Cornell University Press.

Gosselin, Peter. 2001. "House Members Scold Greenspan." *Los Angeles Times*, July 19, A18.

Gramlich, Edward. 1976. "Impact of Minimum Wages on Other Wages, Employment, and Family Incomes." *Brookings Papers on Economic Activity* 2 (76): 409–51.

Greenhut, Melvin I., and George Norman, eds. 1995. *The Economics of Location*. 3 vols. Brookfield, Vt.: Edward Elgar.

Griffin, Keith. 2000. Problems of Poverty and Marginalization. Unpublished manuscript, University of California–Riverside.

Hansmann, Henry, Daniel Kessler, and Mark McClellan. 2003. Ownership Form and Trapped Capital in the Hospital Industry. In *The Governance of Not-for-Profit Firms*, edited by Edward L. Glaeser, 45–69. Chicago: University of Chicago Press.

Hinkin, Timothy R., and J. Bruce Tracey. 2000. "The Cost of Turnover: Putting a Price on the Learning Curve." *Cornell Hotel and Restaurant Administration Quarterly* 41 (3): 14–21.

Hirsch, Werner Z. 1991. *Privatizing Government Services: An Economic Analysis of Contracting Out by Local Governments*. Monograph and Research Series, no. 54. Los Angeles: Institute of Industrial Relations, University of California.

——. 1995. "Contracting Out by Urban Governments: A Review." *Urban Affairs Review* 30 (3): 458–72.

Howes, Candace. 2005. "Living Wages and Retention of Homecare Workers in San Francisco." *Industrial Relations* 44 (1): 139–63.

International City/County Management Association. 2003. *Profile of Local Government Service Delivery Choices, 2002–2003*. Washington, D.C.: International City/County Management Association.

Jekanowski, Mark D. 1999. "Causes and Consequences of Fast Food Sales Growth." *FoodReview: Food Away from Home: America's Changing Food Choice* 22 (1): 11–16.

Katz, Lawrence, and Alan B. Krueger. 1992. "The Effects of the Minimum Wage on the Fast-Food Industry." *Industrial and Labor Relations Review* 46 (1): 6–21.

Kiefer, Nicholas, Thomas J. Kelley, and Kenneth Burdett. 1994a. "A Demand Based Approach to Menu Pricing." *Cornell Hotel and Restaurant Administration Quarterly* 35 (1): 48–52.

——. 1994b. "Menu Pricing: An Experimental Approach." *Journal of Business and Economic Statistics* 12 (3): 329–37.

Krugman, Paul. 1998. "Moral Economics: What the Campaign for a Living Wage Is Really About." *Washington Monthly* 30 (9): 42–44.

Kurtz, Cynthia. 2000. *Agenda Report: Living Wage Ordinance—One Year Status*. Submitted to the Pasadena City Council and the Community Development Commission on February 7. Available at http://www.cityofpasadena.net/councilagendas/agendas/fe_07_00/10a.pdf.

Lazear, Edward P. 1999. "Personnel Economics: Past Lessons and Future Directions." *Journal of Labor Economics* 17:199–236.

Levin-Waldman, Oren M. 1999. Revisiting the Minimum Wage as a Tool for Assisting the Poor. Unpublished manuscript, Jerome Levy Economics Institute, Bard College, Annandale-on Hudson, N.Y.

Levine, David. 1992. "Can Wage Increases Pay for Themselves?: Tests with a Production Function." *Economic Journal* 102 (414): 1102–15.

Lewis, Robert C., and Stowe Shoemaker. 1997. "Price-Sensitivity Measurement: A tool for the Hospitality Industry." *Cornell Hotel and Restaurant Administration Quarterly* 38 (2): 44–54.

Luce, Stephanie. 2002. " 'The Full Fruits of Our Labor': The Rebirth of the Living Wage Movement." *Labor History* 3 (4): 401–9.

———. 2004. *Fighting for a Living Wage: The Politics of Implementation*. Ithaca: Cornell University Press.

Malani, Anne, Tomas Philipson, and Guy David. 2003. Firm Behavior in the Nonprofit Sector: A Synthesis and Empirical Evaluation. In *The Governance of Not-for-Profit Firms,* edited by Edward L. Glaeser, 181–215. Chicago: University of Chicago Press.

Manning, Alan. 2003. *Monopsony in Motion*. New York: Cambridge University Press.

Mason, Maryann, and Wendy Siegel. 1997. *Outsourcing: Thinking through the Outsourcing Decision*. Chicago: Chicago Institute on Urban Poverty.

Mehren, Elizabeth. 2000. "In America's 'Boom Time', A Record Cry for Food. *Los Angeles Times*, December 18, A20.

Miller, Hilary S. 1994. "Price Ranks Fourth among Consumer Concerns, Study Finds." *Beverage Industry* 85 (6): 18.

Milward, H. Brinton, and Keith G. Provan. 2000. "Governing the Hollow State." *Journal of Public Administration Research and Theory* 10 (2): 359–79.

Mincer, Jacob. 1974. *Schooling, Experience and Earnings*. New York: Columbia University Press for the National Bureau of Economic Research.

Mishel, Lawrence, Jared Bernstein, and Heather Boushey. 2003. *State of Working America: 2002–2003*. Ithaca: Cornell University Press.

National Restaurant Association. 1992. *Price-Value Relationships at Restaurants.* Washington, D.C.: National Restaurant Association.

Neumark, David, and Scott Adams. 2000. Do Living Wage Ordinances Reduce Urban Poverty? Working Paper no. W7606, National Bureau of Economic Research, Cambridge, Mass.

———. 2003a. "Detecting Effects of Living Wage Laws." *Industrial Relations* 42 (4): 531–64.

———. 2003b. "Do Living Wage Ordinances Reduce Urban Poverty?" *Journal of Human Resources* 38 (3): 490–521.

Neumark, David, Mark Schweitzer, and William Wascher. 2004. "Minimum Wage Effects throughout the Wage Distribution." *Journal of Human Resources* 39 (2): 425–50.

Neumark, David, and William Wascher. 2000. "Minimum Wages and Employment: A Case Study of the Fast-Food Industry in New Jersey and Pennsylvania: Comment." *American Economic Review* 90 (5): 1362–96.

New Mexico Department of Labor. 2005. *Labor Market Report* 7 (3).

Niedt, Christopher, Greg Ruiters, Dana Wise, and Erica Schoenberger. 1999. The Effects of the Living Wage in Baltimore. Working Paper no. 119, Economic Policy Institute, Washington, D.C.

Nissen, Bruce. 1998. *The Impact of a Living Wage Ordinance on Miami-Dade County.* Miami: Research Institute on Social and Economic Policy, Center for Labor Research and Studies, Florida International University.

Nissen, Bruce, and Jen Wolfe Borum. 2006. *A Difference That Matters: The Impact of the Miami-Dade Living Wage Ordinance on Employees Covered by the Ordinance.* Miami: Research Institute on Social and Economic Policy, Center for Labor Research and Studies, Florida International University.

Owen, Laura. 1995. "Worker Turnover in the 1920s: The Role of Changing Employment Policies." *Journal of Economic History* 55 (2): 23–46.

Pack, Janet Rothenberg. 1989. "Privatization and Cost Reduction." *Policy Science* 22 (1): 185–203.

Parrott, James A., and Brent Kramer. 2006. *States with Minimum Wages above the Federal Level Have Had Faster Small Business and Retail Job Growth.* New York: Fiscal Policy Institute.

Pendergast, Canice. 1999. "The Provision of Incentives in Firms." *Journal of Economic Literature* 37:7–63.

Peterkin, Betty. 1964. "Family Food Plans, Revised 1964." *Family Economics Review,* October.

Pollin, Robert. 1998. "Letter." *Washington Monthly* 30 (3).

——. 2000. *Santa Monica Living Wage Study: Response to Peer Reviews and Business Critics.* PERI Research Report no. 5. Amherst, Mass.: Political Economy Research Institute, University of Massachusetts. Available at http://www.peri.umass.edu/fileadmin/pdf/research_brief/RR5.pdf.

——. 2002. "What Is a Living Wage? Considerations from Santa Monica, California." *Review of Radical Political Economics* 34 (fall): 267–73.

——. 2003. *Testimony on Proposed Santa Fe, New Mexico Living Wage Ordinance.* PERI Research Report no. 6. Amherst, Mass.: Political Economy Research Institute, University of Massachusetts.

Pollin, Robert, and Mark D. Brenner. 2000. *Economic Analysis of Santa Monica Living Wage Proposal.* PERI Research Report no. 2. Amherst, Mass.: Political Economy Research Institute, University of Massachusetts. Available at http://www.umass.edu/peri/pdfs/RR2.pdf.

Pollin, Robert, Mark D. Brenner, and Stephanie Luce. 2002. "Intended versus Unintended Consequences: Evaluating the New Orleans Living Wage Ordinance." *Journal of Economic Issues* 36 (4): 843–75.

Pollin, Robert, Mark D. Brenner, and Jeannette Wicks-Lim. 2004. *Economic Analysis of the Florida Minimum Wage Proposal.* Washington, D.C.: Center for American Progress and Political Economy Research Institute.

Pollin, Robert, and Stephanie Luce. 1998. *The Living Wage: Building a Fair Economy.* New York: The New Press.

——. 2000. *The Living Wage: Building a Fair Economy.* Rev. ed. New York: The New Press.

Pollin, Robert, Stephanie Luce, and Mark Brenner. 1999. *Economic Analysis of the New Orleans Minimum Wage Proposal.* PERI Research Report no. 1. Amherst, Mass.: Political Economy Research Institute, University of Massachusetts. Available at http://www.peri.umass.edu/fileadmin/pdf/research_brief/RR1.pdf.

Pollin, Robert, and Jeannette Wicks-Lim. 2005. *Comments on Aaron Yelowitz, "Santa Fe's Living Wage Ordinance and the Labor Market."* PERI Working Paper no. 108. Amherst, Mass.: Political Economy Research Institute, University of Massachusetts. Available at http://www.peri.umass.edu/fileadmin/pdf/working_papers/working _papers_101–150/WP108.pdf.

——. 2006. *Economic Analysis of the Arizona State Minimum Wage Proposal.* Washington, D.C.: Center for American Progress and Political Economy Research Institute. Available at http://www.americanprogress.org/issues/2006/10/pdf/az_min_wage.pdf.

Potter, Nicholas. 2006. *Measuring the Employment Impacts of the Living Wage Ordinance in Santa Fe, New Mexico.* Albuquerque: Bureau of Business and Economic Research, University of New Mexico.

Raff, Daniel, and Lawrence Summers. 1987. "Did Henry Ford Pay Efficiency Wages?" *Journal of Labor Economics* 5 (4): S57–86.

Reich, Michael, and Peter Hall. 2000. *Raise the Bottom or Race to the Bottom?: Economic Development and the Low Wage Labor Market in California.* Berkeley: Institute of Industrial Relations, University of California–Berkeley.

Reich, Michael, Peter Hall, and Fiona Hsu. 1999. *Living Wages and the San Francisco Economy: The Benefits and Costs.* Berkeley: Institute for Industrial Relations, University of California–Berkeley.

Reich, Michael, Peter Hall, and Ken Jacobs. 2003. *Living Wages and Economic Performance.* Berkeley: Institute for Industrial Relations, University of California–Berkeley.

——. 2005. "Living Wage Policies at the San Francisco Airport: Impacts on Workers and Businesses." *Industrial Relations* 44 (1): 106–38.

Revkin, Andrew, 1999. "A Plunge in Use of Food Stamps Causes Concern." *New York Times*, February 25, 1.

Reynis, Lee. 2004. *Santa Fe Living Wage Baseline Study.* Albuquerque: Bureau of Business and Economic Research, University of New Mexico.

Reynolds, David, Rachel Pearson, and Jean Vortkampf. 1999. *The Impact of Detroit's Living Wage Ordinance.* Detroit: Wayne State University Labor Studies Center.

Reynolds, David, and Jean Vortkampf. 2000. *Impact of Detroit's Living Wage Ordinance on Non-Profit Organizations.* Detroit: Wayne State University Labor Studies Center.

Rickman, Dan S., and R. Keith Schwer. 1995. "A Comparison of the Multipliers of IMPLAN, REMI, and RIMS II: Benchmarking Ready-Made Models for Comparison." *Annals of Regional Science* 29 (4): 363–74.

Robbins, Kent. 2002. Request for City Council Action: Living Wage-Job Linkage-Neighborhood Employment Report. Memo to city council members Lisa Goodman and Barbara Johnson, July 15, Minneapolis, Minn.

Ryan, John A. 1906. *A Living Wage: Its Ethical and Economic Aspects.* New York: Macmillan.

Sander, Richard, and Sean Lokey. 1998. *The Los Angeles Living Wage: The First Eighteen Months.* Norcross, Ga.: Fair Housing Institute.

Sclar, Elliott D. 1997. *The Privatization of Public Services: Lessons from Case Studies.* Washington, D.C.: Economic Policy Institute.

——. 2000. *You Don't Always Get What You Pay For: The Economics of Privatization.* Ithaca: Cornell University Press.

Sen, Amartya. 2000. *Development as Freedom.* New York: Random House.

Simons, Tony, and Timothy Hinkin. 2001. "The Effect of Employee Turnover on Hotel Profits: A Test across Multiple Hotels." *Cornell Hotel and Restaurant Administration Quarterly* 42 (4): 65–69.

Spriggs, William E. 1993. "Changes in the Federal Minimum Wage: A Test of Wage Norms." *Journal of Post-Keynesian Economics* 16 (2): 221–39.

Spriggs, William E., and Bruce W. Klein. 1994. *Raising the Floor: The Effects of the Minimum Wage on Low-Wage Workers.* Washington, D.C.: Economic Policy Institute.

Stabile, Don. 1993. *Activist Unionism: The Institutional Economics of Solomon Barkin.* Armonk, N.Y.: M. E. Sharpe.

Steel, Brent S., and Carolyn Long. 1998. "The Use of Agency Forces versus Contracting Out: Learning the Limits of Privatization." *Public Administration Quarterly* 22:229–51.

Stiglitz, Joseph. 1987. "The Causes and Consequences of the Dependence of Quality on Price." *Journal of Economic Literature* 25:1–48.

Tolley, George, Peter Bernstein, and Michael D. Lesage. 1999. *Economic Analysis of a Living Wage Ordinance*. Chicago: RCF Consulting.

U.S. Department of Agriculture. 2000. Reaching Those in Need: Food Stamp Participation Rates in the States. Available at http://www.fns.usda.gov/oane/menu/published/FSP/FILES/Participation/FSPart2000sum.htm

Van Slyke, David M. 2003. "The Mythology of Privatization in Contracting for Social Services." *Public Administration Review* 63 (3): 296–315.

Weisbrot, Mark, and Michelle Sfroza-Roderick. 1996. *Baltimore's Living Wage Law: An Analysis of the Fiscal and Economic Costs of Baltimore City Ordinance 442*. Washington, D.C.: Preamble Center.

Wicks-Lim, Jeannette. 2005. Mandated Wage Floors and the Wage Structure: Analyzing the Ripple Effects of Minimum and Prevailing Wage Laws. PhD diss., University of Massachusetts, Amherst. Available at http://www.peri.umass.edu/fileadmin/pdf/Wicks_Lim_Dissertation.pdf.

Woods, Robert H., William Heck, and Michael Sciarini. 1998. *Turnover and Diversity in the Lodging Industry*. Washington, D.C.: American Hotel and Lodging Association.

Worcester, Barbara A., 1999. "The People Problem." *Hotel & Motel Management* 214 (4): 38–40.

Wysocki, Bernard, Jr. 1997. "Chicken Feed: Minimum Wage Is Up, but a Fast-Food Chain Notices Little Impact—Economic Boom Lifts Profit; Firm's Main Problem Is Hiring, Retaining People—Pressures on Job Are Rising." *Wall Street Journal*, October 27, A1.

Yelowitz, Aaron. 2005a. *How Did the $8.50 Citywide Minimum Wage Affect the Santa Fe Labor Market?* Washington, D.C.: Employment Policies Institute.

——. 2005b. *Santa Fe's Living Wage Ordinance and the Labor Market*. Washington, D.C.: Employment Policies Institute.

Zabin, Carol, Michael Reich, and Peter Hall. 1999. *Living Wages at the Port of Oakland*. Berkeley: Institute for Industrial Relations, University of California–Berkeley

Zavodny, Madeleine. 2000. "The Effect of the Minimum Wage on Employment and Hours." *Labour Economics* 7 (6): 729–50.

Acknowledgments

We are grateful to the many people who, in various ways, have made significant contributions to our work in this book and to keeping our minds and spirits challenged, if not always fresh, while we were working.

To begin with, we thank Fran Benson and Cameron Cooper of ILR/Cornell University Press and two anonymous referees for their support and constructive suggestions.

Thank you also to the many people who worked as research assistants on these studies, including Joseph Bakanauskas, Sophia Bertocci, Michael Burns, Corrado Cotumaccio, Nasrin Dalirazar, Simon Doolittle, Liana Fox, David Harper-Clark, Lynn Hatch, Nuria Malet, Josh Mason, Mary Orisich, Ozgur Orhangazi, Lee Palmer, Kim Price, Michele Rudy, Olga Shemyakina, and R. B. Stewart.

Other researchers who have generously shared their ideas and attempted to steer us from error include Scott Adams, Michael Ash, Jared Bernstein, Carolina Briones, Jeff Chapman, John DiNardo, Andrew Elmore, Jerry Epstein, David Fairris, Richard Freeman, James Heintz, John Halle, Larry Katz, David Neumark, Michael Reich, Mimi Turchinetz, and Christian Weller.

Both chapter 4 on New Orleans and chapter 5 on Santa Fe grew out of legal cases examining the legitimacy of citywide living wage measures. We greatly benefited from the collaboration of Mark Moreau and Charles Delbaum of the New Orleans Legal Assistance Corporation and Tom Weisskopf of the University of Michigan in New Orleans; and from Carmen Cheung, Lauren McMillen, Solomon Klein, and Sidney Rosdeitcher of Paul,

Weiss, Rifkind, Wharton, and Garrison in Santa Fe. Paul Sonn of the Brennan Center for Justice at New York University Law School provided expertise for both trials and many other living wage cases.

We acknowledge the following publications for permission to republish edited versions of materials for which they hold the copyright: *Washington Monthly* for chapter 3; the *Journal of Economic Issues*, published by the Association of Evolutionary Economics, for chapter 4; and the *Review of Radical Political Economics*, published by the Union for Radical Political Economics, for chapter 7. In the first endnote of each chapter that is based on a prior publication, including these three chapters, we provide the full citation for that prior work.

We have dedicated this book with respect to all the organizers of the living wage movement. A few of them have worked closely with us while we produced the chapters in this book, moving us off our comfort zones many times over. They are Danny Feingold, Jen Kern, Madeline Janis, Carol Oppenheimer, and Morty Simon.

The work in this book comes out of a specific place, which is the Political Economy Research Institute (PERI) at the University of Massachusetts–Amherst. PERI functions because the administrative director, Judy Fogg, knows what she is doing, enabling us to appear reasonably efficient in the process.

We close with some personal acknowledgments.

Bob Pollin: I am grateful to Chaim Fersthman and Ariel Rubinstein of the Economics Department of the University of Tel Aviv for inviting me to present the lecture that evolved into chapter 2 of this book. I deeply appreciate all the support of my parents, Irene and Abe Pollin. My daughters, Emma and Hannah, encouraged me to get into this work when they were teenagers, and the realities of their adult lives have encouraged me equally to see this project in a broader context. My wife, Sigrid, has been my constant loving companion through all of this, including some of the final editing stages in Narragansett, Rhode Island, between kayaking trips down the Pettaquamscutt River.

Mark Brenner: I first thank the many mentors, friends, and colleagues I have had the privilege of working with over the past decade, first at the University of California–Riverside and then at the University of Massachusetts–Amherst. I am also deeply indebted to my parents, David and Martha Brenner, and my sister, Susan Ferrell, for teaching me the values that are at the core of the living wage movement, as well as the audacity to act on them. Finally, I extend a special thanks to the thousands of activists who are the heart and soul of the Labor Notes network. You have given me hope that another world is possible and the courage to be a part of building it.

Jeannette Wicks-Lim: I want to thank three people who guided me into this trajectory of work. First, I thank Dorothy King, who showed me how really hard organizing could—sometimes—harness the political and economic resources to create a more just economy. Second, I am grateful to Frank Thompson of the University of Michigan, who convinced me that an economics degree could actually be useful. He also advised me to attend the University of Massachusetts, where I was fortunate to meet Bob Pollin. Thank you, Bob, for engaging me in this work and for our current collaboration. I am also grateful to my wife, Ali, who supports me in all ways possible—practically and emotionally—so that I can do this work at all. My son, Mason, inspires everything I do. Last but not least, I thank my parents, Byung Hoon and Choon Hee Lim; I am thankful for all your support in my endeavors.

Stephanie Luce: It is the beauty of this movement that it is impossible to thank everyone I have met through this work because there are so many people involved in living wage campaigns. I am grateful for the opportunity to be a part of it. I also thank my comrades who teach me to think politically and who inspire me to keep hoping and working for a better world.

Index

About the Authors

ROBERT POLLIN is professor in the Department of Economics and founding codirector of the Political Economy Research Institute at the University of Massachusetts–Amherst. His research centers on macroeconomics, conditions for low-wage workers in the United States and globally, and the analysis of financial markets. His books include *An Employment Targeted Economic Program for South Africa* (with Gerald Epstein, James Heintz, and Leonce Ndikumana; UNDP and Edward Elgar, 2007); *Contours of Descent: U.S. Economic Fractures and the Landscape of Global Austerity* (Verso, 2003); *The Living Wage: Building a Fair Economy* (with Stephanie Luce; The New Press, 1998); and the edited volumes *Globalization and Progressive Economic Policy* (with Dean Baker and Gerald Epstein; Cambridge University Press, 1998) and *The Macroeconomics of Saving, Finance, and Investment* (University of Michigan Press, 1997). He writes and consults extensively throughout the United States on the viability of living wage policies. He has worked with the United Nations Development Program in Bolivia, South Africa, and Kenya. He has also worked with the Joint Economic Committee of the U.S. Congress and as a member of the Capital Formation Subcouncil of the U.S. Competitiveness Policy Council.

MARK BRENNER is codirector of Labor Notes, a nonprofit organization that has been the voice of union activists who want to "put the *movement* back in the labor movement" since 1979. He is a research scholar at the Political Economy Research Institute at the University of Massachusetts–Amherst and a staff economist for the Center for Popular Economics and the Real Cost of

Prisons Project. He received his PhD in economics from the University of California–Riverside in 2000, and before joining Labor Notes was an assistant research professor at the Political Economy Research Institute. There his research examined the dynamics of low-wage labor markets and the effectiveness of poverty-reduction strategies in both developed and developing countries. He has written widely in both popular and academic venues on workplace health and safety, the economics of living wage policies, and the state of contemporary unions. He has also consulted for the International Labour Organization and the United Nations Development Program in Africa and Asia.

JEANNETTE WICKS-LIM is an assistant research professor at the Political Economy Research Institute (PERI) at the University of Massachusetts–Amherst. She completed her PhD in economics at the University of Massachusetts–Amherst in 2005. Wicks-Lim specializes in labor economics with an emphasis on the low-wage labor market and has an overlapping interest in the political economy of race. Alongside her research on minimum wage and living wage laws, she consults other researchers, policy makers, organizers, and students interested in understanding the economic impacts of these laws. Her publications include "Measuring the Full Impact of Minimum and Living Wage Laws," in *Dollars and Sense* (2006); "Decent Work in America" (with James Heintz and Robert Pollin; a PERI report, 2005), and "Promoting Women's Economic Progress through Affirmative Action," (with M. V. Lee Badgett; 2001, in *Squaring Up: Policy Strategies to Raise Women's Incomes in the United States*, edited by Mary King). Prior to coming to PERI, Wicks-Lim was a visiting professor at Marlboro College, in Marlboro, Vermont. She has also worked as a research assistant for the Economic Policy Institute and a research associate for Monitoring the Future at the Institute for Social Research at the University of Michigan, Ann Arbor.

STEPHANIE LUCE is an associate professor and research director at the Labor Center, University of Massachusetts–Amherst. She received her M.A. in industrial relations and PhD in sociology, both from the University of Wisconsin–Madison in 1999. She is the author of *Fighting for a Living Wage* (Cornell University Press, 2004), and coauthor of *The Living Wage: Building a Fair Economy* (with Robert Pollin; The New Press, 1998). In addition to her work on living wages, she has also researched the effects of globalization on jobs and workers, including work with Kate Bronfenbrenner tracking the global movement of jobs. Her other research interests include international labor standards, women and work, and labor-community coalitions.